TYRANTS OF THE HEART:

A Psychoanalytic Study of Mothers and Maternal Images in James Joyce

TYRANTS OF THE HEART:

A Psychoanalytic Study of Mothers and Maternal Images in James Joyce

Michael Zimmerman

Tyrants of the Heart:
A Psychoanalytic Study of Mothers and Maternal Images in James Joyce

Copyright © 2017 by Michael Zimmerman

International Psychoanalytic Books (IPBooks),
30-27 33rd Street, #3R
Astoria, NY 11102
Online at: www.IPBooks.net

All rights reserved. No part of this book may be used or reproduced in any manner whatsoever including Internet usage, without written permission of the author.

Cover Painting: Venus and Adonis by Nicolas Mignard

Interior book design by Maureen Cutajar

ISBN: 978-0-9980833-7-7

To Lily
My Flower of the Rockies, My Alberta Rose

Table of Contents

INTRODUCTION
1

CHAPTER I
The Anonymity of Mothers in James Joyce
7

CHAPTER II
Stephen's Mothers in *Ulysses*: Notes Toward the Autobiography of James Joyce
19

CHAPTER III
Leopold Paula Bloom: The New Womanly Man
41

CHAPTER IV
The Child is Father to the Man: A Strange Murmuring Wine of Blood
63

CHAPTER V
Stoom: The Contransmagnificandjewbangtantiality of Son and Father
87

CHAPTER VI
Blephen: The Contransmagnificandjewbangtantiality of Father and Son
107

CHAPTER VII
Portraits of the Artist: Consubstantiality in a Different Light
131

EPILOGUE
Middler the Holy Ghost
165

CADENZA
Psychoanalysis and the Study of James Joyce (By way of Another Literary Discussion in the National Library)
183

APPENDIX
Gabriel Conroy's Individuating Rhythm and Joyce's use of Autobiography
197

BIBLIOGRAPHY
221

Secrets, silent, stony sit in the dark palaces of both our hearts: secrets weary of their tyranny: tyrants willing to be dethroned.

—Stephen, musing on his student,
Sargent, in "Nestor" *Ulysses* (p. 28)

I can psoakoonaloose myself any time I want (the fog follow you all!) without your interferences or any other pigeonstealer.

Finnegans Wake (p. 522, ll. 34-36)

Introduction

In a number of articles I published when I began my training as a psychoanalyst at the San Francisco Psychoanalytic Institute, now the San Francisco Center for Psychoanalysis, I became intrigued by James Joyce's concern with mothers and maternal images. I found that writing "Stephen's Mothers in *Ulysses*" crystallized my sense that *amor matris*, to use Stephen Dedalus's phrase, the ambiguous "mother love" (a mother's love for her son or a son's love for his mother or both at once), was a way into many of the mysterious, unfathomed, even unfathomable passages in *Ulysses*.

As I continued my training, while simultaneously teaching English literature at San Francisco State, I became more and more aware that the way I enjoyed teaching—the close, systematic textual analysis of literature, *explication de texte*—was dovetailing with the ways I was learning to listen to, and to muse about, my patients. In effect, I was learning that by focusing on the inner lives of patients and literary characters—on what Paul Schwaber in his psychoanalytic reading of *Ulysses*, *The Cast of Characters* (1999), calls "minds in action"—I was doing much the same thing. I was trying to pay the closest attention to the repeated thoughts, feelings, images, and associations that make human beings unique.

Reading *The Cast of Characters*, particularly Schwaber's second chapter, "'What the Hell Are You Driving at?'" that is subtitled "Stephen Dedalus' Shakespeare," I was stunned to find that many of the passages he quoted and the themes that he drew from them were passages and themes (particularly the loss of a mother) that I had quoted and developed in my essay,

"Stephen's Mothers in *Ulysses*" (1975). Despite the seemingly endless varieties of psychoanalysis being practiced today, perhaps, I thought happily, some analysts (who also teach literature) do share common ground in the sense that we find significance in the same things we hear from a patient on the couch or from a character on Joyce's pages.

A major difference between my approach and Schwaber's is that he appears to avoid using elementary psychoanalytic ideas that seem all but called for in the elucidation of a character's psychology. At times, however, this avoidance leads Schwaber to unnecessary impressionism, to literary criticism as appreciation rather than the rigorous psychoanalytic study of character. For example, although he seems aware that Stephen's highly personal interpretation of Shakespeare reflects Stephen's own conflicts, Schwaber does not develop his intuition: "specific links between his Shakespeare theory and his rendered life prove hard to discern, other than an obvious wish to write greatly."

I try throughout to avoid viewing Bloom and Stephen, as well as Joyce, through the prism of prefabricated "ideas" that some consider Freudian—"oedipal conflict," "castration complex," "masochism," and so on, jargon phrases that no psychoanalyst would use while talking with a patient (or that an empathic literature professor would use in his classroom). This approach is predicated on what a "Freudian" critic often incorrectly believes a given diagnostic label contains, on a preformed notion of how the label should be applied. This habit of mind, which is actually pre-Freudian, reduces a complex, various, dynamic life into something that is oddly static. Rather than isolate psychopathic entities, I explore the recurrent wishes, fears, and fantasies that comprise what Joyce, in an early essay, "A Portrait of the Artist" (1904), called the "individuating rhythm" of a character's life. I do use such phrases as "conscious," "pre-conscious," and "unconscious" (with, I hope, understandable definitions), and I also use Freud's ideas about "identification" and "introjection," again, I hope, in a clear and non-jargonistic manner.

Before Paul Schwaber's *The Cast of Characters*, the most important psychoanalytic study of Joyce was Mark Shechner's *Joyce in Nighttown* (1974). More systematic than Schwaber's book, it is a lively, insightful, and rhetorically spirited work, but it is concerned mainly with the theme of fathers-and-sons, "oedipal conflicts" in Joyce's characters and in Joyce himself. At times, "oedipal conflict" becomes something close to a preformed notion. In a review-article, Wolfgang Lederer noted, "there is no father (worth mentioning) in *Ulysses* [so] why call the theme oedipal? Because there is an unresolved bond to the mother? Must that be oedipal? Can it not be something in its own right, and not just a variation?"

I have addressed myself to these questions and have discovered that *Ulysses* (as well as *A Portrait of the Artist as Young Man*) do not characteristically concern themselves with *triangular* relationships between a son, his mother, and his father. Instead, *dyadic* relationships are central, involving a son and his mother. As Lenehan says of Bloom, he's not "one of your common or garden" and surely Joyce's other characters are not common or garden-variety neurotics either, any more than Joyce is.

Tyrants of the Heart uncovers conflicts in Bloom and Stephen (and indirectly in Joyce) that have not been studied before, unresolved problems in the course of development that antedate "oedipal" ones. It focuses on the problematic nature of "amor matris," mother love, the love of mother for son and of son for mother.

When we sense that Joyce was a much more profound student of the unconscious than his psychoanalytically-oriented admirers have previously realized—when we sense that he was transforming a variety of early, all but ineffable unconscious conflicts into the health of high art—we begin to understand Freud's famous remark that he didn't discover the unconscious: the poets did.

I should add that I hope by putting page references in the text, I will encourage my readers to become students again. Studying Joyce's words closely, they should quickly discover whether their understanding agrees or disagrees with mine (an echo of my clinical practice, I realize, where I try to be aware of where, and when, my patients find an interpretation on the mark or off).

My reading of the theme of mother love in the first two chapters, "The Anonymity of Mothers in James Joyce" and "Stephen's Mothers in *Ulysses*: Notes for the Autobiography of James Joyce," leads me to the next chapter, "Leopold Paula Bloom: The New Womanly Man" where I explore Bloom's multiple feminine identifications and the possible sources of Bloom's confusion in body image and wavering genitality. In Chapter IV, "The Child is Father to the Man," I speculate on the connection between Bloom's womanliness and two possible traumas in his early years—"infantile debauchery" with a "dissolute granddam."

In "Stoom: The Contransmagnificandjewbangtantiality of Son and Father" and "Blephen: The Contransmagnificandjewbangtantiality of Father and Son," Chapters V and VI, I concentrate on the "Circe" section of *Ulysses*, what Joyce called "the best thing he had ever written," "a new Inferno in full sail." I discuss the consubstantiality, the mysterious oneness, of Bloom and Stephen who find themselves in Bella Cohen's brothel. I also explore, in Joyce's phrase, their "fusion," i.e., "Stoom" or "Blephen," and as I do, I develop more fully the theme of mother love. Using Stephen's interpretation of Shakespeare's "Venus and Adonis," I speculate on an early disappointment in love in Joyce's very different "cornfield" where "love lies ableeding"—an Adonis-like experience of a fatal tusking that Stephen shares with Bloom (and with Shakespeare).

And in the last chapter, "Portraits of the Artist," I focus on Joyce's intuitions about the consequences of an early disturbance in amor matris in the artist' gestation. I pay special attention to his insights into the nature of the Dedalean artist in *A Portrait of the Artist as a Young Man*, thus exploring another aspect of the consubstantiality of Father and Son—the shared artist-ness of Stephen and Bloom.

"Middler the Holy Ghost," the Epilogue, is an interpretation of the perpetually enigmatic Man in the Macintosh in which we see how Joyce completes his secularized version of the Trinity: Father and Son are joined by the Holy Ghost. In the Cadenza, my recreation of the dramatic scene in the National Library in the "Scylla and Charybdis" chapter of *Ulysses*, I discuss with Stephen, Buck Mulligan, and others the nature of my psychological approach in *Tyrants of the Heart*. Finally, the Appendix, "Gabriel Conroy's Individuating Rhythm and Joyce's Use of Autobiography," shows how Gabriel's psychological conflicts (and strengths) echo Stephen's in Chapter VII (and likely many of Joyce's).

* * *

Introduction

A version of "The Anonymity of Mothers in James Joyce" was first published as "Joyce's Mothers" in *Dialogue: A Journal of Psychoanalytic Perspectives*; a version of "Stephen's Mothers in *Ulysses*" originally appeared in the *Journal of the Philological Association of the Pacific Coast*; and the first part of "Leopold Paula Bloom: The New Womanly Man" was originally published in *Literature and Psychology*. Each has been revised for the present study. "Middler the Holy Ghost" was delivered in a somewhat different version at a conference of the James Joyce Society at the University of New Mexico at Albuquerque under the title "Joyce's Personal Catholicism and the Meaning of the Man in the Macintosh."

I've used the following, pre-1941, editions of *Dubliners, A Portrait of the Artist as a Young Man* and *Ulysses* due to the legal advice I received about how to avoid a "slight" chance of entanglement with the Joyce Estate: James Joyce, *Dubliners,* with an introduction by Padraic Colum (New York: The Modern Library, Inc., 1926); *A Portrait of the Artist as a Young Man*, with an introduction by Herbert Gorman (New York: The Modern Library, Inc., 1928); *Ulysses* (Paris: Shakespeare and Company, 1926); and *Finnegans Wake* (New York: The Viking Press, 1939).

CHAPTER I

The Anonymity of Mothers in James Joyce

> "'O that I could nestle in your womb like a child born of your flesh and blood, be fed by your blood, sleep in the warm secret gloom of your body!'"
> —James Joyce, Letter to Nora Joyce, September 2, 1909, quoted by Richard Ellmann, *James Joyce*

One of the most autobiographical of all modern writers (if indirectly), and surely the most profound student of the dark underside of consciousness, James Joyce seems almost reluctant to describe the mother of his semi-legendary, semi-fictionalized version of his youthful self, Stephen Dedalus. In fact, Mrs. Dedalus's spectral quality as a character is striking. *A Portrait of the Artist as a Young Man* begins at such an early time in Stephen's childhood—we seem to be both inside and outside his mind as he hears and simultaneously recreates a nursery story—that we expect a fully drawn portrait of the mother to stand beside the thinly disguised self-portrait. But Mrs. Dedalus is not reading to her, perhaps, two-year-old son. Mr. Dedalus is, and as his father embellishes a famous Connemara folk tale, Joyce hints that Simon Dedalus is one of Stephen's first maternal images and possibly the most important.

The novel opens with Simon's bedtime words to the boy and closes with Stephen's famous words to him—or to a mythic version of him. Here is Simon Dedalus in full rhetorical flight:

> Once upon a time and a very good time it was there was a moocow coming down along the road and this moocow that was coming down the road met a nicens little boy named baby tuckoo....His father told him that story: his father looked at him through a glass: he had a hairy face.[1]

It is the father, not the mother, who tells Stephen-Tuckoo stories at the beginning of *Portrait*, and at the end, it is Stephen Dedalus who tells his mythic forbear, Daedelus, a story about going down the great road of life. He feels ready, he imagines, to fly by the nets of "nationality, language, religion" that hold the artist's soul from flight (*Portrait*, p. 238). Yet this young artist-manqué also asks to be stood up and stood by, as if he were a nicens little boy of two or so, ready to surge upward into the world, to independence and a mastery of reality. In his last diary entries, Stephen chants:

> *April 26*....Welcome, O life! I go to encounter for the millionth time the reality of experience and to forge in the smithy of my soul the uncreated conscience of my race.
> *April 27.* Old father, old artificer, stand me now and ever in good stead. (*Portrait*, p. 299)

Although the novel begins and ends with talk by and to a father, this father is curiously maternal—the first source of the mother tongue and the transformation of that tongue into such Dedalean English as nicens little boy and baby tuckoo, English in the son's hands that will eventually become Joycean English. (In the beginning *was* the Word—or Irish

---

[1] James Joyce, *A Portrait of the Artist as a Young Man*, with an introduction by Herbert Gorman (New York: The Modern Library, Inc., 1928), p. 1. Subsequent references will appear in the text and refer to this edition.

words with a Cork accent; and the Word was made flesh; and the Word was with what seemed to be the Son, at least a Son with a uniquely Irish God.) Yet Joyce also seems to be implying that Stephen is still very much the receptive and dependent child as he prepares to leave Ireland and fly toward the sun. He is still enveloped and nourished by a protective presence, a fount of physical and emotional support and well-being. The difference between Baby Tuckoo in the beginning and at the end is not so great as it appears. The baby is passively cared for and "looked at," while the artist-as-a-young man actively elicits and receives parental care, concern, and attentiveness.

When we recall the relatively few details of Stephen's relationship with his mother, we sense something quite similar: Stephen wants to receive nourishment, as well as echoing and mirroring approval from her. In fact, Joyce wants us to see that Mrs. Dedalus *is* more or less anonymous in her relation to the artist-to-be and not as an interesting and autonomous creature in her own right. She is important to him (and thus to us) only if she cares or does not care for him, comforts him or fails to comfort him. She changes the wet bedding for Stephen when he is an infant and puts on an oil-sheet; she plays the piano for him to dance as he grows older; she tries to make peace at the Christmas dinner that is also Stephen's homecoming from school (and, tumultuously, his initiation into the raging Parnellite-anti-Parnellite war in Ireland); she scrubs her son's neck, ears, and nose when he is at the university. We feel her presence (spectral as it might be) as Stephen apparently felt it— either cooking or cleaning or not cooking and cleaning, supporting Stephen wholeheartedly or not supporting him, sustaining her son or failing to sustain him, present or absent, idealized or uncaring. Since a large aspect of Joyce's artistic economy in *Portrait* is to dramatize other characters only insofar as they reveal important truths about Stephen's artist-ness, we may assume that Joyce makes Mrs. Dedalus more or less shadowy, seemingly anonymous in her lack of three-dimensionality, to indicate a deep strain of narcissistic self absorption (and hostile dependency) in his young man.

2. A Swoon of Sin

As Stephen grows older, he continues to respond to his mother in an essentially self-engrossed way. He experiences her, in the words of Peter Blos in another context, as the "active dispenser of frustration or comfort."[2] Basically, Stephen wants only to receive—to feel that all her care is given to him. Upon winning an "exhibition," an essay prize, he does appear to give of himself to her in early adolescence, treating his mother (and his similarly anonymous siblings) to meals, the theater, groceries, delicacies, dried fruit, and other presents. However, we sense that he is still trying to evoke his mother's pleasurable reaction for his own good. There is very little genuine kindness and empathy in his behavior. Mrs. Dedalus's delight in his academic achievements gives Stephen a feeling of well-being. He now knows how to draw these responses from his mother, but his aim is still a passive and narcissistic one—to receive her love, to bask in her pleasure in him.

At the time of his adolescent "swoon of sin," Stephen repeats this mother-and-son relationship with the prostitute. Deep-seated passive wishes appear to be more powerful than any active element in his sexuality. In nighttown, he is attempting to satisfy a genital longing that Joyce describes as a baffled prowling beast (*Portrait*, p. 112). Stephen arranges things so that he might be held and caressed, much as the prostitute might hold and caress the huge silent doll that she placed seated in an armchair beside her bed:

> Her round arms held him firmly to her and he, seeing her face lifted to him in serious calm and feeling the warm calm rise and fall of her breast, all but burst into hysterical weeping. Tears of joy and relief shone in his delighted eyes and his lips parted though they would not speak. She passed her tinkling hand through his hair, calling him a little rascal.
> —Give me a kiss, she said.
> His lips would not bend to kiss her. He wanted to be held firmly in

---

[2] Peter Blos, *On Adolescence* (New York: The Free Press of Glencoe, 1963), p. 21.

her arms, to be caressed slowly, slowly, slowly. In her arms he felt that he had suddenly become strong and, fearless and sure of himself. But his lips would not bend to kiss her.
(*Portrait*, pp. 113-114)

Stephen, we remember, did not know how to answer the question put to him by his taunting classmates years earlier, "Tell us, Dedalus, do you kiss your mother before you go to bed?" (*Portrait*, p. 10). To answer "yes" would imply that he was still a baby, but "no" would imply that he was withholding love or was unloving. Here, Stephen is still frozen and unbending, yet we begin to feel that throughout his life he wants to be kissed, to be loved. Self-absorbed dependency is very strong indeed in this little rascal at the warmly rising, calmly falling breast. Like a mother as she is perceived by her infant, the prostitute is the source of physical warmth, pleasurable skin sensations, gentle soothing and cuddling; and like a very young child cradled firmly by round arms, Stephen finds that those bodily sensations are inseparable from the fulfillment of pervasive longings for security and assurance, for bolstered self-esteem, independence, and omnipotence. This experience of undifferentiated physical and psychological pleasure—of feeling strong, fearless, and sure of himself in her arms—culminates in oblivion: the glorious bliss that one associates with the satiated infant at the breast:

It was too much for him. He closed his eyes, surrendering himself to her, body and mind, conscious of nothing in the world but the dark pressure of her softly parting lips. They pressed upon his brain as upon his lips as though they were the vehicle of a vague speech; and between them he felt an unknown and timid pressure, darker than the swoon of sin, softer than sound or odour. (*Portrait*, p.114)

There is a complex relationship with a motherly presence here. Although Stephen holds himself aloof and will neither speak to the prostitute nor kiss her, it is clear that with *his* parted lips he hopes to encourage her to part *her* lips and to give him the pleasure available through the activities of her tongue, lips, and mouth. Actively receptive—anxious yet eager to be penetrated—Stephen, it seems, is experiencing as much delight in oral, as in genital, satisfaction in this relationship with a maternal figure. He is also learning a somewhat different mother tongue—the "vague" speech of his sexuality—from this later version of his mother. Finally, he feels the "unknown and timid pressure" of a dark softness that enters him between lips that may be regarded as either his or hers because of the ambiguous "them." At the climactic moment, Stephen appears to have become a sexually initiated young woman as well as a young man. For an instant, at least, he seems to be something like a youthful version of what we will hear Leopold Bloom called in Chapter III, a "new womanly man."[3]

When Stephen goes to the university, he still regards his mother as the active dispenser of emotional sustenance and comfort, a major source of strength, fearlessness, and self-assurance whom his lips will not bend to kiss. Not novelistically alive, not well-rounded, in the sense of being endowed with an active emotional, psychological, and social life (by either Joyce or Stephen), she becomes one of Stephen's earliest creations, someone who satisfies his deepest needs. In the manner of a young child, he feels that he and she still comprise some sort of unspoken unity. To him, anyone or anything, including his faith, that interferes with her availability at a moment of need, is a dangerous intrusion. Gradually, whatever gets between the child-turned-undergraduate and his mother becomes the target of his aggressive impulses. Stephen's angry possessiveness—and his defense against it with serene dutifulness—becomes clear at the time of his mother's opposition to his educational plans. Mrs. Dedalus apparently hoped that he would choose the seminary:

> Yes, his mother was hostile to the idea, as he had read from her listless silence. Yet her mistrust pricked him more keenly than his father's pride and he thought coldly how he had watched the faith

---

[3] James Joyce, Ulysses (Paris: Shakespeare and Company, 1926), p. 466. Subsequent references will appear in the text and refer to this edition. We will explore Stephen's wish to be at one with his mother—and with maternal figures—in the next chapter.

which was fading down in his soul ageing and strengthening in her eyes. A dim antagonism gathered force within him and darkened his mind as a cloud against her disloyalty: and when it passed, cloud-like, leaving his mind serene and dutiful towards her again, he was made aware dimly and without regret of a first noiseless sundering of their lives. (*Portrait*, p. 191)

The oedipal connotations are clear, to be sure. The young man resents whatever intrudes on his fantasy that he and his mother are at one with each other—that there *was* a kind of mystical union that has now been noiselessly sundered. But there is more than an echo of an early form of a triangular relationship. The harshness of such phrases as "mistrust," "disloyalty," and "dim antagonism"—together with Stephen's feeling that his life and his mother's had been merged—suggests the presence of pre-oedipal, as well as oedipal, elements in his relationship with her. The gathering thunderhead of antagonism within Stephen, hidden in his growing coldness, hints at barely suppressed narcissistic rage at his mother's mistrust and disloyalty, her failure to sustain him perfectly by mirroring him perfectly. His later refusal to fulfill her request that he do his Easter duty by confessing and taking communion also seems to contain unconscious retaliatory impulses for her supposed disloyalty, as well as the conscious desire to avoid the dark and ineffable consequences of paying "false homage to a symbol behind which are massed twenty centuries of authority and veneration" (*Portrait*, p. 287).

It seems that Stephen's long-suffering mother comes alive for him *only* when she mirrors him, when she reflects and reinforces his emerging identity as an artist-to-be. She ceases to be alive for him—and a part of him seems to become lifeless as well—when she fails to support him in every way, when she opposes his increasing anti-clericalism. The "noiseless sundering" that he attributes to moral and spiritual differences between himself and his mother—this rending of what to him is an almost mystical union—hints at the psychological cost of the frustration of his very deep dependence on her. Going to the university against her wishes seems to have plunged him into the feelings of loneliness and abandonment that we will see more vividly in the next chapter where he experiences her loss as the loss of a part of himself. (Later, we will see how Joyce himself echoed Stephen's anxiety and depression when he felt in 1909 that Nora had betrayed him, had all but destroyed what he felt to be *their* transcendent oneness, because she had slept with others *before* they fled to Italy in 1904.)

3. The Virgin Womb of the Imagination

As a university student, Stephen's identification with another active, giving, and "good" mother resolves his anxiety temporarily. Joyce also implies that in large measure his young man becomes an artist by becoming one with a pure, idealized, virginal mother within himself. Put somewhat differently, the artist-to-be becomes conscious of his identification with the Virgin's womb—"the virgin womb of the imagination." During a moment of inspiration that comes to Stephen just before waking in his bed at home, the son feels he is nothing less than the Virgin Mother herself:

> His mind was waking slowly to a tremulous morning knowledge, a morning inspiration. A spirit filled him, pure as the purest water, sweet as dew, moving as music. But how faintly it was inbreathed, how passionlessly, as if the seraphim themselves were breathing upon him!...The instant of inspiration....flashed forth like a point of light and now from cloud on cloud of vague circumstance confused form was veiling softly its afterglow. O! In the virgin womb of the imagination the word was made flesh. Gabriel the seraph had come to the virgin's chamber. (*Portrait*, pp. 254-255)

In contrast to the delightfully garrulous and increasingly hapless father, the more or less wordless mother *is* "absent" in *Portrait*; but Joyce's imagery allows us to see how Mrs. Dedalus has played a crucial, if unwitting, role in the gestation of her son's artist soul. Identified with a highly idealized, highly mythicized version of his mother—feeling that he *is* the Blessed Mother's womb—he wakes inspired. Receiving what to Stephen seems to be divine inspiration, the ejaculation-like flashing forth of a point of light, he presses forth from the dewy womb of his imagination a Villanelle to the Temptress. It is far from being a technically brilliant performance, to be sure, but despite Joyce's mocking of Stephen's adolescent pretentiousness (the imagery of a wet dream is almost comically intrusive), we do get to read Stephen's first genuinely creative poetry:

> *Are you not weary of ardent ways*
> *Lure of the fallen seraphim?*
> *Tell no more of enchanted days. (Portrait,* p. 255)

At the novel's end, we can begin to perceive the full extent of Stephen's dependence on a loving protector, an idealized supplier of support and self-esteem. This time, the all-powerful, mythicized parent is Daedalus, the archetypal Artist in Greek mythology, whom Stephen invokes in the famous phrases I quoted earlier: "Old father, old artificer stand me now and forever in good stead" (*Portrait,* p. 299). Daedalus is meant to serve the same function as Mrs. Dedalus. Blended in with, or mirrored back by, either his mother or his mythic father—feeling that he exists in some sort of *unio mystica* with either figure—Stephen feels alive, vital, real.

4. Bloom Got Her So Cheap

There are other mothers in Joyce, of course. Like Mrs. Dedalus, Ellen Higgins, Leopold Bloom's mother, is inconspicuous too. In fact, physically she is totally absent. Wordless, all but a ghost, she died sometime before Leopold Bloom's father committed suicide. Again, with Mrs. Dedalus in mind, we may infer that the seeming anonymity of a mother paradoxically hints that her apparent absence will be momentous in her son's life. In Chapters III and IV, we will discover the ways Leopold Bloom, the "new womanly man," manages to reunite himself with her psychologically—and hilariously. In "Circe," where Bloom's unconscious fantasy life is presented as living theater, after he exclaims in Bella Cohen's brothel, "O, I so want to be a mother," he gives birth to "*eight male yellow and white children*" (*Ulysses*, pp. 466-467).

Lunita Laredo, Molly's Jewish mother, is spectral, too. We infer she died quite early in Molly's life, and her daughter is ambivalent about her. Molly is convinced that Bloom "got [her] so cheap" because of either the ambiguous taint of her mother's Jewishness, or the hint of sexual corruption, or both (*Ulysses*, p. 701).

As we read "Penelope," we see, again, that a child can find many ways to erase the pain of an absent mother or a maternal figure. Molly has taken into herself one of Lunita Laredo's defining characteristics, wondering whether she, like her mother, is somehow a fallen woman. But Molly's unconscious maternal identifications, like Bloom's and Stephen's, are also inseparable from her creativity. She has created a daughter, too, of course. But she also creates out of the virgin womb of her imagination. (Her birthday is, supposedly, the Virgin's[4].) There's a "touch of the artist" in Molly (just as there is in Bloom, according to Lenehan in the "Wandering Rocks" episode of *Ulysses*, p. 225). Not only does she sing on concert tours with Blazes Boylan, but she also sings her own heart-stopping version of one of the most touching leitmotifs in *Ulysses*—"Love's Own Sweet Song."

In "Penelope," as does her husband in "Lestrygonians," she recreates in moving, lyrically effervescent prose poetry the scene on Howth Head, sixteen years earlier, in 1888, when she gave Poldy a bit of seedcake out of her mouth as they plighted their troth. Feeding her lover as a mother bird feeds her young and as Eve fed the lover whose blood was hers— Richard Ellmann reminds us that in *Finnegans Wake* the apple in the Garden is referred to as "seedfruit"[5]—Joyce seems to be implying that Molly is doing what Stephen believes the artist does: she is recreating life out of life (*Portrait*, p. 200). Filled with the memory of love, Molly is rebearing Dante's "Earthly Paradise,"[6] a timeless time (or no-o'clock, the

---

[4] Don Gifford and Robert J. Seidman, *Notes for Joyce: An Annotation of James Joyce's Ulysses* (New York: E. P. Dutton & Co., Inc., 1974), p. 142.

[5] Richard Ellmann, *Ulysses on the Liffey* (New York: Oxford University Press, 1972), p. 169.

[6] *Ibid.*

"time" of "Penelope") where there is no sin. It is love, for Joyce, not just deprivation and despair, that "empowers the imagination to overcome time."[7]

Although Stephen at the end of *Portrait* is exultant about his impending flight from his homeland—an Icarus-like flight it turns out—he is not filled with this kind of love. In fact, he will remember in *Ulysses* his mother's wish that someday he might learn the word all men know (but he doesn't)—the word love, presumably. Yet despite his lovelessness (which is painfully obvious in the "Telemachiad"), Joyce allows us to infer that in the near future Stephen will learn the word that empowers the imagination (joined with memory) to make time past both timeless and radiantly alive.

The final "words" in *Portrait* are "Dublin 1904," and then, underneath, "Trieste 1914." Most readers assume that Joyce wrote them, his signature, his implicit assertion that he began the book in Dublin in 1904 (where he did begin revising the manuscript, *Stephen Hero*). He took this manuscript with him and Nora Barnacle into exile and completed it (as he vowed to do) in a decade, publishing it (serially) in *The Egoist* as the Great War began. But it is also possible to read these dates as Stephen's final diary entries. Joyce could very well be implying that a Stephen-Icarus version of himself somehow arose from the failure of his first flight as Daedalus's son, a doomed, premature attempt to soar to the sun, past the bird-destroying "nets" of "nationality, language, religion" (*Portrait*, p. 238). By 1914, it was clear that he had recovered from his fall, due, perhaps, to a new found ability to love and to be loved that flowered in Trieste in 1904 and afterward. And that gift (which Molly celebrates so rapturously) allowed him to become James Joyce—to write and to publish a mythicized autobiography.

If we assume that both interpretations of the last words of *Portrait* are possible, we can say that Stephen and Joyce are blended at the end of the book, collaborating in the creation of Stephen's Daedalean nature. "Stephen Dedalus" is not a symbol invented by Stephen such as the "angel of mortal youth and beauty" that he makes out of the wading

---

[7] *Ibid.* p. 174

Dublin girl at the end of Chapter IV of *Portrait*. With his strange last name, Joyce is objectifying the fact that for Stephen, as for Joyce, the artistic calling *is* a calling, a voice coming from beyond, resounding down through the generations from his Greek father, Daedalus, to his curiously maternal father, Simon Dedalus, and, finally, into the ear of another artist-to-be, on another labyrinthine island, this one located in the Irish Sea.

In the next chapter, we will examine in *Ulysses* the recurrent rhythm in Stephen's life that we have seen in *Portrait*—a fall springing from the loss of a mother (this time to death) that is also something close to a *felix culpa,* a fortunate fall, in his partial recovery of her in other maternal images and objects.

CHAPTER II

Stephen's Mothers in *Ulysses*: Notes Toward the Autobiography of James Joyce

> He watched her pour into the measure and thence into the jug rich white milk, not hers. Old shrunken paps. She poured again a measureful and a tilly. Old and secret she had entered from a morning world, maybe a messenger. She praised the goodness of the milk, pouring it out. Crouching by a patient cow at daybreak in the lush field, a witch on her toadstool, her wrinkled fingers quick at the squirting dugs. They lowed about her whom they knew, dewsilky cattle. Silk of the kine and poor old woman, names given her in old times.
> —"Telemachus" (*Ulysses*, p. 14)

In his self-mocking yet highly serious discourse on Shakespeare in "Scylla and Charybdis," Stephen Dedalus says, "*Amor matris*, subjective and objective genitive, may be the only true thing in life" (*Ulysses*, p. 199). The translation of the Latin, "love of the mother," is ambiguous for Stephen. It could mean the mother's love for her child (subjective), or the child's love for his mother (objective), or both. But despite the ambiguity, Stephen seems ready to agree with Cranly's assertion in Chapter V of *Portrait*, "—Whatever else is unsure in this stinking dunghill of a world a mother's love is not" (*Portrait*, p. 285).

Amor matris takes on a striking immediacy in "Nestor," when Stephen mothers a graceless, physically weak pupil with his lessons. Seeing himself in Cyril Sargent, Stephen thinks of the boy's mother: "She had loved his weak watery blood drained from her own. Was that then real?" (*Ulysses*, p. 28). Somewhat later he muses, "*Amor matris*: subjective and objective genitive. With her weak blood and wheysour milk she had fed him and hid from sight of others his swaddling bands" (*Ulysses*, p. 28).

Here, Stephen seems to regard "mother love" as proceeding from a literal enwombing to nursing to safeguarding her infant son's earliest days in the outer world. Her "love" for the child in her womb—the inseparability of her "weak blood" and that of the foetus in her placenta—reappears in another kind of fusion, the oneness between her "wheysour milk" and his sucking mouth as she feeds him at her breast.[8] The ambiguity of the phrase suggests that the love of the child for his mother is also the desire to exist in some sort of *unio mystica* with her, where the boundary between the child and the mother is dissolved. Perhaps the surest thing in this stinking dunhill of a world, not just for Stephen and Cranly but for Joyce himself, is a mother's capacity to enwomb her child, not just biologically but psychologically, and the child's psychological need to be enwombed, a wish that can last a lifetime. Richard Ellmann writes:

> In the letters he sent to Nora in that discomposed summer of 1909, there are many testimonies that Joyce longed to reconstitute in his relation with [Nora] the filial bond which his mother's death had broken. Explicitly he longs to make their relationship that of child and mother, as if the relationship of lovers was too remote. He covets an even more intimate dependence: 'O that I could nestle in your womb like a child born of your flesh and blood, be fed by your blood, sleep in the warm secret gloom of your body!'[9]

---

[8] Both Molly and Leopold Bloom seem be trying to re-experience a similar form of mother love in "Penelope." Molly remembers her "great breast of milk with Milly enough for two....I had to get him to suck them they were so hard he said it was sweeter and thicker than cows then he wanted to milk me into the tea" (*Ulysses*, pp. 708-709).

[9] Richard Ellmann, *James Joyce* (New York: Oxford University Press, 1965), p. 303.

Stephen's Mothers in *Ulysses*: Notes Toward the Autobiography of James Joyce

If we look closely at the maternal figures who flow, one after the other, through Stephen's mind in *Ulysses*, we will see that Joyce, by a repetition of images and the use of allusion and dramatic irony, is underscoring the theme of mother love in the phrase's double sense. He is implying, not only that Irish mothers often seek to enwomb their sons, to satisfy their every wish in what they hope is a totally selfless, totally loving way. He is also implying that there is a deep-seated wish in Stephen to recapture a state of primal unity with his mother, a Joycean wish for an even more intimate dependence than the relationship of lovers.[10] At the end of the chapter, I will again speculate on the psychological significance of Stephen's mothers to Joyce's own psychology on or about June 16, 1904. But now let me turn to Stephen's first maternal image.

We get a glimpse of his deep love for his mother—fleeting, to be sure—when Stephen remembers singing Yeats's "Who Goes with Fergus" to his dying mother, hoping to alleviate her suffering:

> A cloud began to cover the sun slowly, shadowing the bay in deeper green. It lay behind him, a bowl of bitter waters. Fergus' song: I sang it alone in the house, holding down the long dark chords. Her door was open: she wanted to hear my music. Silent with awe and pity I went to her bedside. She was crying in her wretched bed. For those words, Stephen: love's bitter mystery. Where now? (*Uysses*, p. 9)

Arising in a sickroom in Cabra in 1903, mother love unites for an instant a son's heart to his mother's in "silent awe and pity," her heart and breath to his. Through the "long dark chords," the mystery of lyric poetry itself, the pulsing chords seem to enter both of them simultaneously. Almost as if he were a mother singing a lullaby to her sick child, Stephen all but binds himself to the crying figure in the wretched bed as he weds love and memory to the poetic imagination. With mouth, lips, and tongue, he recreates the song from "The Countess Cathleen" that his mother longs to hear. As he refashions through his own art Yeats's

---

[10] Cf. Michael Balint, *The Basic Fault: Therapeutic Aspects of Regression* (London: Tavistock Publications Ltd. 1968), pp. 66-67.

song of comfort to the Countess (who has sold her soul so that her people might have food)—as the artist as a young man recreates life out of life for a loving audience of one—he momentarily repairs the breach in their union that her dying is sundering.

A year later, Stephen recaptures the oneness with his mother that his artful singing evoked. He blends memory, his eye for revealing detail, and his imagination until Mrs. Dedalus's soul all but appears before our eyes; we perceive her *"quidditas,"* her *"whatness"* (*Portrait,* p. 250). Where now? he asked. To Mulligan. she is "beastly dead," but to Stephen, recalling her past, she is alive *within him*, in his mind's eye, and thus inseparable from him. Stephen resurrects her in his imaginative (and loving) recreation of the everyday details of her everyday life. Just as Bloom and Molly, when they each recreated (in lyric prose-poetry) their moment of love on Howth sixteen years earlier, transforming a Dublin promontory into the Earthly Paradise, so too Stephen dramatizes Joyce's insight that despite love's bitterness, love does not die for those with a touch of the artist, for those who can imaginatively transform the mundane into something wondrous and strange—the ordinary into the extraordinary:

> Her secrets: old feather fans, tasselled dancecards powdered with a gaud of amber beads in her locked drawer. A birdcage hung in the sunny window of her house when she was a girl. She heard old Royce sing in the pantomime of Turko the terrible and laughed with others when he sang
>
> > *I am the boy*
> > *That can enjoy*
> > *Invisibility.*
>
> Phantasmal mirth, folded away: muskperfumed.
>
> > *And no more turn aside and brood*
>
> Folded away in the memory of nature with her toys. Memories beset his brooding brain. Her glass of water from the kitchen tap when she had approached the sacrament. A cored apple filled with brown sugar, roasting for her at the hob on a dark autumn evening. Her

Stephen's Mothers in Ulysses: Notes Toward the Autobiography of James Joyce

shapely fingernails reddened by the blood of squashed lice from the children's shirts. (*Ulysses,* p.10)

In his moving evocation of his mother's very soul as she lay dying, Stephen is actually offering us an example of what he meant by an epiphany—something he didn't offer Cranly—in his lecture on beauty in *Stephen Hero*. Here, in Stephen's beautifully observed images—the old feather fans and tasseled dance cards, the glass of water from the kitchen tap, and the cored apple roasted for her on the hob on a dark autumn evening—he deepens and enlarges our sense (and Lynch's) of the "*quidditas,*" the "*whatness of a* thing" that the artist can bring forth from the commonest objects.[11]

Another sign that Stephen is still emotionally fused with his mother, although she was buried almost one year before, is his sharp exchange with Buck Mulligan over Mulligan's wisecrack at the time of Mrs. Dedalus's death. We realize that for Stephen, Mrs. Dedalus was like the air to him—less a person than a life-sustaining, all-supporting environment that was inseparable from him and that he took completely for granted until it was gone. When Mulligan tells Stephen that he didn't mean to offend the memory of Mrs. Dedalus in his "*O, it's only Dedalus whose mother is beastly dead*" (*Ulysses,* p. 8), "Stephen, shielding the gaping wounds which the words had left in his heart, [says] very coldly:

—I am not thinking of the offence to my mother.
—Of what, then? Buck Mulligan asked.
—Of the offence to me, Stephen answered. (*Ulysses,* p. 9)

Stephen is offended not only because Mulligan has callously disregarded Stephen's feelings as a bereaved son but also because an offence to the mother is also an offence to the son if he feels that they are psychologically all but one. Joyce's image makes the very close tie between Stephen and his mother even more painfully clear. Her death *is* a death to him, a violent wrenching of his very being that leaves "gaping wounds in the heart."

---

[11] See Appendix, pp. 215 ff.

Joyce also reveals *amor matris*—Stephen's unwitting desire to remain inseparable from her—in another image of a heart-sickening wound. As he watches Mulligan dress a bit later, the phrase "agenbite of inwit" appears in his stream of consciousness—Middle English for "remorse of conscience"[12] (*Ulysses,* p. 17). Stephen's biting conscience gnaws on him in a dream:

> In a dream, silently, she had come to him, her wasted body within its loose graveclothes giving off an odour of wax and rosewood, her breath bent over him with mute secret words, a faint odour of wetted ashes. Her glazing eyes, staring out of death, to shake and bend my soul. On me alone. The ghostcandle to light her agony. Ghostly light on the tortured face. Her hoarse loud breath rattling in horror, while all prayed on their knees. Her eyes on me to strike me down.... Ghoul! Chewer of corpses! (*Ulysses,* p. 10)

Chewing on his deadened flesh, his now ghoulish mother becomes an endlessly hungry, tooth-filled mouth, all but feeding on him, an endless source of food (Stephen *is* depressed). In "Circe," the corpsechewer returns in a different guise. In Bella Cohen's brothel, where Joyce presents the unconscious world of his characters directly, dramatically, Stephen is fused with his dead mother, having exchanged identities with her. In his nightmare, his is the lifeless, cancer-ridden body bitten and devoured by murderous grinning claws. The astrological Cancer the Crab, punishing him for matricide, gnaws on his heart. Horribly bound to her pinching and clawing, Stephen seems to be linked forever to his mother in his guilt:

> STEPHEN
> (*Panting.*) The corpsechewer! Raw head and bloody bones!
> THE MOTHER
> (*Her face drawing near and nearer, sending out an ashen breath.*)

---

[12] Don Gifford and Richard J. Seidman, *Notes for Joyce: An Annotation of James Joyce's Ulysses* (New York: E. P. Dutton & Co., Inc., 1974), p. 13.

Beware! (*She raises her blackened, withered right arm slowly towards Stephen's breast with outstretched fingers.*) Beware! God's hand! (*A green crab with malignant red eyes sticks deep its grinning claws in Stephen's heart.*) (*Ulysses*, p. 544)

It is the offending organ, Stephen's unloving and thus murderous heart, that is ravaged by the vengeful Crab. In this horror, late at night, where *lex talionis* rules, Stephen is united with his mother as if he were still her baby in the womb.

We are presented with a metaphoric recapitulation of the problematic nature of Stephen's mother love, as well as a foreshadowing of the appearance of a second mother, as he faces the sea and gazes at the "fraying edge of his shiny black coatsleeve" (*Ulysses*, p.5):

Pain, that was not yet the pain of love, fretted his heart... Across the threadbare cuffedge he saw the sea hailed as a great sweet mother by the wellfed voice beside him. The ring of bay and skyline held a dull green mass of liquid. A bowl of white china had stood beside her deathbed holding the green sluggish bile which she had torn up from her rotting liver by fits of loud groaning vomiting. (*Ulysses*, pp. 5-6)

If we return to Stephen's poignant "Where now?"—the question he asks when he recalls his mother crying at the words "love's bitter mystery" from Yeats's song—we may say that the mother who once stirred love in him because of her love for him is not dead; she is as close as the sea, that ancient maternal symbol. Put somewhat differently, for Joyce, a mother's love for her son is as true, sure, and timeless as the sea—and as frightening, since she can die and her love can die with her.[13]

In fact, a motherly creature is approaching the Martello tower at this very moment—a nameless old milkwoman who, to a son who has lost

---

[13] Even before her death, Stephen seems frightened by the sea—"A faint click at his heart, a faint throb in his throat told him once more how his flesh dreaded the cold infrahuman odour of the sea" (*Portrait*, p. 194).

mother love, is at first glance decidedly empty of the milk of human kindness: "He watched her pour into the measure and thence into the jug rich white milk, not hers. Old shrunken paps" (*Ulysses*, p. 14). Before Stephen can find a loving mother in this world—someone who will enwomb him psychologically and whom he can enwomb in song and poetry—he will need to free himself from the pain of the loss which frets his heart, a feeling of abandonment that often causes him to view maternal figures as creatures he can too quickly scorn.

In Joyce's metaphors, Stephen's guilt—the "threadbare cuffedge" of his "shiny black coat-sleeve," the suit of mourning (which is really melancholy) that he has been wearing for almost a year—blocks his view of the sea. It stands between him and a mysterious power that supports one's weight effortlessly, a fluid medium that has no sharp boundaries separating the individual from it.[14] Filled with overwhelming feelings of self-hating remorse, displacement, and homelessness, he can only view the sea—and other maternal images—in the light of the dying Mrs. Dedalus. Her "bowl of white china" holding "green sluggish bile" becomes the "dull green mass of liquid" in Dublin bay. No wonder Stephen is uneasy in the presence of the old milkwoman, asking whether she, like the ghost of Mrs. Dedalus, is there to "upbraid" (*Ulysses*, p. 14).

2. Silk of the Kine

The milkwoman, however, is not only old shrunken paps, someone from whom, at first, Stephen "scorned to beg...favour" (*Ulysses*, p. 14). Joyce immediately also asks us to see her connection to the theme of mother love. As soon as she enters the dark room, she comes forward to stand at Stephen's elbow. Standing next to Stephen-Telemachus—next to a dispossessed son? a prince?—she seems to bring light out of the lair-like darkness: "That's a lovely morning, sir.... Glory be to God" (*Ulysses*, p. 13). But the most obvious echo of *amor matris* is her gift for nourishing and sustaining thirsty sons. She generously pours out "rich, white milk"—a "measureful and a tilly" (*Ulysses*, p. 13). Apparently, as we have

---

[14] Cf. Balint, *op. cit.*, pp. 67-72.

seen before, she strikes such easy, natural relations with the cows that to Stephen her supply seems inexhaustible: "Crouching by a patient cow at daybreak in the lush field, a witch on her toadstool, her wrinkled fingers quick at the squirting dugs. They lowed about her whom they knew, dewsilky cattle" (*Ulysses*, p. 14).

Endowed by Stephen with his mother's characteristics, Joyce implies that the milkwoman is some sort of second mother. As the nameless woman with shrunken paps and wrinkled fingers "bows her old head" to a "voice that speaks to her loudly, her bonesetter, her medicineman" and to 'the voice that will shrive and oil" her, the milkwoman seems to be the transmigrating soul of the dying Mrs. Dedalus, surrounded by doctor and priest (*Ulysses*, p. 14). Her pious praise of God; her nationalistic delight in Gaelic (a language she doesn't know); her generosity with shillings—all these qualities recall Stephen's mother, too.

To Stephen's mythicizing mind, she is another kind of mother as well. "Silk of the kine and poor old woman, names given her in olden times," he thinks to himself—traditional epithets for Ireland (*Ulysses*, p. 14). She is "silk of the kine"—the most beautiful of cattle—and she is a "poor old woman" in appearance only. In folklore and legend, Ireland looks poor and unattractive to all but those who truly love her. To them, she looks like a young girl with the walk of a queen.[15]

The milkwoman is not simply the Motherland, though. She is the Motherland betrayed, "A wondering crone, lowly form of an immortal, serving the conqueror and her gay betrayer, their common cuckquean" (*Ulysses*, p. 14). As Stephen knows, her supposed lovers have betrayed Ireland, as a female cuckold, for centuries. As an impoverished queen surrounded by false lovers, she also is Penelope. If we assume that *amor matris* is a true thing in this world, then Ireland's true lover, her artist-son in waiting, is standing nearby (though as a dispossessed and betrayed Telemachus he is not yet ready to celebrate her).

Stephen-Telemachus is drawn to this common yet queenly cuckquean, this woman in disguise who is profoundly maternal, fundamentally regal, and archetypically Irish. As I mentioned earlier, he

---

[15] Gifford and Seidman, *op.cit.*, p.12.

"scorned to beg her favour," yet he seems to want her favour (*Ulysses*, p. 14). He listens in "scornful silence" as she bows her head to Mulligan's boisterous voice, yet he thinks to himself "me she slights" (*Ulysses*, p. 14). He seems to pity her, too, when he refers to her as "that poor old creature" (*Ulysses*, p. 16). To be sure, this hint of attraction—this mix of scorn, awe, and pity—is not the mother love, the enwombing fusion, which Stephen regularly yearns for. But Joyce does imply that the potential for such a fusion exists within Stephen. He seems destined by his very nature as an artist-to-be to recreate life out of life—to carry dear, dirty Dublin within his imagination for a lifetime and, projecting it out into the world, to reveal (in beautifully wrought prose-poetry) that the poor old woman is also the silk of the kine.

Joyce underscores the significance of Stephen's relationship with the milkwoman with another series of images. In a mocking discussion of her, Mulligan tells Stephen, "You put your hoof in it now" (*Ulysses*, p. 16). Later in the morning, bearing Mr. Deasy's letter about the foot and mouth disease, Stephen muses to himself that Mulligan will probably dub him the "bullock-befriending bard" (*Ulysses*, p. 35). For Joyce, Stephen really does know his way around Irish cattle. Silk of the kine—the most beautiful of cows—would only breed with the most prized of bulls, and Stephen is linked many times with bulls. In 'Scylla and Charybdis," he recalls the epithet his classmates chanted at him as he walked toward The Bull, the sea, and the full realization of his artistic calling in Chapter IV of *Portrait*: "*Bous Stephanoumenos*," they cried out in schoolboy Greek—Stephen of the bull-soul (*Portrait*, p. 196).[16] They then added, "*Bous Stephaneforos*"—"the ox as garland-bearer for sacrifice" (*Portrait*, p. 196).[17]

Stephen *is* a garland-bearing, sacrificial bull, at least in his soul. Of course, he will not realize this, the fate of those who sing truly of the poor old woman, until by metempsychosis he merges with Joyce's soul

---

[16] Don Gifford, *Joyce Annotated: Notes for Dubliners and Portrait of the Artist as a Young Man*, 2nd ed. revised and enlarged (Berkeley: University of California Press, 1982), p. 220.

[17] *Ibid.*

and tries to publish *Dubliners*. With constant rejections, attempts at censorship, and delays from his would-be publishers, Joyce will feel that he has been all but sacrificed to the narrow-minded conventionality of the Irish tribe.

Yet the bull-souled artist-to-be will also experience the joy of union with a noble creature, a queen, no less, who isn't disguised as a poor old woman. In "Circe," he remembers that Queen Pasiphaë, placed inside Daedalus's wooden cow, had sexual intercourse with the prize bull that Poseidon gave King Minos of Crete: "*Et exaltabuntur cornua iusti*. ["And the horns of the righteous *shall* be exalted"[18]] Queens lay with prize bulls. Remember Pasiphaë for whose lust my grandoldgrossfather made the first confession box" (*Ulysses*, p. 533).

One day, Joyce seems to be implying, Stephen of the bull-soul shall be exalted. Like Poseidon's gift, he is the prize bull (as yet unrecognized) of an ancient island kingdom. When he finds a way to avoid the self-sacrifice of his crippling despair, lovelessness, and guilt, he will, perhaps, fulfill his high destiny. United with the silk of the kine, the beautiful cow that is also an embodiment of Ireland and a lusty queen, he will exchange the garland of a ritualized death for the victor's laurel. The union of Poseidon's garland-bearing bull and Pasiphaë, we remember, issued first in the child-devouring Minatour but ultimately in the labyrinth. And that cunning art is as much Joyce's as Daedalus's. It holds blood-lusting hatred at bay, reduces its terror and destructiveness, and brings light out of darkness—forms of joyful life out of various kinds of death.

This union will take place some time past June 16, 1904. Early in the morning, Stephen faces a morally problematic mother, a creature who is being milked for an extra shilling or two. But when this day is over, the milkwoman—or her avatar—will re-appear. In the next section we will see that in the beautiful cow and lusty queen—in Molly Bloom's womb of the imagination—Stephen (inseparable from Leopold Bloom as well) will nestle, the two of them fused with each other and with Molly in some sort of eternal *unio mystica*.

---

[18] Gifford and Seidman. *op.cit.*, p. 421.

3. A Great Breast of Milk

Joyce takes pains to show us that his final mater—the singer of the Yes-filled rhapsody that concludes *Ulysses*—is truly none of your lean kine. She is the most dewsilky creature, true silk of the kine. Molly is pleased she was the source of rich milk for her child and husband, as well as for the child-in-the-husband:

> I had a great breast of milk...enough for two what was the reason of that he said I could have got a pound a week as a wet nurse all swelled out...hurt me they used to...he said it was sweeter and thicker than cows...and it was so much smoother the skin much an hour he was at them Im sure by the clock like some kind of big infant I had at me they want everything in their mouth...I can feel his mouth (*Ulysses*, pp. 708-709)

A woman who gives milk bountifully, she is the reincarnation of the milkwoman in other ways, too. Worrying about being "an old shrivelled hag" and squatting to urinate on the undersized one-handled "chamber," she recalls the old crone crouching on her toadstool in the early morning (*Ulysses*, p. 730). Molly also has the "lowly form of an immortal." She is, after all, not just the eternal Weib on a lumpy, old jingly bed in 7 Eccles street. She is also the Virgin (her birthday, September 8, is also Mary's, and the eight sentence-paragraphs of Molly's soliloquy underline the connection). Again, like the milkwoman, she is old (or at least worried about becoming old), yet she is young at thirty-four (though not young enough: she takes a year off her age). She is poor yet queenly, the common cuckquean of a conqueror and gay betrayer (Buck Mulligan), and she is also Penelope faithfully awaiting her true love, her Ulysses as he was sixteen years earlier, the one man who could make her feel she was embraced in her true radiance.

But perhaps the most important similarity between this swelled-out woman and the woman with the milk jug is their instinctive mothering of Stephen. Just as the milkwoman seemed to move naturally to Stephen's side (an echo, perhaps, of Pallas Athena mentoring Telemachus), so Molly unites herself with him out of mother love. She thinks of him first as a son—"Simon Dedalus son"—and recalls seeing him eleven years earlier at the time of her own son's death (*Ulysses,* p. 722). When we remember that Stephen was eleven at the time of Rudy's death, Molly's syntax and ambiguous pronoun reference all but make Stephen synonymous with Rudy: "I saw him driving down to the Kingsbridge station with his father and mother I was in mourning thats 11 years ago now yes hed be 11" (*Ulysses,* p. 727). She loves Stephen as an "innocent boy," "a darling little fellow in his lord Fauntleroy suit and curly hair like a prince on the stage" (*Ulysses* pp. 727-728). She also blends herself in with him as a young poet: "Im sure itll be grand if I can only get in with a handsome young poet at my age" (*Ulysses,* p. 729). In fact, Molly enfolds Stephen within herself because of his gift for language and song: "I can tell the Spanish and he tell me the Italian" (*Ulysses,* p. 732); "we can have music and cigarettes I can accompany him first I must clean the keys of the piano with milk" (*Ulysses,* p. 734).

Joyce's syntax deepens our sense of *amor matris,* subjective genitive, as well. The long quasi-paragraph of prose poetry in which Molly fantasizes about a life with Stephen is the penultimate one in her monologue, the seventh. Devoted to her insides, especially to her womb, it begins "who knows is there anything the matter with my insides or have I something growing in me" (*Ulysses,* p. 723). While she is menstruating, Stephen is paradoxically growing inside her. Joyce's paradox suggests that Molly is creating Stephen, feeding him with the blood of her womblike imagination. She is sustaining him with milk, too, for that matter, milk for the piano keys that will unite them in song (like the song that momentarily united Stephen with his dying mother). As I have mentioned, Stephen is not the only one gestating in Molly. She can produce milk "enough for two" (*Ulysses,* p 709). Penelope's womb also contains the "childman weary" (Bloom), her Ulysses curled up in a foetal position at the foot of the bed (*Ulysses,* p. 692). But Poldy (Bloom-Ulysses) seems to blend with Stephen in Molly's enfolding mother-love. The childman, weary after his Dublin odyssey, is also the "manchild in the womb" (*Ulysses,* p. 692), Bloom-and-Stephen. In "Ithaca," Joyce has his own phrases for this fusion: "Stoom," Stephen fused with Bloom, or

"Blephen," Bloom fused with Stephen (*Ulysses*. p. 639). As I said earlier, since no clear time is assigned to her soliloquy, we may say it is "no o'clock."[19] Molly is carrying Blephen with her into eternity.

It seems that *amor matris*, subjective genitive, is the only true thing in life—and out beyond life, too, in the "everchanging tracks of neverchanging space" (*Ulysses* p. 692). (For Dante—Joyce's favorite poet, aside from Shakespeare—love was at the heart of the universe as well.) But what about mother love, objective genitive? Is Stephen prepared to do something to gain entry into the dark realm of timelessness and spacelessness that is Molly's dreamy imagination? Is Joyce hinting that it is not his Ulysses but his homeless son who will find a new path home?

In "Circe," Joyce tells us in his stage-directions that Stephen brings himself out of time as he cries "Nothung!" and smashes the chimney of the gas-jet: "(*He lifts his ashplant high with both hands and smashes the chandelier. Time's livid final flame leaps and, in the following darkness, ruin of all space and toppling masonry.)*" (*Ulysses*, p. 545). Stephen himself is combining images from Blake—time's livid final flame at the dawn of eternity—with a vision of the fall of Troy (shattered glass and toppling masonry).[20] But at midnight, in Bella Cohen's brothel, *Joyce's* use of the symbolism suggests that, in actuality, Stephen is bringing about a new world, a world associated with Blakean timelessness. "Every Mortal loss is an immortal gain. The ruins of Time build mansions in Eternity," Blake wrote in his famous letter to William Haley in 1800.[21] Joyce might be implying that Stephen, that mythicized version of his youthful self, is in the process of converting the deadening loss of a mother to an immortal gain, a future in the womb-imagination of an eternal Weib, a suitor-defying, language-blessed Penelope.

"*Nothung*" or "Needful," the magic sword planted in an ash-tree in Wagner's *Ring*, shatters in Siegmund's hands but is reforged by the son, Siegfried, because the son is fearless.[22] Stephen yearns to be fearless

---

[19] Richard Ellmann, *Ulysses on the Liffey* (New York: Oxford University Press, 1972), p. 163.
[20] Gifford and Seidman, *op.cit*., p. 425.
[21] *Ibid.*
[22] *Ibid.*

(despite being needful) by the end of the day. Facing the vengeful ghost of his mother—conscious of his unconscious and murderous self-hatred—he first cries, *"Non serviam!"* and then," No! No! No! Break my spirit all of you if you can! I'll bring you all to heel!" (*Ulysses*, p. 545). Joyce seems to be asking us to infer that as the livid final flame of June 16, 1904, leaps, Stephen may no longer be so paralyzed by matricidal guilt as he was before. Bringing that inner Fury to heel, he is capable of a more or less guiltless aggressiveness symbolized by his gesture with his ashplant. He is also capable of another kind of aggression that for Joyce is both adult and honorable. In his fight with Privates Carr and Compton, he affirms that he will fight outer and inner oppression—Blake's "priest" and "king" (*Ulysses*, p. 589)—with his mind rather than with physical violence. (In his memorable phrases, he tells Cranly that the only arms he will allow himself to use are "silence, exile, and cunning" (*Portrait*, p. 291).

This hard-won power in Stephen—the phallic assertiveness that does not need to brutalize the beloved (as Blazes Boylan brutalizes Molly in her memory of intercourse with him earlier in the day) or to degrade the enemy (as the Citizen tries to degrade Bloom in "Cyclops")—this hard-won power suggests he might be on the way to feeling that he is not only a hapless son, a betrayed, dispossessed Telemachus. Echoing Stephen's own delight in high literary speculation, we may enlarge his important question in "Scylla and Charybdis," "can the son who has not a father be a son?" (*Ulysses*, p. 199). We may ask, "Can a son who has neither a father nor a mother be a son?" Since "paternity may be a legal fiction" for Stephen (*Ulysses*, p. 199)—there seems to be very little patricidal guilt in Stephen, though there is shame—and since his mother may very well cease being the intensely guilt-producing presence she once was, Stephen has neither father nor mother. No longer only an inhibited, embittered, displaced son, he is the son-becoming-man, still enlivened by mother love but, like Telemachus, ready to return to his rightful place in his mythic father's house in Eccles street.

At midnight, when Stephen offers his final version of Aesop's riddle about the fox burying his grandmother, we see most clearly the new path he will take to the mother in the future. Throughout the day, skulking, roaming Stephen, like the dog-fox-pard on Sandymount strand, is a tattered mongrel digging in the ground. Stephen, like the mongrel, is also "looking for something lost in a past life," but for Stephen it is a maternal figure he has buried (*Ulysses*, p. 45). Rooting furiously in the sand, the dog-fox-pard is "vulturing the dead," according to Stephen (*Ulysses*, p. 46). One way to recapture that lost unity with a slain mother is to vulture the dead—a species of cannibalism where he chews on the corpse but, in the very eating, loses the loved-hated object. But by the end of the day, Stephen perhaps is close to realizing that feeding on his mother in his matricidal guilt—as she simultaneously feeds on him in his self-murderousness—is fruitless. In "Circe," he chants this riddle:

> The fox crew, the cocks flew
> The bells in heaven
> Were striking eleven
> 'Tis time for her poor soul
> To get out of heaven. (*Ulysses*, p. 523)

Foxes are now cocks; different kinds of cocks are surly flying about in Bella-Circe's brothel; and a poor soul is implored to get down to nighttown—now. Surrounded by this dizzying, ringing (and comically uproarious) phallicism, Stephen gives the answer to the riddle: "Thirsty fox...Burying his grandmother. Probably he killed her" (*Ulysses*, p. 524). Like the fox in the fable, thirsty Stephen has been unable to reach the grapes that would satisfy him by vulturing the dead. He seems just about ready to say he will foreswear those grapes anyway, since they were probably sour—or ashen. Armed with a potent ashplant and a lyric voice, Stephen, we may infer, is ready to discover that the truly succulent fruit is near at hand—in one of Dublin's "poor souls" who somehow got out of the heaven of the Virgin Mother, a maternal figure who is down to earth, not in it.[23]

---

[23] Bloom, we learn in "Penelope" (and in "Circe," too), adores everything about Molly's melony buttocks. In "Calpyso," recalling old acquaintances, Citron and Mastiansky, and Jaffa, too, he associates her with all the fruit of the Promised Land: "Oranges... Citrons....

Stephen's Mothers in Ulysses: Notes Toward the Autobiography of James Joyce

4. Vulturing the Dead

Molly, of course, is the great maternal figure in *Ulysses*. Born, as I have mentioned, on what to some is Mary's birthday, September 8—Bloom recalls, "For her birthday perhaps. Junejulyaugseptember eighth" (*Ulysses*, p. 160)—she muses about Stephen and Bloom throughout the night and on into June 17. She is weaving, in the virgin womb of *her* imagination, a Penelope-like web of reminiscence, longing, and desire. A son-and-pard, Blephen or Stoom, is the creature in the womb-imagination of the woman who is not only the reincarnation of Mary-Penelope but Gea-Tellus. The thirsty son at eleven in the morning is inseparable from the man who moves with the "Step of a [gentle] pard" late at night (*Ulysses*, p. 209). Within her womb-imagination, then, we have a Dublin, 1904, version of the Son consubstantial with the Father, a son-and-father comprising one person. (I will develop this theme in Chapters V and VI.)

Almost as if to underscore their consubstantiality, Joyce tells us that "Stephen then Bloom, in penumbra urinated" with their gazes "elevated to the projected luminous and semiluminous shadow" of Molly on the roller blind screen (*Ulysses*, p. 659). We are being asked to recall that the thirsty dog-fox-pard in "Proteus" urinated before he "delved" in the sand for his grandmother-mother (*Ulysses*, p. 46). Joyce is also asking us to recall that at the end of "Proteus," Stephen urinated and "took the hilt of his ashplant, lung[ed] with it softly [in the sand], dallying still" (*Ulysses*, p. 49). Delving and dalliance rather than the earlier form of attention-getting spraying may eventually bring the dog-fox-son-pard inside this final mother who is not just down to earth but, as Gea-Tellus, is synonymous with it. Put somewhat differently, mirroring a kindly and protective and assertive father (Bloom saves Stephen from a beating in Bella Cohen's), Stephen, we may infer, will someday discover his capacity to be a loving man with an unbudging moral authority within.

To be sure, Joyce does not describe Stephen regaining any womb phallically in *Ulysses*, but he does know from his own experience that a

---

Molly in Citron's basketchair. Nice to hold, cool waxen fruit, hold in the hand, lift it to the nostrils and smell the perfume" (*Ulysses*, p. 60).

talented son who feels dispossessed, lonely, and betrayed—a son who was often treated as a prince by his mother—can shed his Telemachus-like self. Sometime past June 16, 1904, the date of his first promenade with Nora Barnacle, Joyce said that Nora "made me a man."[24]

Let me conclude this chapter by continuing to use the bold, autobiographical-biographical criticism that Stephen used in his interpretation of *Hamlet* (and that Joyce enjoyed using as well). We may infer that in Stephen's mothers, Joyce is fictionalizing, among many other things, a true and sure thing, a perennial rhythm, in his own life, *amor matris*, subjective and objective genitive. Is it wildly speculative to assume that with the painful death of his mother, Joyce became convinced. at least unconsciously, that he had killed this embodiment of intense, even excessive, mother love by his refusal to be the Catholic she wanted him to be—to confess, to take communion, perhaps to become a priest? He might very well have felt that he was a "woman-killer" in Nora's reproachful phrase.[25]

Recreating life out life—recreating artistic life out of his own unconscious life—Joyce perhaps understood how quickly one could project one's own murderousness onto a mother who seemed to die on you. It seems he knew from the inside that Stephen would feel that THE MOTHER is the destroyer; *she,* not he, is the woman-killer. Again, from his own uncanny understanding of his own inner life—from his apparently genuine capacity, in *Finnegans Wake*-speak, to psoakoonaloose himself anytime he wanted—Joyce would know that a once loving mother could turn into a Fury. With her soul transmigrating to her son's guilt-ridden unconscious filled with the "agenbite of inwit," this "ghoul," "corpsechewer," would seek horrible vengeance on Orestes-like Stephen, convincing that son that cannibalism is all but the condition of life in Ireland. She is the "old sow that eats her farrow" or, again in "Circe," she is OLD GUMMY GRANNY, the quintessence of maternal hatefulness, homicidal fury, and death (*Ulysses,* p. 557).

For Joyce, maternal images could be deadly snares. He, too, felt that

---

[24] Quoted by Ellmann, *James Joyce,* p. 163.
[25] Quoted by Ellmann, *James Joyce,* p. 304.

his soul was in peril unless he could fly by the nets of nationality, language, and religion that Stephen describes to Cranly in Chapter V of *Portrait*—Motherland, Mother Tongue, Mother Church. But this habit of mind—of seeing mothers as threatening, even, in his darkest moments, as cannibalistic—is not just a sign of emergent misogynistic impulses and matricidal wishes projected outward. It hints at an archaic form of love as well. Just as the fox in the riddle vultures the vulturing dead—and thus seeks to regain a lost oneness with the mother—so Joyce as an artist battens on the dead.

With something like a prehensile eye, an uncanny ear for the curve of speech (almost dog-and-fox-like in its aural acuity), and, it seems, an almost perfect recall of olfactory and tactile experience, he seems to ingest those who no longer walk the earth, to incorporate them within himself. Feeding in memory on these visual and auditory stimuli, Joyce summons from heaven those Dubliners he once walked among in 1904 and earlier, endows them with their essential "whatness," and sets them living again on the earth—Dubliners once more alive in their unique language, nationality, and religion. (He does seem to be a secular version of the Resurrection and the Life as I will argue in the Epilogue.) Reborn in his imagination (and ours), Joyce is united with a whole variety of mothers—Ireland (which he said he never left); the English language (which he rescues from her Sassenach betrayers and refashions into his own self-born mother tongue, Joycean English); and, finally, the greatest fruit of *his* Mary-like womb (his complete works). Unlike Stephen's often stumbling guilt- and shame-ridden path back to his mother—it really is sour grapes since the more ravenously he feeds on her, the more rapidly she diminishes as a complex, "live," "real" human being—Joyce's path doesn't leave him (or us) with the taste of wet ashes in the mouth. Rather, reading Joyce, we often feel the joy that Bloom felt when he received a different kind of food from Molly, an echo of a famous apple, when they plighted their troth in what was an Eden for both of them on Howth Head sixteen years earlier:

Ravished over her I lay, full lips full open, kissed her mouth. Yum. Softly she gave me in my mouth the seedcake warm and chewed.

> Mawkish pulp her mouth had mumbled sweet and sour with spittle.
> Joy: I ate it: joy. Young life, her lips that gave me pouting. Soft,
> warm, sticky gumjelly lips. (*Ulysses*, p. 167)

Joyce met a maternal figure on June 16, 1904, but, unlike the milkwoman, she was to be truly nourishing and sustaining, a source of milk and mentoring in whose womb, as I mentioned earlier, he could imagine sleeping, nestled like a child born of her flesh and blood. At first, Nora appeared to slight a dispossessed son. This maid in a cheap rooming house who would over a lifetime help him repossess his homeland as a man, a father, and an artist did not keep an appointment to meet Joyce on June 14.[26]

However, Joyce was convinced that Nora's easy acceptance of him on June 16 was absolutely instinctive and natural.[27] In the milkwoman and Molly, Joyce recreates Nora's "curve of an emotion," the "individuating rhythm" that, he argued in his 1904 essay, "Portrait of the Artist," will be the very heart of characterization in the fiction of the future, his fiction.[28] As a maid in Finn's Hotel (actually an "exalted rooming house"[29]), Nora's life as a poor, uneducated servant to Dublin lodgers, with an air of something secret, timeless, and queenly in her bearing, recalls the milkwoman's life.

Nora simultaneously calls to mind Molly as well, another relatively poor, uneducated woman of untutored naiveté and superstitious piety who can, like the milkwoman, also bow her head to medicine men and priests (but with no reverence). Like Nora, Molly can at the same time admire, if not quite fathom, a quiet-voiced man of thought and knowledge (even if Bloom's wisdom, unlike Joyce's, often seems *Reader's Digest* at heart). Again, like Nora (and the milkwoman), Molly can also serve—or more accurately appear to serve—a gay betrayer. (Far from being the boorish Blazes Boylan, Joyce did not quite become Nora's gay

---

[26] Quoted by Ellmann, *James Joyce*, p. 162.
[27] Quoted by Ellmann, *James Joyce*, p. 165.
[28] Ellmann, *James Joyce*, p. 150.
[29] *Ibid.*, p. 162.

betrayer in his wished-for affair with Amalia Popper in Trieste in 1913, but he did ironically identify himself with Casanova in the nom d'amor he used in his account of it in his notebook—*Giacomo Joyce*).[30] Like Nora, Molly can at the same time that she appears to be serving a suitor remain faithful to a wandering "Jewgreek [who] is [a] greekjew" from Dublin (*Ulysses*, p, 475).[31] Finally, Molly, like Nora, is indistinguishable from the "poor old woman," Ireland herself, from Penelope, and from the Virgin—the ordinary embodiment of extraordinary radiance.

Apprehending luminously the immortality in Nora's lowly form, Joyce could feel that he and she were one flesh, one blood (he did seem to believe that, common-law or not, marriage *was* a sacramental rite where two mysteriously became one). It was in the womb of this Irish Penelope-and-Mary that he imagined himself nestling as son-and-father. Fused to this mother, he found his perennial themes—the Family, the Self, the Nation, and their endless interpenetration. Quickened by those themes, he found that he possessed within the power to be his own mother and the mother of a world without end—"the virgin womb of the imagination [where] the word was made flesh" (*Portrait*, p. 255).

---

[30] *Ibid.*, p.353.

[31] In 1909, Vincent Cosgrave told Joyce (who was in Dublin while Nora remained behind in Trieste) that Nora had had an affair with him while she and Joyce were courting in 1904, before they expatriated themselves. Horrified, depressed, and half mad, Joyce only gradually convinced himself that Nora hadn't "betrayed" him. He became convinced that Nora was truly and only his when she agreed to return his autoerotic letters with autoerotic letters of her own. Cf. Ellmann, *James Joyce*, pp. 288-290 and James Joyce, *Selected Letters of James Joyce*, ed. Richard Ellmann (New York: The Viking Press, 1975), pp. xxiii-xxiv, pp. 180-181.

CHAPTER III

Leopold Paula Bloom: The New Womanly Man

(In motor jerkin, green motorgoggles on his brow.) Dr Bloom is bisexually abnormal. He has recently escaped from Dr Eustace's private asylum for demented gentlemen. Born out of bedlock hereditary epilepsy is present, the consequence of unbridled lust. Traces of elephantiasis have been discovered among his ascendants. There are marked symptoms of chronic exhibitionism. Ambidexterity is also latent. He is prematurely bald from selfabuse, perversely idealistic in consequence, a reformed rake, and has metal teeth. In consequence of a family complex he has temporarily lost his memory and I believe him to be more sinned against than sinning. I have made a pervaginal examination and, after application of the acid test to 5427 anal, axillary, pectoral and pubic hairs, I declare him to be virgo intacta.
—Dr Malachi Mulligan, sex specialist, "Circe" (*Ulysses*, p. 465)

(Reads a bill of health.) Professor Bloom is a finished example of the new womanly man. His moral nature is simple and lovable. Many have found him a dear man, a dear person.... He was, I understand...a very posthumous child. I appeal for clemency in the name of the most sacred word our vocal organs have ever been called upon to speak. He is about to have a baby.
—Dr Dixon, "Circe" (*Ulysses*, p. 466)

Tyrants of the Heart

And it is a baby—or, rather, *"eight male yellow and white children"*—that Bloom then proceeds to have in Circe's den, Bella Cohen's brothel, where men are converted into swine (*Ulysses*, pp. 466-467). After exclaiming, "O, I so want to be a mother" and tightly embracing the midwife who helped deliver Molly of her short-lived son, Rudy, the new womanly man offers the viewers of Joyce's comic (and nightmarish) drama a stunning obstetrical performance (*Ulysses*, p. 467). Outshining Molly (who produced only two live babies), he produces a whole flock of living, healthy, respectably dressed sons—all "handsome," "valuable," "wellmade," and "wellconducted." Not only are their faces made of valuable metals, their names reflect their worth as well: they are *"Nasodoro"* (Nose of Gold), *"Goldfinger," "Chrysostomos"* (Goldenmouthed), *"Maindorée"* (Hand of Gold), *"Silversmile," "Silberselber"* (Silver Self), *"Vifargent"* (Quicksilver), and *"Panargyos"* (All Silver).[32]

Like his dead son Rudy, another mother lode buried deep within the earth these past ten and a half years but often recalled by his still-grieving parents, Bloom's latest composite son-and-heir is of incalculable worth to the doting father. Underscoring their great value for Bloom, Joyce tells us that these same sons hold positions of high public trust and that each speaks five languages fluently. These precious substances that were once inside Bloom's body are now outside and can't be put back. But if we assume that their maternal father (with the help of James Augusta Joyce, his own maternal father-and-creator) gave them their unique names—*"Each has his name printed in legible letters on his shirtfront"*—then these children are also identifiable possessions (*Ulysses*, p. 467). Although they exist in the external world as *"managing directors of banks, traffic managers of railways, chairmen of limited liability companies, vice chairmen of hotel syndicates,"* they are not Joyce's sons but Bloom's and are indistinguishable from the most ardent desire of their polyphiloprogenitor. Bloom's touching lower middle class wish for wealth, power, and status shows in the names he has given them (*Ulysses*, p. 467). Chrysostomos and his brothers are the royal treasure of their queenly

---

[32] Don Gifford and Richard J. Seidman, *Notes for Joyce: An Annotation of James Joyce's Ulysses* (New York: E. P. Dutton & Co., Inc., 1974), p. 395.

sire—cherished capital produced and sent out into the world—rather than autonomous and independent individuals. These creations (inside and outside him at the same time) are both his and not his.[33] (They are also works of art, symbolically, but I will return to the theme of Bloom's natural artistry later.)

Joyce complicates and deepens our understanding of Bloom's womanliness by hinting at a connection between these well-made and valuable midnight artifacts—these objects in the world that are infused with Bloom's subjectivity—and other well-formed and precious products of his body that are more or less subjective objects. Some sixteen hours earlier, he also appeared to embrace something more or less tightly before yielding and allowing somewhat different but equally costly possessions to see the light of day. Enthroned "asquat on the cuckstool" of the jakes of 7 Eccles street, Bloom "allowed his bowels to ease themselves quietly as he read, reading still patiently, that slight constipation of yesterday quite gone. Hope it's not too big bring on piles again. No, just right. So. Ah! Costive one tabloid of cascara sagrada. Life might be so. It did not move or touch him but it was something quick and neat. Print anything now...He read on, seated calm above his own rising smell. Neat certainly (*Ulysses*, p. 66).

That second "it" merges Bloom's relatively quick and neat, not too big or painful, bowel movement and Mr. Beaufoy's easily produced (it *is* pornographic hackwork) three-and-six *Masterstroke,* just as Joyce's own masterstroke joins together the dark matter brought forth from within Bloom's body and vaguely ill-gotten wealth. It seems that feces and literary creations (dirty or not, slightly pornographical or not) are all but synonymous for Bloom and Joyce, and, at least in their creators' dreaming minds, worth real British gold and silver. Like that late evening gold-and-silver octoplicate birth, Bloom's early morning production of a

---

[33] See Otto Fenichel, *The Psychoanalytic Theory of Neurosis (*New York: W. W. Norton and Company, Inc., 1945), pp. 281-282, for a discussion of the psychoanalytic concept of possession. Also, see "Transitional Objects and Transitional Phenomena," in D. W Winnicott, *Through Paediatrics to Psycho-Analysis* (New York & London: Brunner-Routledge, 1992), pp. 229ff.

somewhat different Nasodoro, Goldfinger, and Silversmile is valuable (his fecal column is as precious to its creator as Beaufoy's "first column" or "second" is to him); it is the result of a successful mining expedition deep within the bowels of a dark, hidden place; and, most significantly, it is a treasured part of the self that has been externalized, projected into the outer world as an object. Joyce is implying that, in Bloom's unconscious, feces, babies, literary creations, and wealth are interchangeable. Bloom is as womanly on the cuckstool as he is in the ministering presence of the midwife, Mrs. Thornton.

2. Womanly Full

Bloom's wondrously neat and quick delivery of a creation in the morning and his easy delivery of valuable babies at midnight are not the essence of his womanliness, however. It seems that giving birth is an adequate condition of womanliness for Joyce but not the necessary one. At bottom, it is Bloom's simultaneous physical and psychological satisfaction in being filled full—his psychophysiological delight in the receptive pleasures of the body—that constitutes his fundamental femaleness. The rectum is, of course, an excretory, as well as a hollow organ, yet he does not seem to expel his dark matter actively in "Calypso." He wants to "keep it a bit," we remember. Apparently, Bloom is taking pleasure in being filled up as he reads quietly, patiently. "Restraining himself," "yielding but resisting," he finally yields (with his "last resistance yielding"), pleasurably stimulated by the moving columnar mass within (*Ulysses*, p. 66).

Joyce focuses more sharply on his womanliness when, later, in 'Circe," Bloom mistakes a phrase in BELLO'S torrent of ridicule. (Joyce weds his technique in "Circe," the stream of unconsciousness, to his theme, the living theater that is a brothel, filled with often piggish agonists and protagonists. And he capitalizes the names of his characters to underscore the fact that we are eavesdropping on their unconscious fantasies, wishes, and thoughts.) Bloom thinks that BELLO-Circe is mocking his behavior as a female impersonator in the high school play, *Vice Versa*: "you took your seat with womanish care, lifting your billowy flounces,

Leopold Paula Bloom: The New Womanly Man

on the smoothworn throne" (*Ulysses*, pp. 504-505). But Bloom also thinks that BELLO is referring to the other smoothworn throne on which he seated himself in the jakes, the "cuckstool," an obsolete phrase for a chair used to punish "dishonest tradesmen" and other miscreants. These wrongdoers were forced to sit upon it at their front door where they were hooted at and jeered by the community.[34] Flustered and ashamed, Bloom replies, "Science. To compare the various joys we each enjoy. (*Earnestly.*) And really it's better the position....because often I used to wet" (*Ulysses*, p. 505).

Apparently, Bloom often did not like to "do it standing," as BELLO puts it. At the time that Molly weaned Milly, Bloom seems to have broken yet another smoothworn throne, this time the commode in the bedroom of 7 Eccles street on which he sat to urinate. After reminding him of the shameful things she has seen in the bedroom, the embarrassed NYMPH in the picture above their bed elicits the following reflection from crestfallen Bloom. To the accompaniment of a "brightly cascading waterfall" (the chamber music that echoes ironically in the title of Joyce's collection of poetry, *Chamber Music*), BLOOM tells us:

> That antiquated commode. It wasn't her weight. She scaled just eleven stone nine. She put on nine pounds after weaning. It was a crack and want of glue. Eh? And that absurd orangekeyed utensil which has only one handle. (*Ulysses*, p. 514)

While Molly was preoccupied with her newborn baby and, presumably, was sexually and emotionally removed from him, Bloom, as we have seen, discovered ways to "compare" their "various joys." Seated on the antiquated commode inside the house or asquat on the cuckstool in the jakes outside, he seems to have taken pleasure in what he assumes to have been a Mollyesque delight.[35]

---

[34] Gifford and Seidman, *op. cit.*, p. 59.
[35] Molly might have unknowingly satisfied her future husband's overpowering (and apparently lifelong) wish to sit where a woman has sat, to feel "the warm impress of her warm form," when they first met (*Ulysses*, p.518). In "Sirens," Bloom recalls, "First night

In another exchange in "Circe," when his "grossoldgrandfather" VIRAG cynically responds to the "piping hot" urination of another woman (either Zoe or Florry or Kitty), Joyce implies what that pleasure was: "Hot, Hot! Ware Sitting Bull," warns THE VOICE OF VIRAG (*Ulysses*, p. 518). Bloom replies:

> It overpowers me. The warm impress of her warm form. Even to sit where a woman has sat, especially with divaricated thighs, as though to grant the last favours, most especially with previously well uplifted white sateen coatpans. So womanly full. It fills me full. (*Ulysses*, p. 518)

The accompanying sounds of the waterfall at Poulaphouca summarize Bloom's experience of his emergent womanliness—impulses which he regards as "womanly," impulses which seem to overpower his "maleness" whenever he comes into contact with the "warm impress" of a woman's "warm form":

THE WATERFALL
Phillaphulla Poulaphouca
Poulaphouca Poulaphouca. (*Ulysses*, p. 552)

As BLOOM is seated on the same cuckstool-throne that a woman sat on, imagining her seated with divaricated thighs framed by sateen garments, Joyce seems to be implying that BLOOM feels the same way a woman feels, a woman who is "phillaphulla" with "poulaphouca." "Poula" can be variously read as "pooly" (or urine) that BELLA scornfully attributes to BLOOM, or it can refer to the "poo" of the child's stool, or, perhaps, it takes its meaning from both at once. For Leopold Paula (Poula?) Bloom, the visual or tactile impress of a woman's warm bottom on her throne apparently causes him to experience his own bottom as

---

when first I saw her at Mat Dillon's in Terenure.... Musical chairs. We two the last. Fate. After her. Fate. Round and round slow. Quick round. We two. All looked. Halt. Down she sat. All ousted looked. Lips laughing. Yellow knees" (*Ulysses*, p. 264).

womanly. He begins to feel a gathering sensation of his own hollowness, a hollowness that he enjoys being filled full.

As he experiences that filling, his joy is indistinguishable from what he takes a woman's joy to be when she is being filled full with "phouca," when she is being fucked. It seems that womanliness is catching for Bloom. Physical proximity often leads to a kind of fusion with a woman, and, as we shall soon see, Joyce appears to enjoy dramatizing the many different ways—tactile, auditory, but especially visual—in which Bloom becomes one with her. (Later, in Chapter IV, I'll speculate on a psychological mechanism that sheds more light on Bloom's lifelong habit of incorporating a female or parts of a female into his identity.)

Musing on the difference between man and woman in "Sirens," and quickly identifying with the woman, Bloom ponders the differences between the ways women and men sing: "They can't manage men's intervals. Gap in their voices too. Fill me. I'm *warm, dark, open*" (italics mine) (Ulysses, p. 270). His use of "gap," something absent, to describe a female singer's supposedly physiological inability to manage male "intervals"—the difference in pitch between two tones—intensifies our sense of Bloom's never ending fascination with the female body, particularly the warm, dark openings that exert an almost magnetic attraction.

Bloom's erogenous delight in those organs that incorporate things extends to his eyes and nose, too. In the jakes, we remember, he takes in *Matchum's Masterstroke* visually from above, at the same time that he takes in (and expels) a different kind of dirty matter from below. He reads, "seated calm above his own rising smell" (*Ulysses*, p. 66). All but inseparable from his pleasure in an active receptivity—in a wished-for, resisted, then, finally, a willed "yielding" to dark presences that make him feel womanly full—is the less strenuous delight of a simple, thoughtless letting go, a passive giving up of himself, the foregoing of all restraint. A passive letting flow seems to characterize his urination as well. Bloom does not forcefully make water. He does not so much "scout it out straight whistling like a man almost easy" as Molly recalls she could do (*Ulysses*, p. 723). Instead, he presides (as a fantasized woman) over his own gentle waterfall. Having glanced back through what he had read, he feels his "water flow quietly" (*Ulysses*, p. 66).

Joyce is associating BLOOM'S miraculous obstetrical performance in Bella Cohen's counting house, his gentle labor of love in the Eccles street counting house, and his mild exertions on the cracked commode. If we allow our consciousness to flow with Joyce's stream of consciousness—if we sense these images simultaneously—we see that Bloom wears many hats in addition to the hat with the missing "t" in the sweatband label, "Plasto's high grade ha" (*Ulysses*, p. 55). We can begin to fathom their brand names as well. Using one of Joyce's central images, we may say that Bloom is doubly crowned. He wears a queen's within a king's, or, better, the queenly crown can sometimes supplant the kingly one. In the light of day—in his own conscious mind—he is not a woman but a man, the king in his counting house. But in the jakes (or on the commode), Bloom is in the dark, a king momentarily shut off from the light of day. Overwhelmed by sorrow, he queens it over his warm, dark openings, taking a womanly pleasure in his feelings of fullness. And what calm delight there is in that retained inner treasure, that gently produced "pouly"—a smelly yet radiant trove of gold and silver guineas and shillings!

Deep within Circe's palace—in the mind's midnight—Joyce makes BLOOM'S womanliness as clear as it has ever been in *Ulysses*. The artist "presents his image in immediate relation to others," to use Stephen's definition of dramatic form in *Portrait* (p. 251). Not only does he dramatize it, Joyce makes it broadly comical. In one portion of Bloom's mind, he is not a man but a woman. The king in Circe's counting house, counting out the money he sadly doesn't have, is changing into the queen in her parlor or, rather, the queen bee enjoying the bread and honey of generation, an abundance of yellow and white goodness formerly housed within the body. Whether at eight o'clock in the morning or at midnight, the womanly man can only be called regal in the calm and graceful manner with which he manages pressing matters that easily enter his hollow space below and then, not too big, leave it easily, too. Ah! "Neat certainly."

3. A Soft Qualm Regret

Does Joyce offer us clues about what arouses Bloom's womanliness? How and when does manly Bloom become womanly Bloom? What does the king in his counting house feel before he feels himself becoming the queen in her parlor? In "Calypso" (and later in "Circe"), Bloom suffers attacks of painful anxiety, "A soft qualm regret, flowed down his backbone, increasing" (*Ulysses*, p. 65). Bloom, it seems, can be reduced to that frightening feeling of paralysis by a womanly performance, either while on the cuckstool in the jakes or in Mrs. Thornton's capable arms.

The flowing qualm is first stirred by feelings of separation from the women he loves and who love him. In "Calypso," thoughts of physical separation from his fifteen-year-old daughter, Milly, who has just celebrated her first birthday away from home at the seaside in Mullingar working as a photographer's assistant, lead to thoughts of even more dreadful loss (*Ulysses*, p. 64). Thinking of Milly leads him to Mrs. Thornton, the midwife who helped deliver Milly and who "knew from the first poor little Rudy wouldn't live....She knew at once. He would be eleven now if he had lived" (*Ulysses*, p. 64). Remembering the death of the baby brings Bloom back to regretful thoughts of Milly and the sad realization that, with her initiation into adult sexuality, he will soon be as painfully separated from his now-womanly daughter as he is from his wife.

Bloom is conflating Milly and Molly not only in their sexual allure but in their connection to Blazes Boylan, someone who has gotten between him and his wife and, apparently, between him and his daughter as well:

Seaside girls. Torn envelope. Hands stuck in his trousers' pockets, jarvey off for the day, singing. Friend of the family. Swurls, he says. Pier with lamps, summer evening, band.
 Those girls, those girls
 Those lovely seaside girls
Milly too. Young kisses: the first. Far away now past. Mrs Marion. Reading lying back now, counting the strands of her hair, smiling, braiding. (*Ulysses*, pp. 64-65)

After sneaking a glance at the letter, Bloom knows that Boylan has addressed Molly familiarly, intimately, as "Mrs Marion"(Bloom), instead of the proper Mrs Leopold Bloom (*Ulysses* p. 59). Since the song about those lovely seaside girls is a kind of metonym for Blazes throughout *Ulysses*—and since Bloom feels cut off from one seaside girl by her stay in Mullingar (which Boylan apparently helped arrange) and from the other by her affair with Boylan—we can easily imagine Bloom's pain. Cut off from those lovely seaside girls who no longer love him alone, Bloom's body, as we have seen, registers a gathering enervation as the soft qualm flows within him:

> Will happen, yes. Prevent. Useless: can't move. Girl's sweet light lips. Will happen too. He felt the flowing qualm spread over him. Useless to move now. Lips kissed, kissing kissed. Full gluey woman's lips. (*Ulysses*, p. 67)

"Qualm" is a "fit of sickening fear, misgiving, or depression; a sudden sinking of heart."[36] Joyce seems to be implying that a sudden sinking of the heart, an access of regret, is flowing down Bloom's backbone and increasing, and as that frightening feeling of heart-sickness spreads through him, he is paralyzed. Frozen to the chair in his kitchen table—helpless and powerless in his passivity—Bloom "can't move." Yet he does rise again. Unconsciously, he manages to contain that spreading anxiety and depression that momentarily fixes him in a death-in-life state.

His paralyzing despair begins to recede and dissolve in a new mood, a "yielding mood." As Bloom thinks of a girl's "sweet light lips," "kissed, kissing kissed" (presumably Milly's), he is apparently thinking of another young girl's lips, Molly's, sixteen years earlier. In "Lestrygonians," as I mentioned previously, recalling the moment he and eighteen-year-old Molly sealed their love high up on Ben Houth, he muses (allow me to indulge myself in returning to Bloom's poetry): "Young life, her lips that gave me pouting. Soft, warm, sticky gumjelly lips....She kissed me. I was kissed.... Kissed, she kissed me" (*Ulysses*, p. 167-168).

Apparently, in "Calypso," anxious Bloom is fantasizing not only about Milly's and Molly's lips being kissed. He is also merging Milly-Molly's

---

[36] *The Shorter Oxford English Dictionary on Historical Principles,* rev. and ed. by C. T. Onions, 3rd ed. (Oxford: At the Clarendon Press, 1959), p. 1635.

"lips kissed, kissing kissed" with his own. (As I mentioned in Chapter II, Stephen seems to feel that he and the prostitute are at one in the fusion of *their* lips.) The remembered, now-present, sensation of his lips being kissed by Molly's full, gluey, sticky gumjelly lips makes her lips (and Milly's) indistinguishable from his. Bloom seems to be consciously and unconsciously identifying himself with the lost and lovely seaside girls of his youth, particularly with their all-yielding lips.

Becoming womanly, feeling his lips becoming the lips of Milly-and-Molly, he is ready to be kissed. No longer feeling "separated" from them—no longer feeling separated from their love—his qualm begins to disappear. Only a minute later, once he is seated calmly above his own rising smell and quietly flowing water—"reading lying back now" like Molly reading in bed—Bloom does move something. Feelings of qualm and uselessness disappear, and his previous brush with death-like immobility is all but forgotten. Taking womanly delight in the relatively passive and receptive joys of a warm, dark hollowness at the other end of the alimentary canal being filled full, Bloom seems to have stiffened his backbone.

In "Circe," Bloom also feels a flowing qualm spreading over him before becoming womanly and bearing eight healthy sons. But at midnight, it is less a soft splash of "regret" and more a flooding of mortal terror. Once again, a separation from a woman who once loved him leads to an attack of sickening anxiety in Bloom, but here the attack is massive, and Joyce is explicit about the complicated nature of that paralyzing dread. A mysterious, powerful, all-knowing woman, "THE VEILED SIBYL," once idolized Bloom: "I'm a Bloomite and I glory in it. I believe in him in spite of all. I'd give my life for him, the funniest man on earth" (*Ulysses*, p. 491). She does have the last laugh, too. She leaves him laughing—by dying. "Giving" her life for Bloom, THE VEILED SIBYL stabs herself, melodramatically gasps "My hero god!" and dies (*Ulysses*, p. 464).

As if to emphasize the traumatic effect of this violent (albeit comic) abandonment on Bloom—and perhaps to suggest that Bloom tried to undo its psychological effects by constantly returning to it, converting what he passively experienced into something he actively "created"—

Joyce comically multiplies it in the manner of what Freud called the "primary process," the often magical "thinking" of the unconscious.

> *(Many most attractive and enthusiastic women also commit suicide by stabbing, drowning, drinking prussic acid, aconite, arsenic opening their veins, refusing food, casting themselves under steamrollers, from the top of Nelson's pillar, into the great vat of Guinness's brewery, asphyxiating themselves by placing their heads in gas ovens, hanging themselves in stylish garters, leaping from windows of different storeys.)* (*Ulysses*, p. 464)

One result of the loss of this attractive, enthusiastic, worshipful prophetess—a mighty and wise woman who believed in him despite his shortcomings—is a swiftly flowing qualm. At its deepest level, it is synonymous with a dangerous loss of self-esteem in Bloom, self-esteem wrapped up in being worshipped by her. With her self-destruction, her hero-god is devastated. (In Chapter II, we saw that the "gaping wounds" in Stephen's heart opened up when his worshipful mother abandoned him.) Before her bloody "suicide," BLOOM apparently believed in himself as blindly as the mysterious woman believed in him. He was a semi-deity, or, more accurately, he became identical with her, blended in with her, a male sibyl. BLOOM offers stunning oracular answers to such a vexing question as, "What am I to do about my rates and taxes?" Or "What is the parallax of the subsolar ecliptic of Aldebaran?" (*Ulysses*, p. 461). He could explain his Fabian socialist schemes for "*social regeneration*" so convincingly that "*All agree with him* (*Ulysses*, p. 463). And he could even sing one of "the old sweet songs" "*With rollicking humour*," a truly heroic feat given his association of the song with Blazes Boylan (*Ulysses*, p. 463). As Hoppy Holohan says (more truly than he knows), "There's nobody like him after all" (*Ulysses*, p. 464).

Bloom was able to glorify himself when he felt glorified by a nameless and faceless woman who spoke sibylantly. But with the loss of that idealizing figure—actually, as we shall soon see, the mother as an infant might perceive her—Bloom feels that he is the lowest of the low. No longer participating in her sibyline magic, he begins to regard himself as totally worthless. From feelings that there's no self like the Bloomite self after all—omnipotent and omniscient—Bloom rapidly collapses into feeling that he is the most abject and empty of men.

As the qualm spreads, melancholy Bloom gives himself over to a torrent of self-accusations that Joyce externalizes. A "mob"—the self-reproaching chorus within him, always ready to take center stage—begins to jeer, "Lynch him! Roast him! He's as bad as Parnell was. Mr. Fox!" (*Ulysses*, p. 465). In the cruelty of his unconscious conscience, this suddenly "bad" man feels he has channeled Parnell (the famous Anglo-Irish statesman and adulterer who used the nom de guerre "Mr. Fox" when writing Kitty O'Shea, his married mistress). The qualm that begins to flow when he feels abandoned by a doting, powerful woman is more than just the sickening feeling of self-diminishment and self-loathing; it is also the spreading impulse to self-punishment.

MOTHER GROGAN, who had previously removed her boot to throw at this good man who has turned almost immediately wicked—this prophet become a "beast" and an "abominable person" (*Ulysses*, p. 463)—finally does throw it at BLOOM. And then a flood of "*objects of little or no commercial value, hambones, condensed milk tins, unsaleable cabbage, stale bread, sheeps' tails, odd pieces of fat*" sail about the head of this shameful miscreant (*Ulysses*, p. 465). In the midst of all this cabbage-in-the face carrying on, Joyce is seriously implying that with the "death" of THE VEILED SIBYL, Bloom is tempted to "die." For an instant, at least, he seems all but ready to bring down on his own head the death-by-stoning that the ancient Jews sometimes inflicted on abominable human beasts.

In "Circe," then, as well as in "Calypso," Bloom's disappointment in a highly idealizing woman—apparently a projection of his own powerfully idealizing impulses—leads to an identification with her. But in "Circe," he doesn't first identify himself with her nurturing abilities—with her capacity to feed hungry lips with "food" from her own body or with her gumjelly kissable lips. Forsaken, Bloom feels a qualmy impulse to become the bloody end that she became, to identify himself (at least fleetingly) with her most disappointing single feature—her bodily "damage," "mutilation," and "death."[37] Finally, however, he doesn't give

---

[37] In "Cyclops," the nameless narrator, one of the pubcrawlers in Barney Kiernan's,

himself over to self-murder and its variations. Bloom doesn't get himself hamboned to death; nor does he shoot himself, open his veins, or leap from the top of Nelson's pillar. He becomes THE VEILED SIBYL in her most positive aspect. (Apparently, he has powerfully opposed feelings about this woman deep within his mind; there are two sibyls in the dark underside of Bloom's consciousness.)

Somewhat earlier in the evening, we recall, Molly arose out of Bloom's mind as a veiled woman, too, wearing a *"white yashmak"* up to her *"large dark eyes"* (*Ulysses,* p. 439). Proceeding to have a baby in Mrs. Thornton's arms as Molly did, Bloom becomes that veiled woman. She is not far away but inside him. In fact, he is the Veiled Woman in both her negative and positive aspects. To give birth is to experience one's body opening up and bleeding, a kind of self-created stab wound from within; but to give birth to a male wonder (to eight little hero-gods, no less, each of whom survives to speak five modern languages fluently) is also to feel worshipful and awestruck. Bloom might be feeling as womanly full with wonder and admiration for those precious little Blooms as the idealizing VEILED SIBYL once felt for him, a "limp [yet amazingly fertile] father of thousands, a languid floating flower," as Joyce foresees (along with Bloom) Bloom's penis in the bath at the end of "Lotus Eaters" (*Ulysses,* p. 83).

At the risk of redundancy, let me summarize these shifting and dovetailing associations. When Bloom feels deserted by the significant women in his life—particularly by a woman who is less than perfectly loyal and worshipful—he begins to suffer from a paralyzing qualm. It can begin to flow with the relatively slight disappointment of a loving

---

recounts a much earlier moment in Bloom's life where he seemed to have imitated a bleeding woman, a prostitute with her period: "One of those mixed middlings he is. Lying up in the hotel Pisser was telling me once a month with headache like a totty with her courses" (*Ulysses,* p. 323). Bloom's impulse to identify with a woman, especially when he feels abandoned, also appears indirectly in J. J.'s French interjection: "—O, by God, says Ned, you should have seen Bloom before the son of his that died was born. I met him one day in the south city markets buying a tin of Neave's food six weeks before the wife was delivered. —*En ventre sa mère,* says J. J." (*Ulysses,* p.323). In the belly of his mother, Bloom seems identified with both the foetus and Molly as he buys baby food (see Gifford and Seidman, *op.cit.,* p. 299).

and much-doted-on daughter going away from home for the first time or with the knowledge that Blazes Boylan is on a first-name basis with his wife. Or the qualm can begin to spread with the bloody withdrawal of a VEILED SIBYL from him as he is flooded with guilt over an unnamable crime once committed or fantasized. At its worst, at the kitchen table early in the morning, the anxiety makes him feel that his body is paralyzed (useless: can't move) or, late at night, that it is in mortal danger (lynch him! roast him!).

Sitting on the smoothworn throne of the jakes with divaricated thighs, like a woman about to urinate or defecate, can be self-soothing. In other words, autoerotic activity involving the bottom and its creations—feeling, touching, seeing, or smelling it and its products—can arrest that spreading qualm regret. Fantasies about becoming a woman in childbirth can staunch it momentarily, too. No matter what its immediate cause—a felt loss of love, or the loss of a loving creature named Milly, Molly, or SIBYL, or the threat of physical punishment—Bloom defends himself against the flowing qualm by being a woman among women, by identifying himself with a maternal figure or, more accurately, with her warm, dark openings which both incorporate and expel.

The most severe anxiety, however, seems to be stirred by the sight of a "mutilated" woman named THE VEILED SIBYL—a woman enveloped in mystery and omniscience who, he feels, once idealized him but then suddenly "made" many fatal bleeding wounds on her body and disappeared. We can be fairly sure that Joyce is moving closer to those very early experiences where Bloom's womanliness may have taken root when we recall that in "Lotus-Eaters," Bloom wondered whether another hero-worshipping woman, Ophelia, killed herself because her hero-god was another womanly man, "Male impersonator. Perhaps he was a woman," who didn't reciprocate her love (*Ulysses*, p. 73).

With Bloom's stream-of-consciousness connection of a female suicide, a self-injured woman, with a womanly (yet princely) man at ten o'clock in the morning, we may guess that we're traveling even further on the royal road to Bloom's unconscious that Joyce has cunningly laid out (and cunningly concealed) at midnight.

4. Infantile Debauchery with a Dissolute Granddam

As I have been suggesting throughout, Joyce seems intuitively aware of the psychoanalytic axiom that following the loss of a very significant person—and feelings of loss can arise from excessive gratification as well as excessive disappointment or a combination of gratification and disappointment—we tend to replace love with identification. Unconsciously imitating aspects of that important love object, we become the person we can no longer possess.[38] Joyce seems to ask us to infer that Bloom was satisfied or frustrated in crucial things almost solely by his mother, at least if we believe Dr Dixon's assertion that he was "a very posthumous child"—literally, a child whose father was dead, absent, or weak. But in "Circe," where does Joyce imply that Bloom suffered from either excessive gratification or excessive disappointment in his mother at a very early age? Do we have any evidence that he identified himself with that very significant woman (or with anxiety-producing aspects of her) whom he felt he lost or was in danger of losing?

Before turning to "Babby," as ZOE calls BLOOM in "Circe"—she is preparing to rock him in his cradle (*Ulysses,* p. 472)—I want to study the ways Joyce's highly allusive and highly inferential style allows us to see ever more clearly a symbolic version of Bloom's mother, a maternal image that seems to be constantly emerging from his unconscious in "Circe." Let me begin by quoting the Bible-pounding, one-man incitement to riot, ALEXANDER J. DOWIE, the evangelist from America, who is convinced that Elijah is coming. His crazy sermon-diatribe does give us clues into the genesis of the womanliness of Joyce's Elijah, "ben Bloom Elijah," as Joyce calls him at the end of "Cyclops," the new womanly man (*Ulysses,* p. 330).

An Americanized Scot—an immigrant from the Old World living on in the New—he declaims violently against Bloom, but Joyce's dramatic irony transforms him into a comic John the Baptist, a genuine, if funny, Precursor fulminating against the anti-Christ:

---

[38] Fenichel, *op.cit.,* p. 331.

> (*Violently.*) Fellowchristians and antiBloomites, the man called Bloom is from the roots of hell, a disgrace to christian men. A fiendish libertine from his earliest years this stinking goat of Mendes gave precocious signs of infantile debauchery recalling the cities of the plain, with a dissolute granddam. This vile hypocrite, bronzed with infamy, is the white bull mentioned in the Apocalypse. A worshipper of the Scarlet Woman, intrigue is the very breath of his nostrils. (*Ulysses* pp.464-465)

Throughout "Circe," as we have seen, Joyce used his own lifelong interest in dreams and their meaning to explore what he would call the "subconscious" of his main characters.[39] Translating Joyce's version of Freud's "dream-work"—especially Joyce's version of "condensation" (the combination of a number of thoughts into economical composites) and "displacement" (substituting one identification for another)—we begin to realize that Bloom does unconsciously harbor a "dissolute granddam" with whom he showed signs of "infantile debauchery."[40]

This granddam is also a dam, Dowie's Scarlet Woman, whom his fiendish libertine worshipped. Zoe Higgins, "*a young whore in a sapphire slip, closed with three bronze buckles,*" has the same last name as the

---

[39] Richard Ellmann, *James Joyce* (New York: Oxford University Press, 1965), p. 559. "Joyce was close to the new psychoanalysis at so many points that he always disavowed any interest in it. 'Why all this fuss and bother about the mystery of the unconscious?.... What about the mystery of the conscious? What do they know about that?'" (*ibid.*, p. 450).

Ellmann also gives us examples of Joycean "dream work": "'Do you know that when we dream we are reading I think it's really that we are talking in our sleep. But we cannot talk as fast as we read so our dream invents a reason for the slowness.'" Or: "'In sleep our senses are dormant, except the sense of hearing, which is always awake, since you can't close your ears. So any sound that comes to our ears during sleep is turned into a dream'" (*ibid.*, p. 560).

[40] Cf. Sigmund Freud, "The Dream-Work," in "The Interpretation of Dreams," *The Complete Psychological Works of Sigmund Freud,* vols. IV-V, trans. James Strachey London: The Hogarth Press, 1981), pp. 277-350 and Charles Brenner, *An Elementary Textbook of Psychoanalysis,* rev. ed. (Garden City, New York: Anchor Books 1974), pp. 149-170. Ellmann reminds us that Joyce's interest in dreams is "pre-Freudian in that it looks for revelation not scientific explanation" (Ellmann, *op. cit.,* p. 89n).

maiden name of Bloom's dam (*Ulysses*, p. 449). Joyce then deepens our sense that Zoe is the transmigrating soul of Ellen Higgins. He gives her a first name that means "Life" in Greek. He also hyphenates it, naming her "ZOE-FANNY" when she describes her own precocious fall into debauchery (*Ulysses*, p. 479). Thus with her name "objectively" combined with Fanny (and we can only assume that the names and stage directions come from the sole source of "objective" reality, James Joyce), Zoe has the first name of Bloom's maternal grandmother as well as the last name of both grandmother and mother.

When Joyce has the enigmatic THE MAN IN THE MACINTOSH say of BLOOM, "His real name is Higgins," we are again asked to infer that Bloom is connected to Zoe-Fanny by blood (*Ulysses*, p. 458). In his stage directions, Joyce reemphasizes that this Scarlet Woman-granddam-dam is (in Bloom's mind) his mother. He uses the same directions to describe both ELLEN BLOOM and ZOE lifting up their garments to reveal a potato secreted on their bodies, the "hard, black, shriveled" potato that his mother first gave her son as a "talisman," an "heirloom," a "relic." ELLEN BLOOM "*hauls up a reef of skirt and ransacks the pouch of her striped blay petticoat*" (*Ulysses*, p. 417). ZOE seems to be imitating ELLEN, as she "*hauls up a reef of her slip, revealing her bare thighs and unroll[ing] the potato from the top of her stocking*" (*Ulysses*, p. 521).

As if Joyce wanted to make sure that we saw the connection, both ELLEN BLOOM (née Higgins) and Zoe-Fanny Higgins react with similar alacrity to Bloom's habit of falling down. ELLEN "cries out in shrill alarm" at the cut in her son's arm that he received after slipping in the mud in a "sprint" with his high school friends (*Ulysses*, p. 417). ZOE (Life) Higgins cries out "Hoopsa" as Bloom again trips awkwardly, this time at the doorway to Bella Cohen's, "*saving him*" with her "*lucky hand*" (*Ulysses*, p. 473). "Hoopsa," we remember, is the cry in "Oxen of the Sun" with which the midwife celebrates a man's first fall earthward—the birth of a male child. Thus, for the briefest of instants, ZOE seems conflated with ELLEN BLOOM as the woman who "gives" life to Bloom—or at least a new lease on it.

If we take these scattered allusions together—ZOE'S not insignificant last and first name, together with her repeating ELLEN HIGGINS' actions—Bloom's connection to Higgins's blood seems almost explicit. The young whore with the bronze belt buckles and sapphire slip seems to be the externalization of one of Bloom's unconscious images of his mother when she was young.

The transmigration of souls is catching in "Circe." Bloom becomes a baby, once again, in the presence of Zoe-Granddam-Mother. After calling ZOE "laughing witch"—the epithet applied to the lewd woman in *Matchum's Masterstroke*—Bloom murmurs, "The hand that rocks the cradle" and becomes an infant in the cradle whom ZOE has maternally called "Babby" (*Ulysses*, p. 472):

BLOOM
(*In babylinen and pelisse, bigheaded, with a caul of dark hair, fixes his big eyes on her fluid slip and counts its bronze buckles with a chubby finger, his moist tongue tolling and lisping.*) One two tlee: tlee tlwo tlone. (*Ulysses*, p. 472)

Counting her bronze belt buckles with his chubby finger and lisping numbers with his tolling tongue, BLOOM seems to have returned to the age of two or so, when the infant begins to speak, to point, and to walk. But the imagery of caul, cradle, and babylinen implies that BLOOM is also younger than two. Again, if we think with the dream-logic of a Joyce (or a Bloom)—minds that easily condense two different ages or things into one thing—then tolling, lisping, moist-tongued Babby is a two-year-old going on one, or earlier.

In other words, Joyce wants us to see that he is dramatizing a perennial psychological rhythm in Bloom, the "individuating rhythm" we have seen before where he identifies himself with a maternal figure, unconsciously incorporating her, or an aspect of her, becoming her. Once again, ALEXANDER J. DOWIE'S preposterous, but uncannily prophetic, language points out a path to understanding that rhythm. "Bronzed with infamy," Bloom seems to be taking on the patina, the coloration, of Dowie's Scarlet Woman. Fingering Zoe's bronze buckles as if they were the removable flower petals in the "Love me. Love me not. Love me" game that THE BUCKLES chant, bewitched Babby appears to be incorporating ZOE'S (i.e., mother's) body or a part of her body into his own by the use of eye, finger, mouth, and language (*Ulysses*, p. 472).

The imagery of bronze, particularly Bloom being "bronzed with infamy," is at the heart of Joyce's symbolism. Earlier in the day, Bloom fixed his eyes on a somewhat different laughing witch whose hand rocked a somewhat different cradle. In "Sirens," he is thinking of the up-and-down movement of the thumb and finger of "bronze"-headed Lydia Douce ("Bronze," one of the barmaids) as she fondles the smooth jutting beerpull in the bar room of the Ormond Hotel. As he connects Bronze to Molly on Howth Head years earlier, he also connects Bronze to a Zoe-like maternal power: "Beerpull. Her hand that rocks the cradle rules the. Ben Houth. That rules the world" (*Ulysses*, p. 288). Eyeing intently Bronze's Zoe-like fluidity—Miss Douce's "liquid of womb of woman eyeball" as she muses on the dead Irish folk hero, the Croppy Boy—Bloom seems bronzed with Bronze, merging with her (*Ulysses*, p. 276). His momentary self-pity in "Sirens" seems to dissolve in her pity; Bloom's sexual longings fuse with her abstracted eroticizing of the beerpull, while simultaneously the eyes of the Croppy Boy, Bloom's eyes, and Bronze's eyes, all become one:

> On the smooth jutting beerpull laid Lydia hand lightly, plumply, leave it to my hands. All lost in pity for croppy. Fro, to: to, fro: over the polished knob (she knows his eyes, my eyes, her eyes) her thumb and finger passed in pity: passed, repassed and, gently touching, then slid so smoothly, slowly down, a cool firm white enamel baton protruding through their sliding ring. (*Ulysses*, p. 274)

Joyce is asking us to connect Miss Douce-Bronze's eroticizing sliding ring of a hand with bronze-buckled Zoe's constantly patting "lucky hand," the hand that saved Bloom from falling and slid over his left thigh toward his "nuts" (*Ulysses*, p. 450). When we do make the connection, we sense that BLOOM is misperceiving the present in terms of the past. He is not only transferring his feelings about Miss Douce earlier in the day to ZOE late at night, but he also seems to be remembering and not remembering momentous early experiences with his mother.

We may infer that Babby once experienced his body in the cradle as a white enamel baton, a plaything being fondled by an abstracted and inward-turning Bronze-Zoe-Mother. Let me emphasize that I am *not* suggesting that Ellen Bloom literally abused her son. What I am suggesting is that Joyce is implying that Bloom's womanliness might have arisen in the "infantile debauchery" of excessive fondling, in Ellen Bloom's "mathering" of her son—Molly's critical word for both Bloom's mistaken belief that he knows just about all there is to know about a woman and his excessive and exasperating mothering of her. Subjected to such stimulation (psychological, not simply physical), he might have felt that he was little more than a polished knob. While his eye was fixed, perhaps, on her Bronze-like "liquid of womb of woman eyeball," hers, perhaps pityingly, like Bronze's, was fixed somewhere else (*Ulysses*, p. 274).

Joyce's crisscrossing references in "Circe" allow us to speculate even further. Bloom's miraculous production of eight babies suggests that he knows what it is like both to give birth and to be surrounded by what seems to be an endless number of babies. Was Ellen Bloom also abstracted as she caressed her son, thinking of another child or two or tlee? Was she musing on an idealized Croppy Boy, a baby (or two or three) who died? As she stroked her living boy to and fro perhaps absent-mindedly yet (to him) "dissolutely," the most significant psychological result seems to have been that Babby experienced his body in a very strange and confusing way.

The picture that Joyce's stage directions give us of Bloom's infant body—and presumably the body image that the baby has of himself—is not so unambiguously male, so obviously a body-phallus as we might first think. With his *"caul"* (he is membrane-topped), Joyce seems to be evoking the fact that *"bigheaded"* Bloom is an uncircumcised male. But he is also enveloped in a *"pelisse"*—the long fur cloak that many Victorian women were particularly fond of. One implication seems to be that a basic maleness is sheathed in femaleness. Bloom is both white enamel baton *and* sliding ring, phallic and vaginal. In BLOOM'S fingering of ZOE'S bronze buckles, Joyce is also hinting (as I have suggested) that the origin of the new womanly man's womanliness possibly arose in an early experience of excessive and exasperating "mathering," "infantile debauchery" with a "dissolute granddam."

"One two tlee: tlee tlow tlone" implies that BLOOM has returned to the age of two or so when the infant with newly acquired language and locomotion begins to surge upward in a love affair with the world. But the imagery of caul, cradle, and babylinen suggests that Bloom is also younger than two. Again, if we "think" with the dream-logic of a Joyce (or a Bloom)—the mind that easily condenses two different ages or things into one thing—then the pre-verbal tolling, lisping, moist-tongued Babby might very well have experienced his mother's abstracted, sliding-ring treatment of him in the first days, year, and year-and-a-half of life as well as later. In other words, Bloom's infant, as well as two-year-old body, might have been stimulated in an overpowering way by a *seemingly* "dissolute" hand constantly sliding over him with the stroking of an earlier version of Bronze-Zoe's hand, an earlier version of the Scarlet Woman who perhaps shared her love with many others named Babby.

When as an infant Bloom first "fixe[d] big eyes" on mother's fluid shape—as well as at the age of two or so when he began to lisp in numbers—he could very well have been suffused with sensory stimulation which he couldn't discharge. But what does the hand of a "laughing witch," rocking a baby in his cradle, have to do with the picture we have of a girlish boy at the age of two or so? Why should mother's gently touching hand lead to girlishness in very young Bloom and womanliness in the man?

In the next chapter, I will discuss Phyllis Greenacre's ideas about the problematic results of a disturbance in the early relationship of mother and child, especially her ideas about "primary identification." Using them, we can fathom more fully Joyce's insights into the connection between Bloom's womanliness and what appear to be two distinct yet related traumas in his early years—the psychological mechanism of his "infantile debauchery" with a "dissolute granddam.

CHAPTER IV

The Child is Father to the Man: A Strange Murmuring Wine of Blood

BLOOM
(Gently.) Give me back the potato, will you?

ZOE
Forfeits, a fine thing and a superfine thing.

BLOOM
(With feeling.) It is nothing, but still a relic of poor mama.

ZOE
Give a thing and take it back
God'll ask you where is that
You'll say you don't know
God'll send you down below.

BLOOM
There is a memory attached to it. I should like to have it.

STEPHEN
To have or not to have, that is the question.

ZOE
Here. *(She hauls up a reef of her slip, revealing her bare thighs and unrolls the potato from the top of her stocking.)* Those that hides knows where to find.

—"Circe" (*Ulysses*, p. 521)

In the previous chapter, we have seen Bloom's lifelong habit of incorporating a woman's body (or parts of that body) visually and tactilely, from urinating or defecating Molly (whose warm impress of her bodily form imprints itself on his body), to the idealizing and self-murdering Veiled Sibyl (whose self-destruction Bloom is tempted to imitate), and finally to Zoe (whose buckles bronze him with infamy). Here, I want to examine Joyce's sharpening focus on what for Bloom is the most exciting and frightening part of a woman's body, her genitals. With the help of Phyllis Greenacre's ideas, I hope to deepen and complicate our understanding of Joyce's attempt to convert into art what he uncovered as he psoakoonaloosed himself. I also hope to avoid the dangers of theoretical systematization and absurd oversimplifications as we trace out Joyce's hints about the mysterious "oona" (Oona? Una?) that seemingly lay half-buried in his unconscious and in Bloom's. But the risk is worth it if we begin to appreciate more fully the psychological depth of his cunning art.

2. The Grey Sunken Cunt of the World

At the start of his odyssey, in "Calypso," Bloom travels to an ever-darkening version of Zion and experiences a terrible benumbing. Mentally voyaging early in the morning (after a sexually frustrating experience with the next-door girl in Dlugacz's shop, the Jewish pork butcher whom he doesn't acknowledge as a fellow Jew), Bloom falls victim to a kind of psychological rigor mortis. This attack of intense anxiety is intertwined with his vision of the death-associated genitalia of a woman. It is symbolized by a liquid body implanted in the Holy Land, a salt sea—a version of the Dead Sea.

Walking alone down Dorset Street—reading gravely the advertisement for "Agendath Netaim," the Zionist colony in Palestine—he recalls, first, a fertile land, a foreshadowing of the Middle Eastern land of gazelles, cedargroves, lakes, fountains and damask roses that he will later see in "Circe":

> To purchase vast sandy tracts from Turkish government and plant with eucalyptus trees. Excellent for shade, fuel and construction.

Orange groves and immense melonfields north of Jaffa. You pay eight marks and they plant a dunam of land for you with olives, oranges, almonds or citrons. (*Ulysses,* p. 58)

Then, he recalls another Promised Land, one that he and Molly created in the places they lived in when they were first married, Saint Kevin's parade, Pleasants street, Arbutus place:

Silvered powdered olivetrees. Quiet long days: pruning, ripening.... Oranges in tissue paper packed in crates. Citrons too. Wonder is poor Citron still alive in Saint Kevin's parade. And Mastiansky with the old cither.... Nice to hold, cool waxen fruit, hold in the hand, lift it to the nostrils and smell the perfume. Like that, heavy, sweet, wild perfume. Always the same, year after year.... Arbutus place: Pleasants street: pleasant old times. Must be without a flaw, he said. Coming all that way: Spain, Gibraltar, Mediterranean, the Levant. (*Ulysses,* p. 58)

"A cloud beg[ins] to cover the sun wholly slowly wholly. Grey. Far" (*Ulysses,* p. 58), and Bloom's associations shift dramatically away from memories of the Zion on Arbutus place and Pleasants street where he once lived happily with his bride. A place of lush Mediterranean fruit, a cither playing, and Molly's heavy, sweet, wild perfume becomes a death-haunted, grey, and poisonous wasteland:

A barren land, bare waste. Vulcanic lake, the dead sea: no fish, weedless, sunk deep in the earth. No wind could lift those waves, grey metal, poisonous foggy waters. Brimstone they called it raining down: the cities of the plain: Sodom, Gomorrah, Edom, All dead names. A dead sea in a dead land, grey and old. Old now. It bore the oldest, the first race. ... The oldest people. Wandered far away over all the earth, captivity to captivity, multiplying, dying, being born everywhere. It lay there now. Now it could bear no more. Dead: an old woman's: the grey sunken cunt of the world. Desolation. (*Ulysses,* pp. 58-59)

Rudy's death almost eleven years earlier was also the death of Bloom's capacity for genital intercourse with Molly. He and Molly knew she would bear no more children. There would be no "multiplying" for them. Cast out of the Promised Land of Pleasants street (and cast down), Bloom is associating Molly with the now barren motherland of the "oldest, the first race," the "oldest people [who] wandered far away over all the earth, captivity to captivity." Bloom imagines her belonging to the wandering Jewish people. In her ambiguous remark about her mother, which I mentioned earlier, she implies that Lunita Laredo was Jewish, thus making her daughter Jewish: "he hadnt an idea about my mother till we were engaged otherwise hed never have got me so cheap as he did" (*Ulysses*, p. 701).

Not only does Bloom's thirty-four-year-old wife turn into a barren old woman, as dead as the dead sea. Even more devastating to this wandering jewgreek is the paralyzing sight of her genitals:

> Dead: an old woman's: the grey sunken cunt of the world. Desolation. Grey horror seared his flesh. ...Cold oils slid along his veins, chilling his blood: age crusting him with a salt cloak. (*Ulysses*, p. 59)

This desolating sight makes Bloom feel that he too is becoming as dead as the once promising, now sterile, Jewish homeland. As "grey horror sear[s] his flesh," he seems identified with that grey sunken cunt; and in his horror, his female identification crystalizes. He momentarily becomes an embalmed version of Lot's wife, "Cold oils slid[ing] along his veins...crusting him with a salt cloak" (*Ulysses*, p, 59).

Bloom has become the fallen woman associated with the "cities of the plain" that appeared in the ranting sermon of the street evangelist ALEXANDER J. DOWIE that I quoted earlier. We remember that he connected Bloom with Sodom and Gomorrah, the "cities of the plain" that Lot's wife looked back upon only to be turned into a pillar of salt. Then Dowie went on to fulminate that Bloom "gave precocious signs of infantile debauchery...with a dissolute granddam" (*Ulysses*, p. 465). (Joyce's comic touch hints at a serious, earlier experience of infantile debauchery, which we will turn to shortly.) At that time, Babby Bloom might very well have been horrified when he saw another sunken cunt. I will suggest that that vision of a woman's "damaged" genitals was also horrifying.

In other words, it is not just the sight of "Sodom, Gomorrah, Edom" that petrifies Bloom, transforming him into Lot's wife. It is his incorporation into himself of the sight of the deadened and deadening motherland of the Jewish people—symbolically, Molly's deadened (and deadly?) "grey" genitalia. This terrible image makes him feel he too is turning into a "sinful" woman, someone who couldn't resist the urge, a kind of inner compulsion, to look on a forbidden sight.

With the emergence of his unconscious identification with the genitalia of a mother whose womb seems to him to be a tomb, Bloom's body image seems to be collapsing along with his sexual identity. Before his own eyes (and ours), he is all but becoming (if he has not already become) what he astonishingly describes Paddy Dignam's corpse becoming in "Hades": "Saltwhite crumbling mush of corpse: smell, taste like raw white turnips" (*Ulysses*, p. 110). A man within the salt-cloaked body of a fallen woman—a saltwhite crumbling inseparable from the sunken cunt of a Jewish wife-and-mother—this seemingly upright pillar of a man suffers from a wavering genitality that can make him feel he is simultaneously male and female.

Let me now turn to Phyllis Greenacre!s ideas about the possible origins of this confusion of body image and sexual identity and allow me to quote her at some length. I ask you to keep in mind the many females Joyce himself grew up with. In addition to three misbirths (and three other sons), his mother had six daughters from the time he was two until he was twelve (see Cadenza, n.134).

In "Certain Relationships between Fetishism and the Faulty Development of the Body Image," Greenacre writes that the image we have of our body develops largely from seeing our own bodies, from endogenous sensations, and from contacts with the outer world, of which feeling one part of our body with another is a "peculiar condensation."[41]

---

[41] Phyllis Greenacre, "Certain Relationships between Fetishism and the Faulty Development of the Body Image," in *Emotional Growth: Psychoanalytic Studies of the Gifted*

She goes on to say,

> not all of our own body is actually visible to us; and in the case of those parts of the body which are not visible to the child himself, the endogenous and contact sensations are supplemented by visual impressions of the bodies of others. Consequently the body image is not based just on the perception of [one's] own body but to a little extent anyway on the visual perception of the bodies of others. (Greenacre, p. 24).

Noting that the face and the genitals are the two "highly differentiated" parts of the body, she writes that our awareness of the face and the genitals and their location in the body image "must be supplemented by the observation of these parts in others" (Greenacre, p. 25). Said somewhat differently, in the first eighteen months or so, we build up our mental representation of our body, especially of the genitals, by visually "incorporating" the genitals of another.

But what happens to the body image of the child who, in his first year or year and a half, continuously experiences some sort of impairment or "dysfunction" in his relationship with his mother—the "infantile debauchery," say, of excessive fondling, handling, cuddling, and stroking by a seemingly seductive but perhaps actually a deeply anxious or guilty or depressed mother. Greenacre hypothesizes that in this "traumatized" infant, in the infant who has been disturbed in his relationship with his mother, there is a prolongation of the state of "primary identification" (Greenacre, p. 24). Suffering "frustration" in his love—and excessive gratification, as I said, can be all but psychologically synonymous with frustration—the infant unconsciously identifies himself with the object of his anxiety.

In building up his body image, the child will continue to take in with his eyes either his mother's body *or* the bodies of his sisters *or* all of

---

and a Great Variety of Other Individuals, vol. I (New York: International Universities Press, Inc., 1971), p. 24. Subsequent references will appear in the text and refer to this book.

them, especially the genitals, for too-long a period. In several of Greenacre's patients, the men with the uncertain or disturbed body images were in very close visual contact with a female, either with the mother or with a sister or sisters relatively close to them in age, when they were boys.

Although there are signs, especially in "Circe," of the adult consequences of primary identification—Bloom's uncertain body image and moments of confusion about the nature of his genitals—that confusion is not due simply to an overly long period of that very early form of identification. Greenacre writes of a second trauma. These later "catastrophies," which the already traumatized child also took in through his eyes, were usually "bleeding injuries" involving the female genitals—multiple births in the home, miscarriages, and menstruating sisters. In a summary of her ideas in, "The Fetish and the Transitional Object," Greenacre writes that it is this *doubly* traumatized child who experiences a "delay in consolidating the body image" (Greenacre, p. 331). This child will often have a confused impression of his own body and of the existence, or danger, of injury to it. First, the child is exposed "frequently or even consistently to awareness of the genitals of the opposite sex, whether of the parent or of a sibling [or siblings]. Such early exposure (in a "maternal environment" of "marginal adequacy") is then combined with him "witnessing or experiencing. . .body injury," especially in the latter part of the second and the fourth year." This "combination of influences results then in an unusually severe castration fear" and a delay in consolidating the body image (Greenacre, p. 331).

Let's accept, at least provisionally and heuristically, the idea that Bloom's "maternal environment" was of "marginal adequacy"; that he was often treated as an anxiety-reducing object (or that he felt that he was); and that because of his prolonged period of primary identification (and subsequent confusion about his sexual identity and the general image of his body), he was likely to be retraumatized by the somewhat later (and repeated) sight of the bleeding female genitals.

Let's turn again to Bloom's exchanges with ZOE for symbolic signs of this second trauma. That trauma, we recall, is a much more disturbing experience for someone whose genitality is already shaky, a man whom Joyce regularly connects with bleeding women (from Gerty MacDowell to Molly). As I have mentioned, early in his marriage, Bloom, according to the nameless debt-collector-narrator of "Cyclops," apparently imitated a prostitute with her period by staying in bed once a month with a headache, "like a totty with her courses" (*Ulysses,* p. 323). In the "Nausicaa" chapter, he intuits that Gerty MacDowell is menstruating—"Devils they are when that's coming on them. Dark devilish appearance. Molly often told me feel things a ton weight" (*Ulysses,* p. 352). And Molly herself is menstruating, irritably, at the end of the book.

After Bloom fingers ZOE'S intriguing bronze petal-buckles, he sees an astonishing sight beneath the sapphire fluidity of her slip. In another quick-change act out of a dream (which we looked at earlier) Joyce again makes it clear that ZOE is all but explicitly the transmigrating soul of Bloom's mother. She "*greedily*" hides near her own genitals the hard, black, shriveled potato-talisman that ELLEN BLOOM stored under her petticoat and gave her son to forestall death and pestilence (*Ulysses,* p. 450).

As ZOE "*cuddl[es] him with supple warmth*," Bloom once more seems to absorb this maternal figure with a kind of prehensile vision (*Ulysses,* p. 450): "*He gazes in the tawny crystal of her eyes, ringed with kohol*," and "*his smile softens*" (*Ulysses,* p. 450). Then, the stage directions allow us to see what enchanted Bloom "*forlornly*" sees—or what Babby might have seen. Said another way, we see metaphorically what he might have seen beneath his mother's undergarment long ago when she was still fondling him. We are seeing, that is, one of the most archaic and, to Bloom, one of the most troubling, unconscious images:

> (*Gazelles are leaping, feeding on the mountains. Near are lakes. Round their shores file shadows black of cedargroves. Aroma rises, a strong hairgrowth of resin. It burns, the orient, a sky of sapphire, cleft by the bronze flight of eagles. Under it lies the womancity, nude, white, still, cool, in luxury. A fountain murmurs among damask roses. Mammoth roses murmur of scarlet winegrapes. A wine of shame, lust, blood exudes, strangely murmuring.*) (*Ulysses,* p. 451)

Again, by means of Joyce's version of a dream-work—here the dreaming mind's use of condensation—parts of ZOE, especially her genitalia, begin to merge with a Middle Eastern landscape. As we shall soon see, this feminized land symbolizes another of Bloom's versions of the Promised Land, his ancestral motherland. Her sapphire slip becomes the burning orient sky with a bronzed cleft. Her kohol-ringed eyelids transform themselves into the filing black shadows of cedargroves that encircle lakes; and those aroma-filled groves then become a resinous growth of hair near a liquid body. (We recall that Bloom associated a "woman eyeball," Bronze's, with a "liquid of womb" in "Sirens.")

The eye shadow-cedargrove-hairgrowth encircling an eye-lake-womb in "Circe" seems to be a dream-like version of a woman's sexual organs—the portal to her womb. But it is not just the strong-smelling hair and the sight of the female genitalia that transfix Bloom. The genitals are associated (by Joycean-Bloomesque displacement) with roses, scarlet, and blood. Under that maternal expanse of *sapphire cleft by bronze* lies a nude luxuriating female body, the *"womancity"* (Jerusalem, we soon discover) that contains a presumably holy wet place—a murmuring, bleeding fountain.

Out of that womb—that vessel of liquid lodged deep within the white nude body of a Dublin odalisque—comes a distressing yet strangely sacramental exudate: *"A wine of shame, lust, blood...strangely murmuring," "among damask roses."* This wine-and-blood flow is saying something, but what? Although it doesn't speak so clearly at this time as it will shortly, Joyce gives us a clue in *"damask."* With its connotations of linen napkins, it first calls to mind Molly's irritated search for "napkins"—probably left, she thinks, in the linen press—as she begins to menstruate in "Penelope." The implication (which Joyce will deepen) seems to be that forlorn Bloom is seeing something usually buried in his unconscious—the bleeding genitals of a mother. But Molly is only the latest in a series of unconscious images of bleeding or wounded or "dying" women that are disinterred in nighttown.

Almost as if to intensify our sense that within Bloom's unconscious there is the simultaneously shameful and sexually exciting image of a curiously abstracted seductress who seems to be bleeding, Joyce rapidly transforms the murmuring wine-and-blood into a second murmur of shame and lust. It exudes through another lip-enclosed, rosy opening in the womancity of Zoe-Mother:

ZOE

(Murmuring singsong with the music, her odalisk lips lusciously smeared with salve of swinefat and rosewater.)
Schorach ani wenowach, benoith Hierushaloim. (*Ulysses*, p. 451)

Murmuring (from "The Song of Solomon") "I am black but comely O ye daughters of Jerusalem," ZOE is not just the transmigrating spirit of ELLEN BLOOM.[42] She is the Queen of Sheba, too, and contains Molly's transmigrating spirit as well. When she arose out of Bloom's mind at the beginning of "Circe," in her *"Turkish costume"* and *"opulent curves," "white yashmak,"* and *"large dark eyes and raven hair,"* Molly, we remember, echoed Flaubert's description of Sheba in *The Temptation of Saint Anthony* (*Ulysses*, p. 417-418).[43] Bloom was "dead gone on" her fat lips (*Ulysses*, p. 717). And he associates those lips with a "nigger mouth" and a veiled "whore" (*Ulysses*, p. 354). "Moorish" and Turkish, Jewish and non-Jewish, Molly *is* comelier to Bloom than the daughters of Jerusalem, despite her dark skin and (to some Dubliners) alien ways (*Ulysses*, p. 360). What all this means is that Bloom is finding crucial aspects of a maternal figure with different names in this womancity. Put another way, in all the women in his life he has found to love—women who now reappear in his seemingly endless nightmare in "Circe"—he refinds someone he first loved.

In the succession of female images that dance witchingly before his eyes, he experiences the most painful anxiety—a very deep fear that was presumably stirred by the first woman in his life. Beneath the yashmak of Molly or the Queen of Sheba—beneath ZOE'S sapphire slip, or the sapphire sky of the motherland—there is a murmuring opening associated with bleeding that simultaneously attracts and repels him. Although this fountain-like mouth seems synonymous with the pleasures of paradise—it does contain echoes of Dante's Rose of Heaven, the scarlet winegrapes of Canaan, and Sheba's comeliness—it is also the place of things forbidden,

---

[42] Don Gifford and Richard J. Seidman, *Notes for Joyce: An Annotation of James Joyce's Ulysses* (New York: E. P. Dutton & Co., 1974), p. 386.
[43] *Ibid.*

repugnant. The veiled opening stirs feelings of swinish lust and the darkest shame as Bloom drinks in ZOE with his eye while she proffers her body to the accompaniment of her singsong of wine and blood. Despite her religious adoration of him (just as ELLEN BLOOM or THE VEILED *SIBYL* adores him)—and despite her seductive rocking, stroking, and caressing—Woman, to Bloom at his most anxious, *is* what ZOE sullenly calls herself, a "bleeding whore" (*Ulysses*, p. 471).

The frightening spectacle of a fountain murmuring among damask roses casts Bloom down as a man and perhaps did so as a boy. That fear seemed to have stopped him from entering the Holy City (except under special safeguards, which I will discuss later) and rendered problematic his relationship with the Promised Land that he yearns to return to. We might imagine that drinking from ZOE'S fount is to participate in a kind of communion service for Bloom, but this communicant is often filled with the most intense worry as the cup passes to him. To communicate, even visually, is to feel that you are in danger of becoming that bleeding goddess yourself.

Is Joyce more explicit about the psychological price Bloom pays for visually incorporating the murmuring wine of a mother's bleeding genitals? Does he allow us at least inferentially to participate in Bloom's experience of such a sight, an experience that can cause Bloom to feel that his own body is also being (or has already been) fatally injured? When the singsong of shame and lust stops exuding from between Zoe-Sheba-Molly-Ellen Bloom's lips, Joyce's stage directions tell us that ZOE sends a "cloying breath of stale garlic" on Bloom. Then, (*"The roses draw apart, disclose a sepulchre of the gold of kings and their mouldering bones.)"* (*Ulysses*, p. 451). At its worst, when the verbal wine of Hebrew no longer bubbles out of Zoe-Sheba-Molly's fat-lipped mouth, the hollow organ becomes synonymous with a kind of death for Bloom, a visual echo of the grey sunken cunt of the world that desolates him earlier in the day. It is indistinguishable from a gloomy resting place sunk deep in the womancity, the "allwombing tomb," to use Stephen's phrase, where kings (as well as Bloom) are reduced to mouldering bones (*Ulysses*, p. 47).

For Bloom, gazing on and entering a woman's opening that glistens like a rose is to risk the psychological equivalent of death. (Little wonder that he hasn't had "complete carnal intercourse with ejaculation of semen within the natural female organ" since "27 November 1893." *Ulysses*, p. 691.) To be sure, as we have seen, ZOE'S mammoth rose-ringed fountain does seem to stir lust and shame in its murmuring. She might even seem comely (if alien in her "blackness"). But the heterosexual impulses of the womanly man can become short-circuited. Bloom seems transformed into something mechanical, numbed by what he sees. Once "fascinated" by the good "accent" of his granddam-dam, he "draws back" from now-cloying, now-asphyxiating ZOE, *"mechanically caressing her right bub with a flat awkward hand"* (*Ulysses*, p. 451). In fact, Bloom seems simultaneously spellbound and repulsed by the sight of the female genitalia; he seems frozen in a state of bodily excitement that cannot be discharged. To enter her rose-garden-and-fountain—or simply to continue gazing on it—is to feel that his body (together with his sexual identity) risks mouldering. It is to feel he is in danger of collapsing, like those dethroned kings of Stephen, into a saltwhite mush of corpse.

This profound fear of physical and psychological disintegration is different from what many students of Freud often label "castration anxiety"—the retaliation which the little boy fears from a powerful man at the height of the "positive" oedipal period (around three or four years of age or so) because of his powerful wishes for erotic intimacy with his mother (combined with his often murderous anger at his potentially castrating rival, his father). But Bloom does not seem to fear the loss of his genitals because of incestuous (and murderous) desires. He is close to experiencing some sort of catastrophic anxiety where his very identity, his sense of who he is, might disappear.

In fact, in "Circe," he often seems to feel (again unconsciously) that he might not have a penis in the first place. On first reading, Bloom's anxiety seems closer to that of a three- or four-year old girl. BELLO coaxingly urges Bloom, "Come, ducky dear. I want a word with you, darling, just to administer correction. Just a little heart to heart talk, sweety. *(Bloom puts out her timid head.)* There's a good girly now"(*Ulysses*, p. 500). Bloom is suffused with feelings of shame and mortification in the presence of a very cruel bisexual mother. (ZOE tells

Bloom that Bella-Bello has a "son in Oxford" and asks Bloom if he is the boy's father. *Ulysses,* p. 449.) The madam is a *"massive whoremistress"* with a *"sprouting mustache"* who, he unconsciously feels, can make him feel penisless (*Ulysses,* p. 496). "Unmanned and mine in earnest," as BELLO tells him, Bloom is also commanded to dress in *"vicelike corsets of soft dove coutille," "nettight frocks, pretty two ounce petticoats and fringes"* (*Ulysses,* p. 503). In the presence of that "Empress," Bloom appears to be an oedipal girl for an instant (*Ulysses,* p. 530). He becomes a *"charming soubrette"* (*Ulysses,* p. 504). He also reveals one aspect of a little girl's "castration anxiety"—the fear of genital injury attendant on her wish to be loved by the one she worships. "*Infatuated*" by the "Hugeness" (*Ulysses,* p. 499) of BELLO (née Bella), the charming soubrette "lies" down before this "Magnificance," *"shamming dead with eyes shut tight, trembling eyelids"* (*Ulysses,* p. 499). Then, desirous but terrified, "enthralled" yet "bleat[ing]" in the manner of a sacrificial lamb, girly Bloom feels her master's "glorious heels, so glistening in their proud erectness" grind *"in on her neck"* (*Ulysses,* p. 500).

However, it is not the little girl's fear of being injured by hugeness's proud erectness (or, just as terrible, being abandoned by someone she loves) that Joyce is dramatizing. Nor is he dramatizing the little boy's fear of *becoming* penisless by a grinding, punitive BELLOesque force. In fact, as I have mentioned throughout, there is relatively little oedipal conflict, male or female, and the concomitant fear of retaliation and loss of love. Bloom's intense anxiety about *already* existing bodily damage—or the threat of grave injury to his body—seems preoedipal in origin. In other words, his confusion about his sexual identity, due to an earlier period of identification with his mother's frightening genitalia, has led to his fear that there is a Bello/Bella within, a body image with the overtones of a dangerous bisexuality, that can obliterate him.

Again, at the risk of redundancy, let me summarize my reading of Joyce's complex patterns of associations. Bloom's anxiety over body damage seems to have arisen before he could form love-and-hate relationships with real others, when he was no more than perhaps two or younger and confused about the image of his own body. And this confusion is due to his body image being intertwined with the image of his mother's body when he was in babylinen and pelisse. Bloom's unconscious sense that he shares his mother's bodily "mutilation" and "injury" is the likely base upon which any later anxiety was built and intensified.

With his big eyes fixed on her, Babby, in possibly his first eighteen months or so, was apparently bronzed with infamy. He mixed up his body with her own in a period of primary identification; and because of his later infantile debauchery with the Scarlet Woman—the repeated vision, that is, of mother's shocking scarlet fountain, perhaps in childbirth, perhaps in stillbirths—Bloom seems to have "caught" her injury. Even before he felt the full intensity of any oedipal conflicts, we may infer that Bloom's body image could break down and his unconscious feminine identification could begin to emerge when he saw or fantasized "damaged" female genitals and, for an instant, misperceived them as his own.[44]

3. Potato Preservative Against Plague and Pestilence (Again)

How does Bloom manage to forestall a collapse of his body image when he sees a woman's genitals? How does he avoid his frightening transformation into her? In "Nausicaa," pausing on Sandymount Strand after visiting Paddy Dignam's widow, he comes close to seeing the genitalia of another seductress. But here he doesn't feel the horrible chill of cold oils sliding along his veins—psychic embalming fluid?—that he felt twelve hours earlier when his Promised Land (inseparable from Molly's body) epiphanized as the grey sunken cunt of the world. Nor does he re-experience what happened to him in nighttown when he seemed to freeze in the presence of Zoe's murmuring fountain of shame and blood. I would suggest that it was because he didn't see Nausicaa's vulva directly

---

[44] In the next section, I will discuss more fully Bloom's constant companion, his Potato Preservative against Plague and Pestilence. Although it seems to be what a fetishist uses to ward off anxiety at the sight of the penislessness of a woman, Bloom doesn't use it as Freud believed a fetishist might use it—as his only non-anxiety-ridden way to have genital intercourse with her.

that he escaped the bodily confusion (and intensifying anxiety) that we have been discussing.

Gazing excitedly at Gerty MacDowell, who soon stretches herself back on the rocks, leaning back "ever so far," as far as she can, he associates her exhibitionism with the temptations of the devil (*Ulysses,* p. 349): "Glad I didn't know [about her lameness] when she was on show. Hot little devil all the same. Wouldn't mind" (*Ulysses,* p. 351). "Devils they are when [menstruation's] coming on them," he tells himself, but despite her menstruation, he is aroused to masturbate (*Ulysses,* p. 352): "Darling, I saw your. I saw all" (*Ulysses,* p. 355). But Gerty's "all" was enclosed in "nainsook knickers," so Bloom didn't see her bleeding genitals directly (*Ulysses,* p. 349).

Keeping in mind his experiences with various symbolic female bodies in "Circe" and "Calypso"—a wine of shame, lust, and blood that exudes from mammoth roses; a wine that murmurs of scarlet winegrapes; a melon- and orange-filled Promised Land that is really a dead sea in a dead land; the grey sunken cunt of the world—we realize that Joyce has given us enough clues about Bloom's erotic "curve of an emotion," the "individuating rhythm" of his unconscious sexual life, to begin to fathom his concentration on Gerty's feet:

> Still she was game. Lord, I am wet. Devil you are. Swell of her calf. Transparent, stretched to breaking point. Not like that frump today....Rumpled stockings. Or the one in Grafton street. White. Wow! Beef to the heel! (*Ulysses,* p. 355)

Focusing on Gerty's packed appendages—the "swell of her calf," the "transparent stockings stretched to breaking point," which he likens to "beef to the heel"—Bloom is warding off the anxiety stirred by her genitalia and simultaneously revealing the way he stabilizes his often insecurely established genitality. Exciting himself by visually incorporating her well-fed hose is a way of *not* incorporating Gerty's "damaged" body (her lameness and menstruation intensify his anxiety at what to him might very well be her bleeding, mutilated genitals). Put another way, seeing Gerty as beef to the heel, concentrating his gaze on her foot,

Bloom is putting a patch on a piece of reality. He is endowing her with a symbolic penis that eliminates her penislessness and thereby reduces his fear that his own genitalia can turn into her bleeding injury.

In "Circe," we remember, Joyce underscores Bloom's lifelong fascination with a woman's feet, appendages that he loves to touch. "*Murmur[ing] lovingly*," he confesses:

> To be a shoefitter in Mansfield's was my love's young dream, the darling joys of sweet buttonhooking, to lace up crisscrossed to kneelength the dressy kid footwear satinlined, so incredibly small, of Clyde Road ladies. Even their wax model Raymonde I visited daily to admire her cobweb hose and stick of rhubarb toe, as worn in Paris. (*Ulysses*, p. 498)

Immediately after, THE HOOF issues a command (Bella possesses a "*plump buskined hoof and a full pastern, silksocked*"), "Smell my hot goathide…Feel my royal weight" and Bloom proceeds to crosslace it lovingly (*Ulysses*, p. 498).

Bloom seems to have found a portable device for reducing the anxiety he feels in the presence of a woman's genitals, the Potato Preservative Against Plague and Pestilence that he secrets on his body. It is a "talisman, heirloom," a gift from his mother, Bloom tells ZOE-ELLEN HIGGINS. This inanimate object associated with a woman's body apparently allows him to sustain his potency. Fondling his "nuts," she becomes alarmed when she feels what she believes to be a "hard chancre," takes the "*hard black shriveled potato*"—his "talisman," his "heirloom"—out of his pocket, and puts it "*greedily into [her] pocket*," actually high up on her thigh (*Ulysses*, p. 450). The preservative's provenance suggests its psychological function for Bloom—to ward off his anxiety at the sight of a woman's genitalia, a fear that causes him to panic about the permanence of his own genitalia, to feel that he is exchanging body parts with her, even to feel he is merging with a dead and barren cunt.

Bloom has carried this hard, black, shrivelled potato in his "*left trouser pocket*" near his genitals, and later, when he asks for it back, Zoe first mocks him with "What's yours is mine and what's mine is my own" and then:

> Give a thing and take it back
> God'll ask you where is that
> You'll say you don't know
> God'll send you down below. (*Ulysses,* p. 520-521)

ZOE seems to regard the heirloom as a private male possession indistinguishable from his "nuts" that, once possessed, will remain hers. ZOE tells him that if he loses possession of it, even momentarily, he will suffer the torments of hell, "down below." When Bloom asks her to return it, she tells him she really didn't take it; she says that he freely gave the potato to her. The back-and-forth possession of this hidden and then not-hidden, present and then absent, preservative suggests its complex psychological function. It preserves Bloom from death "down below"—the catastrophe to his genital integrity at the sight of the mutilated female genitals, Zoe's murmuring bloody fountain. But this occurs only when Bloom "gives" it to her, imagines that what was hidden on a male body to bolster a wavering genitality is now freely transplanted onto a female body where it masculinizes her.

As I mentioned, ZOE has hidden it near her genitals as we see when she reveals its final resting place:

> Here. (*She hauls up a reef of her slip, revealing her bare thigh and unrolls the potato from the top of her stocking.*) Those that hides knows where to find. (*Ulysses,* p. 521)

ZOE'S wisecrack to Stephen, "Hamlet, I am thy father's gimlet" allows us to infer that this "gimlet," this small boring tool, is connected to the potato that Bloom unconsciously gave her (*Ulysses,* p. 525). Yet it is not a permanent gift. Having Zoe replace the word that Hamlet's father used, "spirit," for "gimlet,"—and spirit means ghost to everyone in the play—Joyce makes the "gimlet" into a spirit, a ghost-like thing. It is something that is associated both with a woman (ZOE and his mother) and with Bloom's hellish world down below; it appears in the "real" world and then disappears.

Wisecracking again to Stephen, ZOE says, "Ask my ballocks that I haven't got" (*Ulysses*, p. 526). ZOE remains a nuts-less female momentarily masculinized by Bloom's ghostly potato preservative, a magical object that (both Bloom and ZOE feel) makes what is absent in a woman present. Joyce underlines its psychological function for Bloom by making it inseparable from ZOE'S well-fed hose, her stocking-enclosed foot, a visual echo of Gerty MacDowell's appendage on which Bloom pegged his wavering genitality earlier.

STEPHEN'S joke in all this—"To have or not to have, that is the question"—makes the identity between Bloom's potato amulet and a symbolic penis even clearer (*Ulysses*, p. 521). To have or not to have a penis is a constant question for someone who suffers from the same anxiety as a fetishist but who, *unlike* a fetishist, does not use it as an adjunct to insure adequate sexual performance, *i.e.*, genital intercourse with this anxiety-producing creature. (He doesn't enter Gerty, of course, but masturbates before her—in a quasi-secret way.) Nor has he entered Molly since 27 November 1893, but he does regularly ejaculate on her bottom, an "adorer of the adulterous rump," in BELLO'S disdainful phrase (*Ulysses*, p. 499).

Let's look more closely at Joyce's image of this necessary prop. Why a potato? Almost all of his readers would think of the Great Famine of the mid-1840s when Ireland became the land of "plague and pestilence" as what seemed to be an endemic disease destroyed the potato crop. His mother hopes her gift will ward off the psychological equivalence of the Great Famine and preserve Bloom from the death-in-life that he falls into in "Calypso" as his Promised Land becomes a wasteland. But why hard, black and "shrivelled"? With Bloom's intense anal eroticism in "Circe," it is almost impossible not to regard this "shrivelled" up, hard, black detachable thing that a woman can possess as well as a man, as something fecal. Hidden in a female and then a male body—an exchangeable and emotionally valuable gift that seems simultaneously present and absent—it asks us to think of the significance of Bloom's ever-present anal yearnings.

Although he is mocked as a "dungdevourer" by BELLO, Bloom is not most ashamed about his coprophagous urges (or for that matter about any of his other polymorphous perverse wishes, ranging from the transvestite impulses, masochistic longings, and fetishistic and exhibitionistic desires that Joyce takes fun in displaying) (*Ulysses*, pp. 498ff.). "The most revolting piece of obscenity in all [his] career of crime," he confesses in a gurgle to Bello, is when he "rererepugnosed in rerererepugnant. . ." (*Ulysses*, p. 506). THE SINS OF THE PAST clarify the nature of his self-admitted and regular repugnant nosing around in a woman's "rere":

> By word and deed he encouraged a nocturnal strumpet to deposit fecal and other matter in an unsanitary outhouse attached to empty premises....Did he not lie in bed, the gross boar, gloating over a nauseous fragment of wellused toilet paper presented to him by a nasty harlot, stimulated by gingerbread and a postal order?" (*Ulysses*, p. 505)

Excrementitiousness is what he is most excited about, particularly a seductive woman's feces. Molly recalls that Poldy liked her "muddy boots" and the idea of her "walk[ing] in all the horses dung [she] could find" (*Ulysses*, p. 701). For Bloom, there is something devilishly exciting in a woman dirtying herself, covering her boots (which cover her feet) with fecal matter. Molly also tells us that her husband

> was 10 times worse himself anyhow begging me to give him a tiny bit cut off my drawers...so I let him keep it as if I forgot it to think of me when I saw him slip it into his pocket of course hes mad on the subject of drawers. . .anything for an excuse to put his hand anear me drawers drawers the whole blessed time till I promised to give him a pair off my doll to carry about in his waistcoat pocket" (*Ulysses*, pp. 701-702).

A keepsake, a piece of Molly-esque drawers that he carries around in his pocket, probably as brownstained as the nasty harlot's "wellused toilet paper," it provides what that black talisman-heirloom provides.

Focusing on it, as he focused on the potato, he preserves himself from the desolating sight of a dead sea in a dead land, the grey sunken cunt that can make him feel that he has been turned into Lot's wife, a man whose genitals have turned into a woman's.

Linked to excrement (it is dirt-encrusted, grown in dark soil), the potato is a special kind of symbolic penis for Bloom, an illusory fecal penis. Just as Joyce himself was terribly excited at Nora's apparent possession of a penis when he saw her defecating—seeing "her bum sticking out and a fat brown thing stuck half-way out of her hole"—so Bloom apparently erases the anatomical distinction between the sexes with his potato in hand or with the sight of feces-covered boots or the sight of a woman's calf enclosed in transparent stockings.[45] With these safeguards, magically protected from the horrifying spectacle of a penisless creature, Bloom can magically turn that creature into someone who possesses one and insure his bodily integrity and sexual potency.

---

[45] In the letters he exchanged with Nora in the dark night of his soul, the winter of 1909, meant to stimulate mutual onanism, Joyce himself seemed obsessed with drawers and defecation. He writes Nora about his excitement at recalling the "little brown stain on the seat of your white drawers" (*Selected Letters of James Joyce,* ed., Richard Ellmann [New York: The Viking Press, 1975], p. 184), or he asks, "Are you offended because I said I loved to look at the brown stain that comes behind on your girlish white drawers?" (*ibid.,* p. 189).

Even more exciting to him is the spectacle of Nora defecating, "the most shameful and filthy act of the body. Do you remember the day you pulled up your clothes and let me lie under you looking up at you while you did it?" (*ibid.,* p. 181). Her feces can even appear to be penis-like, a "fearfully lecherous thing ...to see her pretty white drawers pulled open behind and her bum sticking out and a fat brown thing stuck half-way out of her hole" (*ibid.,* p. 191).

Apparently imagining Nora phallicized in this manner reduced the overwhelming anxiety that Joyce lived with in Dublin in 1909 when he felt Nora was not a virgin at the time that they expatriated themselves. He felt she had betrayed (and thus abandoned) him—even before she lived with him. Less anxious, he seemed reassured about her love and his own (now intensified) phallic power.

Cf. Janine Chasseguet-Smirgel, "Loss of Reality in Perversions—With Special Reference to Fetishism," *Journal of the American Psychoanalytic Association,* 29 (1981), 525. She believes that "all perversions are essentially anal-sadistic since the anal universe is a universe where the equation penis=child=feces, as studied by Freud (1917), is to be understood literally.

4. Transparent Stockings Stretched to the Breaking Point and an Ache at the Butt of his Tongue

I have regularly used the phrase "wavering genitality" with Bloom or "confusion" about the nature of his genitals. Does Joyce present us with further images that imply that Bloom's body image *can* momentarily waver, that his genitality is so precariously established as to be in danger of collapsing? Let me return to his tryst with Gerty MacDowell. After masturbating, Bloom gratefully muses in his detumescent state:

> For this relief much thanks. In *Hamlet*, that is. Lord! It was all things combined. Excitement. When she leaned back felt an ache at the butt of my tongue. (*Ulysses*, p. 355)

Joyce underscores Bloom's shaky genital identity with Bloom's allusion to Francisco's "For this relief [from the bitter cold] much thanks" in the first scene of *Hamlet*. In the opening lines, Fernando is announcing one of Shakespeare's major themes (and Joyce's, in "Circe")—the dislodging of identity that can lead to a feeling of self-annihilation. Bernardo, the wrong soldier to issue a challenge, asks Fernando, "Who's there?" Fernando, the guard on duty, should be the one who asks this question to someone entering his post. "Nay," Fernando replies to Bernardo, "answer me. Stand, and unfold thyself."[46]

With his relentless coherence of imagination, Shakespeare presents one of the play's major unifying themes in the first scene: the mystery of identity, the unfolding of the multiple layers of Hamlet's self, conscious as well as unconscious. Throughout the play, we see Hamlet's tragic (even near-psychotic) dislodging of identity—dislodged as future king of Denmark, dislodged as the son of a mother who was, he thought, a loyal wife.

Bloom is a comic version of this unfolding, this collapse of identity. His egregious connection of "butt" with his aching tongue is Joyce's

---

[46] William Shakespeare, *Hamlet*, (I, 1, ll. 1-9), in *The Complete Plays and Poetry of William Shakespeare*, ed. Neilson and Hill (Cambridge, Massachusetts: The Riverside Press, Houghton Mifflin, 1942), p. 1047.

inferential way of hinting at what that collapse might have felt like. As we have seen, eyeing ravenously Gerty's white nainsook knickers, he feels he saw her "all"—"Darling I saw your. I saw all" (*Ulysses*, p. 355). But her genitalia and butt were hidden from view. In the morning, however, he did see that white region on another female, a member of his household whom he also feeds and pampers.

In the opening chapter, "Calpyso," Bloom watches "curiously, kindly" his cat. "Clean to see: the gloss of her sleek hide, the white button under the butt of her tail, the green flashing eyes" (*Ulysses*, p. 53). Bloom seems to understand her language as she cries for her morning milk, "Mkgnao!" then "Mrkgnao!" and finally "Mrkrgnao" (*ibid.*). A short time later, as he prepares to go out, he cares for another creature with early morning needs whose bottom he often eyes. Living in amorous captivity, he asks his Calypso (still half cat-napping in bed) if she wants anything for breakfast. With "a sleepy soft grunt Molly answers:—Mn." He understands her private language as easily as he understood his cat's: "No. She did not want anything" (*Ulysses*, p. 54).

Molly is like demanding pussens in other ways, too. She wants milk with her tea, and she can stir his solicitude with a purring "Mn." He wonders if she wants something to eat, just as he wonders if the cat is hungry: "Nothing she can eat? He glanced round him. No" (*ibid.*). He then imagines that cats understand "what we say better than we understand them. She understands all she wants to" and thinks, self-revealingly, that mice "never squeal. Seem to like it" (*Ulysses*, p. 53). Pussens seems to be Molly's transmigrating soul for Bloom. The pubcrawling cyclopses in "Cyclops" think he is quite mousey, never quite squealing but masochistically accepting Molly's well-known affair, and he does believe she has intuitive ways of understanding things that rival a man's different way of understanding. Most importantly for our purposes here, as a self-appointed member of this feline sorority of two in Eccles street, he is as fascinated by Molly's butt as he is by his cat's, although she is just about fed up. She decidedly doesn't like Bloom constantly embracing her bottom, "where we havent 1 atom of any kind of expression in us all of us the same 2 lumps of lard" (*Ulysses*, p. 730).

BELLO also examines yet another cat's white button region only to pronounce Bloom a dephallicized cat, a "Manx cat":

BELLO
What else are you good for, an impotent thing like you? (*He stoops and peering, pokes with his fan rudely under the fat suet folds of Bloom's haunches.*) Up! Up! Manx cat! What have we here? Where's your curly teapot gone to or who docked it on you, cockyolly? Sing birdy, sing. It's as limp as a boy of six's doing his pooly behind a cart. (*Ulysses*, p. 508)

Before seeing Gerty on Sandymount Strand, needing respite from his docking by the Citizen and his one-eyed tribe, it's easy to imagine Bloom feeling like BELLO'S Manx cat—impotent, limp. Visually incorporating Gerty's white button, her anal-erogenous zone, he perhaps unconsciously senses his genitals becoming feminized as BELLO plunges his arm *"elbowdeep"* into the *"vulva"* of his willingly obedient maid of all work (*Ulysses*, p. 507).

In his passive receptivity, we sense not only Bloom's early identification with his mother's receptive genitalia. We also sense the possible physical substrate of what DR MULLIGAN labels his "bisexual abnormality" (*Ulysses*, p. 465). A more learned physician might describe this substrate as the "passive genital zone."[47] If we accept the possibility that Bloom did incorporate Gerty's white butt visually, he might very well have felt the most powerful erotic sensations in his own butt, not in the shaft or glans, but at "the root of the penis, at the perineum, or in the rectum."[48] Sharpening the descriptions of men with passive anal tendencies who try to describe where their sensations are most intense, Fenichel writes, "[Actually this] point...is not accessible from the outside and ...is equidistant from the root of the penis, the perineum, and the rectum.... ly[ing] in the prostatic part of the urethra."[49] But unlike these

---

[47] Otto Fenichel, *The Psychoanalytic Theory of Neurosis* (New York: W. W. Norton & Co., Inc., 1945), p. 335.
[48] *Ibid.*, p. 83.
[49] *Ibid.*

men, Bloom seems to find prostatic erotogeneity feminizing and thus anxiety-producing.

Unconsciously conflating the sight of Gerty's white-knickered genital region with his early morning sight of the white butt of his cat (which in turn called to mind Molly and her bottom)—and simultaneously incorporating that female bottom visually—Bloom risks feeling "docked," Gerty-ized, dephallicized. But by means of a displacement "upwards"—a defensive maneuver akin to what his fetishistic maneuvers are unconsciously designed to prevent—he manages to overcome the frightening sensation of becoming dephallicized. Bloom unconsciously transfers an ache from the prostate area to, presumably, the thick root of another protrusive organ, his tongue.

It seems that Joyce felt intuitively that there were connections between the distorting mechanisms of dream work—condensation, displacement, a part representing the whole—and the "conversion symptoms" of hysteria: a suddenly paralyzed arm (when a patient was "unconsciously reminded of her feelings toward her father"); a patient's jerking convulsions in her arms (an unconscious portrayal of "the spasmodic contractions of the penis during ejaculation"); a sudden ache at the butt of the tongue.[50] By means of this momentary displacement, Bloom reduces the danger of becoming womanized. With Gerty's arousing and frightening butt no longer a threat to his genital integrity, he can concentrate on her well-fed hose—a patch on the reality of her penislessness—and thereby avoid the frightening spectacle of what truly seeing her "all" would arouse.

Although Joyce is fascinated by the various kinds of womanliness in Bloom, especially his multiple (and hilarious) identificatory habits, he is just as fascinated by Bloom's fatherly nature, particularly in how Bloom plays with Stephen a variation on the theme of the consubstantiality of Father and Son, a theme that Stephen finds endlessly intriguing.

---

[50] *Ibid.*, p. 218.

CHAPTER V

Stoom:
The Contransmagnificandjewbangtantiality of Son and Father

> From before the ages He willed me and now may not will me away or ever. A *lex eterna* stays about Him. Is that then the divine substance wherein Father and Son are consubstantial?
> —Stephen, "Proteus" (*Ulysses*, p. 38)

> *(Stephen and Bloom gaze in the mirror. The face of William Shakespeare, beardless, appears there, rigid in facial paralysis, crowned by the reflection of the reindeer antlered hatrack in the hall.)*
> —"Circe" (*Ulysses*, p. 531)

> Where is poor dear Arius to try conclusions? Warring his life long on the contransmagnificandjewbangtantiality. Illstarred heresiarch.
> —Stephen, "Proteus" (*Ulysses*, p. 38)

> Substituting Stephen for Bloom Stoom would have passed successively through a dame's school and the highschool. Substituting Bloom for Stephen Blephen would have passed successively through the...matriculation, first arts second arts and arts degree courses of the royal university.
> — "Ithaca" (*Ulysses*, p. 639)

Since Bloom is the transmigrating soul of Ulysses and since Stephen is the transmigrating soul of Telemachus, then Bloom must be Stephen's father and Stephen his son. But how can Mrs. Dedalus's son also be Leopold Bloom's? If they do not share the same blood, the same "substance," how can they be father and son? We can begin to fathom Joyce's logic by recalling the many references to their latent oneness throughout *Ulysses*, culminating in the complex symbolism of Shakespeare's face appearing in the mirror in Bella Cohen's brothel as Stephen and Bloom simultaneously gaze into it in "Circe."

Stephen and Bloom know the same thing about Shakespeare's life, and they recall that detail in almost exactly the same words. In the National Library at 2 pm, Stephen muses, "In a rosery of Fetter Lane of Gerard, herbalist, he walks, greyedauburn.... He walks. One life is all. One body. Do. But do" (*Ulysses,* p. 193). Six hours later, in the bar room of the Ormond hotel, while writing to his pen pal, Martha Clifford, under his nom de plume, Henry Clifford, Bloom envisions Shakespeare in the London rose garden of Gerard the herbalist: "In Gerard's rosery of Fetter lane he walks, greyedauburn. One life is all. One body. Do. But do" (*Ulysses,* p. 269). Only the transmigrating soul of Shakespeare, lodged simultaneously in Stephen and in Bloom—one life? one body?—could have had such knowledge in 1904 since this piece of speculation did not come to light until after *Ulysses* was published in 1922.[51]

Just as their memories seem made of the same substance, so are their dream images. In Stephen's dream of the night of June 15-16, "Haroun al Raschid" appeared to him in the "Street of Harlots." As Stephen recalls the sequence in the morning, the famous Caliph of Baghdad held a "melon" with "creamfruit smell" against his face because that was the "rule" and said, "In. Come" (*Ulysses,* p. 46). After midnight, hurrying out of Bella Cohen's into a street filled with harlots to try to save Stephen, BLOOM is described in Joyce's stage directions as *"Incog Haroun al Raschid,"* hastening on by the railings *"with fleet step of a pard"* and with Stephen's *"ashplant mark[ing] his stride"* (*Ulysses,* p. 548).

---

[51] Don Gifford and Robert J. Seidman, *Notes for Joyce: An Annotation of James Joyce's Ulysses* (New York: E. P. Dutton & Sons, 1974), p. 186.

Bloom *is* feeling newly invigorated, empowered, and self-assured at this moment. He also seems to be ironically identified with this enlightened despot, "lover of luxury and pleasure" and "patron of learning and the arts."[52] Thus Bloom gives us the uncanny sensation that he is the actualization of Stephen's dream-image. Later, in "Ithaca," when he invites Stephen into his home, he intensifies the feeling. Stepping out of Stephen's dream, *Incog Haroun al Rachid*, Bloom follows the "rule" (from *Deuteronomy)* by offering the future priest (of art) firstfruits.[53] Using the "viscous cream," ordinarily reserved for Molly's breakfast, to make Stephen a cup of Epps's cocoa, Bloom seems to be offering his guest Eccles street "creamfruit." Just as Stephen imagined the Caliph holding a "melon with creamfruit smell against his cheek," so Bloom, we later learn in "Circe," loved to rub his nose against more than one melon with an attractive smell (*Ulysses*, pp. 499ff.). The narrator of "Ithaca" describes Molly's bottom as "plump mellow yellow smellow melons" (*Ulysses*, p. 690).

Other images deepen our sense that Bloom and Stephen comprise a *unio mystica*. Keyless, dressed in mourning, and carrying an ashplant at the end of "Circe," Bloom seems to be Stephen's double. Consciously and unconsciously, Stephen, still dressed in mourning, has been thinking about a pard all day and on into the night. In the morning, "in growing fear," he focuses on the image in Haines's dream of a "black panther" (*Ulysses*, p. 4). After having been knocked down in the street at the end of "Circe," he mumbles in Bloom's presence "Black panther vampire" (*Ulysses*, p. 569). In "Proteus," he links the black pard with Bloom more directly. Eyeing a mongrel rooting in the sand, he describes him as "a pard, a panther, got in spousebreech, vulturing the dead" (*Ulysses*, p. 46). Stephen seems to know the fourteenth-century belief that the panther

---

[52] *Ibid.*, p. 43. Bloom seems to possess here Odysseus's magic herb, moly, that enables Homer's hero to resist Circe's magic. In Bloom, moly seems to be the magical cause of the mysterious disappearance of the terrifying anxiety, guilt, and sin that unmanned him in BELLA-BELLO's presence. Conscious of what was previously unconscious, he becomes an ashplant-armed protector of his new, replacement son, Stephen. Cf., Cadenza.

[53] *Ibid.*

was born out of an adulterous union of a leopard and a lioness.[54] Leopold-Poldy, an echo of "leopard," is, of course, thinking of Molly's spousebreech all day. Joyce makes it seem that Bloom has stepped out of Stephen's mind.

They seem to share the same substance in other ways, too, these men, black clothed, in mourning: their melancholy memories of a dead parent; their self-soothing autoerotic interludes while lying on, or leaning against, the rocks on Sandymount shore. Bloom's masturbation is explicit, while Stephen's apparent urination seems autoeroticized, inseparable from his sexual fantasies. Speaking to himself, he repeats the phrase "touch," the Victorian euphemism for sexual intercourse: "Touch me. Soft eyes. Soft soft soft hand. I am lonely here. O, touch me soon now. What is that word known to all men? I am quiet here alone. Sad too. Touch, touch me" (*Ulysses,* p. 48). And then he seems to intensify his arousal as he feminizes and eroticizes watery weeds, "writhing weeds [that] lift languidly and sway reluctant arms, hising up their petticoats, in whispering water swaying and upturning coy silver fronds" (*Ulysses,* p. 49). In their sexual guilt (often involving maternal women), their alienation from other Dubliners, their deep loneliness and essential homelessness, Stephen and Bloom often seem convertible into each other, even before they appear in Bella's mirror as a reindeer antlered, hatracked Shakespeare.

But it is in their Shakespeareness—their "divine substance"—that they are most transparently consubstantial, and, as we might expect from Joyce, they are consubstantial in a heretical way. They are two different names for the same thing, two aspects of one being—Sabellius's heresy.[55] Through the consubstantiation of art, Joyce, a heresiarch priest of the eternal imagination, has made these seemingly unrelated and very

---

[54] *Ibid.*

[55] *Ibid.* p. 15. "[Sabellius] maintained that the names 'Father,' 'Son,' and 'Holy Spirit' were merely names for the same thing (or three different aspect or modes of one Being)." Richard Ellmann urges us to remember that Joyce works with "near-identities, not perfect ones, approximating each other at some remove, as a left glove resembles a right"—*The Consciousness of Joyce* (Toronto and New York: Oxford University Press, 1977), p. 58.

different persons one.[56] Stephen and Bloom do not appear to be contransmagnificandjewbangtantial, to use Stephen's jawbreaker, but that is because Joyce was forced by "natural law" to leave their physical and mental properties behind for us readers to see, just as the "accidental" properties of the bread and wine remain behind when they have been transubstantiated by another priest into the body and blood of Christ. Joyce has no need to "reconcile" the two in "Ithaca" since, to use Stephen's phrase from his lecture on *Hamlet*, "there can be no reconciliation. . .if there has not been a sundering" (*Ulysses*, p. 187).

Returning to Bella Cohen's mirror, we first learn that SHAKESPEARE is "beardless," suggesting a lack of maturity, a hint of youthfulness. He is also "rigid" with paralysis, which Joyce soon clarifies in another stage direction:

SHAKESPEARE
(*With paralytic rage.*) Weda seca whokilla farst. (*Ulysses*, p. 532)

This enraged beardlessness in their mirror image suggests a paralyzed anger from an early period in their life. (I'll return to SHAKESPEARE'S garbling of the Player Queen's assertion in *Hamlet* about someone wedding the second who killed the first.) An injury to their hands enlarges our sense of their oneness and their oneness with a youthful Shakespeare. Bloom's "weal" is the result of a slip in the mud while he was sprinting with classmates, "running chaps" or "harriers" (*Ulysses*, pp. 416-417). When we learn that "harriers" also means a pack of hunting hounds and the persons engaged in the hunt, Bloom's scar is also the scar of Ulysses, a boar wound suffered when Ulysses was running or hunting as a boy with an earlier group of harriers.

Stephen's hurt hand is not explicitly connected to a boar's tusking attack, but it is due to youthful athleticism as well, a schoolboy fall in a place

---

[56] Bloom isn't a symbol of Ulysses any more than Stephen symbolizes Telemachus. Ulysses is consubstantial with Bloom just as Telemachus is consubstantial with Stephen. The substance of the body and blood of Ulysses coexists in, and with, the substance of the body and blood of Bloom, while the substance of the body and blood of Telemachus coexists in, and with, the substance of the body and blood of Stephen.

specially set aside for harriers or running chaps. As we shall soon see, Stephen's psychological wound is also due to the attack of a "loving swine," to use Venus's description of the boar in "Venus and Adonis" (which I will turn to shortly). At Clongowes, we remember in *Portrait,* Stephen slipped on the cinderpath as a fellow was coming out of the bicycle house. With his broken glasses, he was unable to write and was unjustly pandied on the hand by the Prefect of Studies. As a somewhat different wild pig, Father Dolan left Stephen with an emotional scar as deep as Ulysses's and Bloom's. STEPHEN'S ambiguous comment on his shared injury reemphasizes their fusion. He mumbles, "See. Moves to one great goal. I am twentytwo too. Sixteen years ago I twentytwo tumbled, twentytwo years ago he sixteen fell off his hobbyhorse. (*He winces.*) Hurt my hand somewhere. Must see a dentist. Money?" (*Ulysses,* p. 528).

STEPHEN'S seemingly offhand, semi-stuporous remarks are in themselves a kind of two-sided mirror in Joyce's often scary nighttown fun-house. In the first part, we have Stephen looking in, yet we see an image of Bloom. If "sixteen years ago," Stephen, "twentytwo tumbled," then, at present, he seems to be thirty-eight, Bloom's present age. On the other side, Bloom peers in, and we see Stephen. At the age of "sixteen," Bloom fell off his "hobbyhorse." He seems to be a child, rather than an adolescent, and the child seems to be Stephen, the figure who tumbled in the first part of the sentence-mirror. Sixteen years earlier, when Stephen *was* six—or if not six at least preadolescent—he did fall off his hobbyhorse. As the leader of the Yorkists, one of the two competing Clongowes teams, the boy who was so good at leading his team to victory in sums was violently pushed off his high horse by Father Dolan as he publicly humiliated him, pandying him before his classmates.

STEPHEN'S musings make it seem that he and Bloom are both injured thirty-eight year olds or injured six-year olds, and that the wound they share (like all psychological injuries) has a life of its own, something that is a recurrent emotional fact, free of time. As a psychological injury, it lasts a lifetime, afflicting someone who is six, sixteen, twenty-two, and thirty-eight.

Blephen's wounds appear in an atmosphere of sexual excitement that is physically threatening at the same time. Prostitutes, especially Zoe

Higgins, are attempting to seduce Bloom and Stephen, while Father Dolan pops up as an ominous jack-in-the-box to ask sadistically, "Any boy want flogging?" (*Ulysses*, p. 526). The emotional weather, taken together with ZOE'S attempts at palmistry, helps to clarify Joyce's symbolism, especially its relation to the enduring anger of a child. Before Stephen sees Shakespeare in the mirror instead of himself, ZOE examines his palm and says "Woman's hand" (*Ulysses*, p. 526). It seems that a problematic sexuality is connected in some way to the place where Stephen was injured. Shortly after, "*peering at Bloom's palm*," she announces "Short little finger. Hen pecked husband," implying that Bloom's sexuality is problematic as well (*Ulysses*, p. 527).[57]

In palmistry, little fingers indicate immaturity or a lack of full development, and "henpecked husband" recalls not only the submission to "petticoat government," the uxoriousness of the new womanly man, but also the abuse that cuckolded Bloom suffers. It seems possible that when Bloom was beardless or immature—and when Stephen was immature as well—each experienced some sort of wound that made each feel unmanned. They might have undergone what seemed to them to be an "attack" that enraged them and that they tried to keep unconscious as they grew up.

2. The Tusk of the Boar Where Love Lies Ableeding

Joyce makes the consubstantialty of Stephen and Bloom even clearer when we recall Stephen's biographical interpretation of *Hamlet* in "Scylla and Charybdis." Stephen tells his audience in the National Library that all of Shakespeare's works, down to the last plays, are the consequences of his seduction by an older woman, Anne Hathaway, and of her later cuckolding of him: "He was chosen, it seems to me. If others have their will Anne hath a way. By cock, she was to blame. She put the comether on him, sweet and twentysix" (*Ulysses*, p. 183). Shakespeare's art is, to Stephen, like all art, the recreation of life out of life.

According to friends, Joyce took Stephen's theory "more seriously" than Stephen did himself, but by crowning Shakespeare with horns—a

---

[57] Gifford and Seidman, *op cit.*, p. 419.

"*reindeer antlered hatrack*"—Joyce is all but making Stephen's theory as "objectively" true as anything that the artistic imagination can make appear to be true.[58] Surely "our knowledge of Stephen involves the knowledge that his mind could only have been recreated reflexively by the mind which created the book."[59] If Stephen is voicing the theory about Shakespeare that Joyce fashioned in 1904 (the same year when Stephen offered *his* reading), then it is in Stephen's metaphors (phrases that come directly from Joyce's imagination) that we might expect to find Joyce's most cherished intuitions about the writer with whom he most consciously identified.

In Stephen's allusions to the myth of Adonis, we have one of the clearest examples of that "law of the Joycean universe" where "every single thing is always on the verge of doubling with another"—where things, as in dreams, simultaneously keep their identities and all but lose them in their resemblances to other things.[60] For Stephen (and, we may assume, for Joyce), the transmigrating soul of Adonis lives on in the young Shakespeare, the soul of Venus in Anne Hathaway. In her seductive "comether," when she was sweet and twentysix," she is "the greyeyed goddess who bends over the boy Adonis, stooping to conquer, as prologue to the swelling act...a boldfaced Stratford wench who tumbles in a cornfield a lover younger than herself" (*Ulysses,* p. 183).

As Stephen imagines her, she is more the unmanning conqueror than tender goddess of love. Bloom, again like Stephen, has her in mind too, thinking of Venus as "manly conscious" in "Lestrygonians" (*Ulysses* p 168). She is mannish in her bold tumbling of the boy, and, significantly, it is her fiercely destructive aggression that Stephen emphasizes, an almost masculine hostility that is inseparable from her seductiveness.

"Overborne in a cornfield," Shakespeare suffers a fatal wound in his capacity for love—his ability to love himself, to love others, and to be loved:

---

[58] Cf., Richard Ellmann, *James Joyce* (New York: Oxford University Press, 1965), pp. 374ff.

[59] William Matthews and Ralph W. Rader, *Autobiography, Biography, and the Novel: Papers read at a Clark Library Seminar,* May 13, 1972 (University of California at Los Angeles: William Andrew Clark 1965), p. 375.Memorial Library, 1973), p. 58.

[60] Ellmann, *The Consciousness of Joyce,* p. 91.

Belief in himself has been untimely killed....he will never be a victor in his own eyes after nor play victoriously the game of laugh and lie down. Assumed dongiovannism will not save him. No later undoing will undo the first undoing. The tusk of the boar has wounded him there where love lies ableeding. If the shrew is worsted yet there remains to her woman's invisible weapon. There is, I feel, in the words, some goad of the flesh driving him into a new passion, a darker shadow of the first, darkening even his own understanding of himself. A life fate awaits him and the two rages commingle in a whirlpool. (*Ulysses*, p. 188)

In Stephen's metaphors, Venus seems to be fused with the boar. Her "invisible" weapon of cuckoldry, which she can sheathe in the one she loves, is her tusk.

Shakespeare's Venus is often like Stephen's. In "Venus and Adonis," the goddess identifies herself with the boar when she sees Adonis's wound in his groin.[61] Venus is convinced that when the boar saw the boy's beautiful face, "He thought to kiss him, and hath killed him so."[62]

"'Tis true, 'tis true, thus was Adonis slain;
He ran upon the boar with his sharp spear,
Who did not whet his teeth at him again,
But by a kiss thought to persuade him there;
And by nuzzling in his flank, the loving swine
Sheath'd unaware the tusk in his soft groin. (*V-A, ll. 1111-1116*)

---

[61] In ancient folklore and rite, we learn in *The Golden Bough*, the pig was a sacred animal of the Earth Mother, an "embodiment of the corn-goddess herself, either Demeter or her daughter and double Persephone": Sir James George Frazer, *The Golden Bough: A Study in Magic and Religion*, Macmillan paperback (New York: Macmillan Publishing Co, Inc., 1978), p. 543.

[62] Willliam Shakespeare, "Venus and Adonis," in *The Complete Plays and Poems of William Shakespeare*, ed. with an introduction and notes by William Allan Nielson and Charles Jarvis Hill (Cambridge, Massachusetts: Houghton Mifflin Co., 1942), p. 1345. Subsequent references to the poem will appear in the text as "V-A," followed by line indications.

Venus goes on to admit, "'Had I been tooth'd like him, I must confess, / With kissing him I should have kill'd him first'" (*V-A*, ll.1117-1118). In the opening of the poem, Venus was "tooth'd like him," or at least tooth'd like the other beasts of prey which hunters seek out. When she encountered Adonis for the first time, she, too, thought to persuade the boy by a kiss that was deadly: "Backward she push'd him, as she would be thrust, / And govern'd him in strength, though not in lust" (*V-A*, ll. 41-42). Then, she "murders with a kiss" his words of resistance (*V-A*, l. 54). Kissing Adonis, Venus all but kills him first. Shakespeare's imagery is of gluttony:

> Even as an empty eagle, sharp by fast,
> Tires with her beak on feathers, flesh and bone
> Shaking her wings, devouring all in haste,
> Till either gorge be stuff'd or prey be gone;
> Even so she kiss'd his brow, his cheek, his chin,
> And where she ends she doth anew begin. (*V-A*, ll. 55-60)

As night begins to fall, Venus again kisses Adonis with a combination of nuzzling and gorging, a devouring lust that is indistinguishable from annihilating the loved one—the ardor of a boar. Feeding gluttonously on the boy, drawing his "lips' rich treasure dry," she seems to be turning into the tusking boar by the end of the poem:

> And having felt the sweetness of the spoil,
> With blindfold fury she begins to forage;
> Her face doth reek and smoke, her blood doth boil,
> And careless lust stirs up a desperate courage; (*V-A*, ll. 553-556)

This foraging goddess, battens on a boy of "unripe years" with such "blindfold fury" that she seems to be more than manly conscious (*V-A*, l. 524). She seems to have turned into her furious lover, Mars, the murderous god of war whose blood boils and whose face reeks and smokes. A goddess of "'increase,'" Venus is simultaneously a loving boar (or vulture or devouring eagle), a deity who can, unawares, tusk Adonis fatally in the groin (V-A, l. 791).

For Stephen, Anne is also a powerful woman who has seduced and betrayed a boy of unripe years, not once but twice. She first betrayed Shakespeare's boyish innocence in a cornfield (thereby plunging him into unmanning guilt and confusion). The second occurred when she tusked him in a different way, by cuckolding him.

In Shakespeare's penultimate image of Venus, she reenacts her deepest wishes symbolically. Looking on Adonis's wide-trenched wound, she makes it appear "three" with her steadfast "dazzling" sight. Then "she reprehends her mangling eye, / That makes more gashes where no breach should be" (*V-A*, ll. 1064-1066). Despite her self-rebuke, she makes another gash in the one she loves. Out of an overwhelming love that springs from earlier loss, she mangles a double for Adonis, a "purple flower" "checkered with white, / Resembling well his pale cheeks" and droplets of blood (*V-A*, ll. 1068-1069). As she "crops the stalk" of the anemone that has sprung up out of Adonis's blood, she compares the "green-dropping sap" to his tears and perceives the flower as both Adonis and a son (V-A, ll. 1175-1176). "'Poor flower,' quoth she, 'this was thy father's guise— / Sweet issue of a more sweet-smelling sire—" (*V-A, ll.177-178*). The anemone is Adonis's sweet issue and, it seems, hers as well. With the anemone now her love-child, Venus's ardor appears to be incestuous.

As she addresses her Adonis-son, Venus unwittingly confesses the dangerous nature of her imperious passion, the destructiveness of a self-engrossed maternal love. She tells the "poor flower" that "it is good / To wither in my breast as in his blood" (*V-A*, ll. 1181-1182). She then offers her withered and cropped lover-son a final resting place within her that summarizes the nature of her love—a "hollow cradle" that also resembles a tomb:

'Here was thy father's bed, here in my breast;
Thou are the next of blood, and 'tis thy right.
Lo, in this hollow cradle take thy rest.
My throbbing heart shall rock thee day and night;
There shall not be one minute in an hour
Wherein I will not kiss my sweet love's flower. (*V-A*, ll. 1183-1188)

Taking his father's place in the bed that is her breast, this "sweet love's flower," this product of his father and of his mother's love for his father, will know no rest: she will rock her lover-son day and night, kiss him every minute.

Using Shakespeare's "Venus and Adonis" to reveal the hidden springs of Shakespeare's art, Stephen is also revealing something close to the psychological substance that he shares with Shakespeare (and thus with Bloom). He seems to be reading his own Venus and Adonis story into Shakespeare. Tumbled as a child in a different cornfield by a woman much older than he, later in his life he attributes to Shakespeare that experience of infantile seduction by a tusked mother-and-wife associated with "increase," with fertility.

But what does "seduced" mean here? Stoom's mother might have been excessively gratifying—kissing, fondling, embracing him constantly, all springing from the fear that she would lose him as Mrs. John Joyce lost her first-born son. Or, again like Mrs. Joyce, she might have been excessively disappointing—seemingly indifferent in her possible depression over her three dead children (a womb that was a tomb?), unwittingly removed in her preoccupation with her many other children (a goddess of increase with ten?) and in her self-preoccupation. (See the previous chapter where I speculate on the possible psychology of Joyce's mother.) Or she might have alternated between excessive gratification and disappointment. Or Stoom might have fantasized that she literally seduced him.

Regardless, Stoom lives with a lifelong store of guilt and rage that he tries to keep out of conscious awareness in a variety of ways. One way is to enact and then to reenact the unconscious conflict due to the original trauma. Unconsciously, he keeps living the Venus and Adonis story, reacting to later women as if they were powerful goddesses and he was a helpless, virginal Adonis. Or he might imagine becoming a kind of male Venus himself, practicing a kind of dongiovannism, ravishing others as he was ravished.

In other words, a Venus seems to have become permanently lodged in Stephen's unconscious—the image of a mother (and wife) who is overbearingly loving (but also simultaneously unmanning). Even more importantly, along with loving feelings, he is left with the anxiety of unconscious rage, the image of himself as murderous as his mother. In that mythic time in an infant's life when a powerful goddess of "increase" *does* seem to be kissing him almost every minute of every hour, he holds her responsible for the seduction. He feels that the situation is wrong or unjust or unfair and blames her for his own feelings of shame, guilt, and confusion.

With the stirring up in him of impulses to retaliate against this woman who has caused him such suffering, he might defend himself from becoming conscious of his rage by unconsciously projecting it onto her and then incorporating this "bad" and "attacking" creature within himself, someone who lives on in his unconscious but who can emerge when his defenses against his murderousness weaken (say, late at night while getting drunk in a brothel).

The sadistic attack upon her is also motivated defensively out of fear of retaliation for the "involvement itself, as if the children are to be punished by the very parents who have initiated these actions."[63] Put somewhat differently, Shakespeare, Stoom, and other heirs of Adonis may be left with "unintegrated extremes of feeling" toward their mothers and with all others "towards whom they react as though they were the mother":

> When these individuals get involved with anyone, they [may] develop intense hatred towards the other, by whom they feel abused; or intense love towards the other, by whom they feel perfectly understood and cared for. These polar feelings are mutually exclusive; when the individual feels hateful he wants to get rid of the other, not remembering that at another time, perhaps just shortly before, the other was loved and valued as perfect.[64]

---

[63] M. D. Faber, "*Oedipus Rex*: A Psychoanalytic Interpretation," *The Psychoanalytic Review*, 62 (Summer, 1975), 249.

[64] Jules Weiss, commentary on Alan Z. Skolnikoff, "Creativity and Therapy," *Dialogue: A Journal of Psychoanalytic Perspectives* (Spring, 1977), 21.

Each of these extreme feelings is intolerable, "the hatred because it leads to murderousness and reflexive self-destructiveness, and the love because it leads to intense intimacy and frightening, primitive, sado-masochistic fantasies."[65]

In "Circe," we will find similar extremes of formerly unconscious feeling in Stephen and Bloom. Joyce first dramatizes the intolerable rage (leading to terrifying murderousness and self destructiveness) that was once projected on a maternal figure, introjected, and then reprojected in the manly conscious madam named Bella/Bello, the transmigrating soul of Circe. Then Joyce hints at an equally intense frightening love, especially when Blephen is in the presence of a manly conscious woman he associates with seductive sexuality and hostility. To Stoom, this woman seems to be Venus as "loving swine," capable of annihilating him at the same time that she is loving him too well.

3. With Paralytic Rage Stoom Chokit a Thursdaymomun

Let us return to the mirror in Bella Cohen's brothel where SHAKESPEARE, *"rigid in facial paralysis....crows with a black capon's laugh....*Iagogo! How my Oldfellow chokit his Thursdaymomun. Iagogogo" (*Ulysses*, p. 531). Dramatizing the nature of SHAKESPEARE'S rigidity, Joyce suggests that the most terrible consequence of his tusking by a boar-like goddess was a "goad of the flesh," an ever-darkening whirlpool of misogynistic rage that can suck everyone into it—including Shakespeare himself (*Ulysses*, p. 188). He soon mutters (*with paralytic rage*) "Weda sec whokilla farst" (*Ulysses*, p. 532). He is refashioning the Player Queen's words, "None wed the second but who kill's the first."[66] He is also refashioning the words of his granddaughter, Elizabeth, who, according to Stephen, also "wed her second, having killed her first" (*Ulysses*, p. 194). Not only Venus-Anne but "all those women"—his mother, sister, two daughters, and grand-daughter—destroyed their men by outliving them:

---

[65] *Ibid.*
[66] Shakespeare, *Hamlet, op.cit.*, p. 1070 (III, ii, l. 190).

All those women saw their men down and under: Mary, her goodman John, Ann, her poor dear Willun, when he went and died on her, raging that he was the first to go, Joan, her four brothers, Judith, her husband and all her sons, Susan, her husband too, while Susan's daughter, Elizabeth, to use granddaddy words, wed her second, having killed her first. (*Ulysses,* p.194)

Stephen's Shakespeare is surrounded by a whole series of Venuses. Repeating the image of a perennial Venus-like tusking, Stephen is unwittingly using dream-logic to underscore the powerful force that maternal seduction (inseparable from one form of emotional tusking or another) exerts in Shakespeare's emotional life (as well as in his own and in Bloom's). Stephen's intellectual heroes are just as wife-dominated. Socrates was "henpecked," and Aristotle, "the allwisest stagyrite was bitted, bridled and mounted by a light of love" (*Ulysses,* p. 411). Transmuting the "facts" of an older Anne and a young Shakespeare into an elaborate vision of a castrating (and cuckolding) Venus, constantly wounding an Adonis with different names down through the ages, Stephen, Joyce is implying, seems to be reading and rereading the facts of his own unconscious life into his creation.

Let us turn to the scene where ZOE examines STEPHEN'S palm and pronounces "Woman's hand":

STEPHEN

(*Murmurs.*) Continue. Lie. Hold me. Caress. I never could read His handwriting except His criminal thumbprint on the haddock.

ZOE

What day were you born?

STEPHEN

Thursday. Today.

ZOE

Thursday's child has far to go. (*She traces lines on his hand.*) Line of fate. Influential friends. (*Ulysses,* pp. 526-527)

Zoe Higgins (whose name, as we have seen, means "life" and whose last name is the same as the maiden name of Bloom's mother) *is* a

Thursdaymomun, this Thursday night, June 16, 1904. While fantasizing about the future of a birthday boy whom she has named and whose hand is resting in hers, ZOE seems to be a whorish mother. She is also a daymomun or Desdemona whom an Oldfellow or Othello chokes after he is goaded by Iago (go). To Stephen, Shakespeare is vicariously avenging himself in his art on an adulterous wife who is also a mother, a seductive and betraying creature who stirred the feelings of a grievously wounded Oldfellow, a castrated, dark-skinned cock of the walk, a "black capon." If we follow Stephen's lead in his reading of Shakespeare—his pleasure in daring, original, boldly intuitive speculation—we may infer that an earlier version of Anne, a seductive and wounding mother, a Thursdaymomun who seemed to be a goddess, stirred the same feelings in Stephen (which he buried) and left him with an unconscious urge either to murder those women he loves when he feels that they too betrayed him or to turn that rage inward, on himself.

Stephen calls this aspect of Shakespeare the "hornmad Iago"; the idealizing and loving self is the "moor":

In *Cymbeline*, in *Othello* he is bawd and cuckold. He acts and is acted on. Lover of an ideal or a perversion, like José he kills the real Carmen. His unremitting intellect is the hornmad Iago ceaselessly willing that the moor in him shall suffer. (*Ulysses*, p. 204)

We may also infer that Shakespeare's creator is himself divided into an unconscious Moor-self and a hornmad Iago-self. These extremes of feeling are as intolerable for Stephen as they are for all children who feel they have been seduced, the unconscious hornmadness leading to terrifying destructiveness and self-destructiveness, the unconscious moorish love leading to frightening, helpless slavishness. This split in his self-image is especially apparent when he is in the presence of a woman who seems to be a Thursdaymomun.

In fact, STEPHEN seems to face two Thursdaymomuns in "Circe," beginning with his first allusion to Wagner's *Ring* and concluding with his last, his enraged cry "*Nothung!*" as he smashes the chandelier (*Ulysses*, p. 545). When we focus our attention on his radically opposed feelings, we perceive not only splits between an Iago-self and a Moor-self, but we also see him splitting the maternal figure into someone either all-good or someone all-bad.

We have already met his first Thursdaymomun, ZOE, the prostitute-life force who imagines the future of her birthday boy while reading his palm. As seducible as an Adonis, STEPHEN reveals hints of moorish feeling, impulses to respond to her as a comforting and reassuring maternal presence. He murmurs, "Continue. Lie. Hold me. Caress" (*Ulysses*, p. 526). In his passive wish to be held, caressed, he calls to mind an earlier time in a brothel where another prostitute was holding him. In early adolescence he experienced his first "swoon of sin." Held firmly in her arms, "he felt that he had suddenly become strong and fearless and sure of himself" (*Portrait*, p. 114). He delighted in being "caressed, slowly, slowly, slowly" (*Portrait*, p. 114). But ZOE also stirs Iago-like feelings, suspicion and anger that seem split off from his more tender wishes to be held and caressed by an all-understanding creature. Buried rage alternates rapidly with his feeling that Zoe can be gently giving.

Still holding his hand, ZOE, as we have seen before, misquotes Shakespeare, saying, "Hamlet, I am thy father's gimlet!" (*Ulysses*, p. 525). Speaking as Hamlet's father, this seductive woman, now endowed with a sharp, puncturing tool, first calls up the mannish Venus who (identified with the boar) tusked her lover-son where love lies bleeding. She recalls something equally significant for Stephen, an earlier experience with a mannish Venus. ZOE tells Stephen-Hamlet accusingly, "I see it in your face. The eye, like that. (*She frowns with lowered head.*)" (*Ulysses*, p. 526). While she frowns, Lynch "*slaps Kitty behind twice,*" echoing ZOE'S words, saying, "Like that. Pandy bat" (*Ulysses*, p. 526). With the rapidity of free association, she metamorphosizes into FATHER DOLAN, the Prefect of Studies who, we remember, pandied Stephen sadistically when he was a schoolboy at Clongowes:

(*Twice loudly a pandybat cracks, the coffin of the pianola flies open, the bald little round jack-in-the-box head of Father Dolan springs up.*)

Tyrants of the Heart

FATHER DOLAN
Any boy want flogging? Broke his glasses? Lazy idle little schemer. See it in your eye. (Ulysses, p. 526)

A caressing, momentarily trustworthy woman can change suddenly into a pandying man, cruel, harmful. Although Stephen does not crow "Iagogo" while choking a Thursdaymomun, we may infer from Joyce's stage directions that Stephen is recalling the same depth of impotent rage that he felt "Sixteen years ago" when he "hurt [his] hand somewhere," when after first gently straightening it, Father Dolan beat him mercilessly on his outstretched palm (*Ulysses*, p. 528). Vengeful Stephen makes Father Dolan dead and buried, his coffin a pianola in a whorehouse. Later, playing the pianola, Stephen all but does a dance on his grave. Even that is not enough to satisfy the desire for vengeance in what we may assume is an unconscious Iago-self. Stephen makes this maiming figure into a ludicrous and harmless jack-in-the-box. In effect, he has decapitated Dolan, just as Stephen seems to have felt morally and psychologically decapitated years earlier when, as the leader of the Yorkists, he was unfairly pandied and humiliated in front of his classmates.

After the pandying at Conglowes, Stephen, in his milder, childhood version of his furious Iago-self, makes Dolan into a lower-class washerwoman: "It was his own name that he should have made fun of if he wanted to make fun. Dolan: it was like the name of a woman who washed clothes (*Portrait*, p. 60).

In Stephen's boyhood, there are other suggestions of the recurrent playing out of the Venus and Adonis myth. As Father Dolan lifts the pandybat to strike, there is a "swish of the sleeve of the soutane" (*Portrait*, p. 54). Stephen hears this sound again when he is pandied, again on the hand. He recalls the attack a short time later in the refectory, the swishing sound returning with the vividness of a waking nightmare. The Jesuit cassock is a kind of gown, and when we reread the scene, with the Prefect of Studies pausing for a moment to touch the fingers to straighten out Stephen's palm, he seems to become a nightmarish washerwoman, beating out in public what he considered to be Clongowes's dirt. In the crashing descent of the pandybat (or "turkey," in schoolboy slang), Father Dolan becomes, for an instant, a kind of turkey vulture or, better, an eagle, a creature with talons that can maim a young Adonis-like boy who felt that he was beloved.

Joyce underscores the connection between Father Dolan and a deadly bird of prey in images of greyish omnipotence. His "whitegrey not young face" and his "baldy whitegrey head with fluff at the side of it" suggest a bald eagle looming over Stephen (*Portrait*, p. 53). Then it attacks. A "hot burning stinging tingling blow" made Stephen's hand crumple together "like a leaf in the fire....crumpled burning livid" (*Portrait*, p. 54). Dolan seems fused with a number of eagles in Stephen's mind: one of those "eagles that will come and pull out his eyes," as Dante chanted to Stephen growing up:

Pull out his eyes,
Apologize,
Apologize,
Pull out his eyes. (*Portrait*, p. 2)

But he is also inseparable from the feasting, gluttonous Venus feasting eagle-like on Adonis's body, wounding him with even more gashes.

A greyish, bisexual deity leaning over an innocent boy with apparent love and tenderness, then betraying his trust by goring him, recapitulates the drama where love perpetually lies ableeding. In his description of Venus-Anne Hathaway bending over Adonis-Shakespeare—the "greyeyed goddess who bends over the boy...stooping to conquer"— Stephen is not only recreating his own experience with ZOE-DOLAN. That tusking, presumably sixteen years earlier by Dolan, seems to be a traumatic repetition of an even earlier tusking by a maternal Venus or Venus-like figure.

Does Joyce hint at a primal love-goring, the first playing out in Stephen's early life of love in a cornfield that ended badly? Before ZOE reads his palm, he extends his hand to her:

STEPHEN
(*Extends his hand to her smiling and chants to the air of the blood oath in the Dusk of the Gods.*)

Hangende Hunger,
Fragende Frau
Macht uns alle kaput. (*Ulysses*, p. 525)

To ZOE'S "Is he hungry?" STEPHEN sings the words of "woeful" Siegmund in Act I of *Die Walküre* to the woman with whom he will commit incest: "Intense desire, questioning wife, destroys us all."[67] ZOE now becomes the transmigrating soul of Sieglinde to Stephen, a married woman who is seductive and questioning with whom Siegmund will elope. This wifely creature with her "intense desire" will bring about a catastrophe so massive that it will destroy the gods themselves.

But STEPHEN (who has many siblings in *Portrait*) is more than a woeful brother (Siegmund). Since the blood oath is sung in *Die Götterdämmerung* by Siegfried (the son of Siegmund and his sister), Stephen has taken on a double role, that of a woeful brother-and-son. He is Siegmund-and-Siegfried. Identified with Siegmund, STEPHEN is a brother who is sexually involved with an intensely desirous wife whose blood he shares. Identified with Siegfried, he is a son who is capable of a mighty rage because he feels mightily wronged.

This seduced son, enraged at a deeply passionate woman with whom he is incestuously involved, is a grown-up Adonis, and the hungry woman who commits adultery seems to be a German Venus-and-mother. (Siegmund and his son, Siegfried, are again evoked in the scene between STEPHEN and THE MOTHER later in "Circe." The nightmarish sequence ends, as we have seen, with STEPHEN crying "*Nothung!*"—"Needful," the name of the magic sword in the *Ring*—raising his magical ashplant-sword in Siegfried fashion, and bringing about a Dublin Dusk of the Gods in nighttown.)

In the next chapter, I want to focus on Stephen's response to his second Thursdaymomun, THE MOTHER. Joyce enlarges and complicates our understanding of the unconscious conflicts that plague Stephen, this woeful son-and-brother consubstantial with the seduced and ragingly murderous Shakespeare-in-the-mirror. I will then discuss Bloom's consubstantiality with Stephen's version of Shakespeare and thus with Stephen himself.

---

[67] Gifford and Seidman, *op.cit.*, pp. 418-419.

CHAPTER VI

Blephen:
The Contransmagnificandjewbangtantiality
of Father and Son

> Touch lightly with two index fingers. Aristotle's
> experiment. One or two. Necessity is that in virtue
> of which it is impossible that one can be otherwise.
> Argai, one hat is one hat.
> —Stephen, "Scylla and Charybdis" (*Ulysses*, p. 184)

Let's look first at Stephen's surrogate mother, the grandmother in the riddle of the fox and grapes that he first asked his students early in the day. In Stephen's recreation of Aesop, the fox is burying his mother-grandmother under a holly tree. In Chapter II, I focused on his inability to reach the grapes by vulturing the dead, by feeding, in his matricidal guilt, on his dead mother in an attempt to unite himself with her. Here I want to discuss more fully another layer of meaning in Stephen's vulturing, his depression-filled, repressed Iagogo murderousness. He repeats his slip about "her poor soul" getting "out of heaven" (*Ulysses*, p. 523). (The line in the original is "'Tis time for my poor soul to go to heaven.'"[68]) Then, STEPHEN

---

[68] Don Gifford and Robert J. Seidman, *Notes for Joyce: An Annotation of James Joyce's*

makes the fox into a thirsty, cunning, crowing animal that has "killed" his "grandmother." I'll quote him again:

STEPHEN

The fox crew, the cocks flew,
The bells in heaven
Were striking eleven
'Tis time for her poor soul
To get out of heaven. (*Ulysses*, p. 523)

STEPHEN, whose thirst *is* unquenchable in Bella Cohen's brothel, then asks, "Why striking eleven?. . .Thirsty fox. (*He laughs loudly.*). Burying his grandmother. Probably he killed her" (*Ulysses*, p. 524). Identified with a crowing fox that murdered a grandmother, Stephen, laughing loudly at the spectacle, calls to mind his mirror image, Shakespeare-in-the-mirror, crowing, as we saw in the previous chapter, out of *his* Iagogo self, over a choked Thursdaymomun. But why would a thirsty fox kill a Thursday mother?

STEPHEN'S next associations join this murdered mother-grandmother planted under a holly tree with "Georgina Johnson": "And so Georgina Johnson is dead and married" (*Ulysses*, p. 524). He also associates her with "Sphinx" (*Ulysses*, p. 525). STEPHEN seems to have equated his dead mother, whom he feels he has "killed," (by not kneeling in prayer at her bedside), with a dead and married prostitute, with the eponymous Sphinx of the Oscar Wilde poem, and with *"la belle dame sans merci,"* Keats's beautiful woman without pity who promises a youth transcendent love but robs him of his vitality instead (*Ulysses*, p. 412).[69] That Venus-like robber then gets blended in with Dolanism, with an unprovoked, sadistic attack. After repeating "Married," STEPHEN recalls the never-to-be forgotten pandying he received from Dolan and becomes, for an instant, Iago himself: "Must get glasses. Broke them yesterday. Sixteen years ago....Hm. Sphinx. The beast that has two backs at midnight. Married" (*Ulysses*, p. 525).

Ulysses (New York: E. P. Dutton & Co,. 1964), p. 22.
[69] *Ibid.*, p. 373.

Blephen: The Contransmagnificandjewbangtantiality of Father and Son

Hornmad Iago's metaphor for adultery was, we remember, "the beast with two backs," and in "Aeolus," Stephen wondered about the "other story" that the Ghost tells in *Hamlet*—the suggestion (according to Stephen) that Claudius (an "adulterate beast") and Gertrude (only "seeming virtuous") committed adultery: "By the way how did he find that out [that Claudius poured poison in the 'porches' of the king's ear]"? He died in his sleep. Or the other story, beast with two backs?" (*Ulysses*, p. 134). We may infer the origins of Stephen's hornmadness in his highly subjective reading of the play. Like Iago—and like his version of Shakespeare in "Scylla and Charybdis"—we may infer that Stephen felt wounded by an adulterous married woman as well, but that woman, unlike Gertrude, was not his legal wife. She was married to his father, and she committed a version of adultery with him. She, too, was "seeming virtuous" because her very young son perhaps experienced her possibly worried clingingness, her excessive (and incestuous-feeling) closeness, as "seductive."

What I am suggesting, with something like the Stephen-like boldness of *his* foray into autobiographical Shakespeare criticism, is that Mrs. Dedalus might have been very much like Mrs. John Joyce (at least in my brief, perhaps wild, analysis of her). I'd guess that Joyce's mother was anxiously protective. Perhaps she was even more protective of her now-first son through her three misbirths, leading him to feel that she was overly close, overly gratifying—"seductive." Between the ages of two and four, when his mother gave birth to his first three siblings (three siblings followed), Joyce might very well have felt like Stephen's Adonis, loved by a Dublin version of Venus.[70] This form of *amor matris* was (to him) so anxiously self-involved as to amount to a wounding, a love that seemed (to him) somehow exploitative. Assuming that Stephen is, among other things, a mythicized version of Joyce, we may speculate that Stephen himself experienced this early childhood trauma where love lies ableeding and then recreated it in his reading of Shakespeare. As with Stephen's Shakespeare, so with Stephen: "Belief in himself has been untimely killed.... he will never be a victor in his own eyes after nor play victoriously the game of laugh and lie down. Assumed dongiovannism will not save him. No later undoing will undo the

---

[70] See Ellmann's description of her many births and misbirths in *James Joyce*, p. 20.

first undoing" (*Ulysses,* p. 188). To return to the multiple interwoven allusions we have been looking at, the "ghost of sin" will soon get out of heaven. The powerful, Sphinx-like woman can wound the boy who seeks to "know" her, to love her, by causing him to feel unforgivably bestial and sinful, becoming what he "would not be."

2. Kinch killed her Dogsbody Bitchbody

In THE MOTHER, the poor soul who returns from heaven to haunt her murderous son, Joyce gives us Stephen's repressed, multi-layered image of Mrs. Dedalus directly, a recapitulation of how she got into Stephen's mind and how his "incorporation" of his mother is connected to his interpretation of "Venus and Adonis." In Bella Cohen's, as the bells are striking eleven, STEPHEN is often unable to distinguish inner from outer reality. In these near-psychotic episodes, Joyce uses STEPHEN'S hallucinations to reproduce what seems to have been a traumatic event. We will first examine Stephen's response to the blow of his mother's death, mourning that thinly veils melancholy. Then, looking closely at the recurrent image of "dogsbody," we will see that his complicated reaction to her death was in turn shaped by (and made more terrible by) a putative trauma from the distant past when he was a young, tusked Adonis.

When we first meet Stephen on June 16, 1904, he is dressed in black. He has been mourning, although, as we shall see, his mourning has passed beyond normal grief. All day he is plagued by the "agenbite of inwit," the "remorse of conscience" (*Ulysses,* p. 16). As Joyce dramatizes Stephen's inner world, he seems to have intuited many of the same things that Freud discovered in "Mourning and Melancholy." One of the great paradoxes that Freud observed in those grieving for someone they lost was the "work of mourning," the painful task of slowly loosening the tie to the dead by focusing on each of the many separate, painful memories that comprise that tie.[71] Stephen, as we have seen, seems on first

---

[71] Sigmund Freud, "Mourning and Melancholia," in *The Standard Edition of the Complete Psychological Works of Sigmund Freud,* vol. xiv, trans. and ed. by James Strachey (London: The Hogarth Press and the Institute of Psychoanalysis, 1981), p. 245.

reading to be doing this work in "Telemachus" when he recalls his mother crying on her deathbed or reimagines the "secrets" of her locked drawer or her "cored apple" or her "glass of water"—or other poignant "memories that beset his brooding brain" (*Ulysses*, p. 10).

Freud also noticed that mourners create a substitute for the lost person within themselves. They "identify" themselves with the departed figure, unconsciously "incorporating" or "introjecting" the dead person, so that the lost person now seems to live inside them. This identification with the lost figure often figures in the unconscious as a "feeding" on the dead person, an "eating" or assimilating of his or her substance, a "vulturing" of the dead. However, mourning is complicated if the relationship to the lost person was extremely ambivalent. Then the introjection is not only an attempt to preserve the loved one but also an attempt to destroy it. If the hostility is in the "foreground," the mourner will suffer from new guilt feelings:

> A case of death is always likely to mobilize ambivalence. The death of a person for whom one had previously wished death may be perceived as a fulfillment of this wish. The death of other persons may cause feelings of joy because death came to somebody else, not to oneself....These reactions create guilt feelings and remorse....The identification with the dead also has a punitive significance: 'Because you have wished the other person to die, you have to die yourself.' In this case, the mourner fears that because he brought about death through the 'omnipotence' of his death wish, the dead person may seek revenge and return to kill him, the living.[72]

Eventually, the mourner usually succeeds in unweaving the separate ties that bound him to the introjected representation of the person who died. With Stephen, though, the sadness seems more intense than that of normal mourners. His mother was buried on June 26, 1903, and he is still wearing black on June 16, 1904. While a sad mourner needs pity and consolation,

---

[72] Otto Fenichel, M. D., *The Psychoanalytic Theory of Neurosis* (New York: W.W. Norton & Company, Inc., 1945), p. 395.

Stephen seems to withdraw from others and attempts to overcome his sadness without their help. And since sadness can be synonymous with a painful, frightening, decrease in feelings of self-worth, Stephen seems to be trying to re-establish his self-esteem privately, internally. The remorse of conscience that has been attacking Stephen ever since his mother's death suggests that mourning has never been completed, that it has quickly passed over into melancholia. Small, relatively tolerable amounts of remorse—little bitings of conscience or breakdowns in self-esteem—are warning signals, signs of a larger remorse in his unconscious, indicating a far more extensive depression within.[73]

A melancholy mourner, ambivalent about his lost mother, Stephen, we may assume, often used her (while alive) as a source of self-esteem. When she "loved" him or praised him or looked favorably upon him—or, as we have seen earlier, when he found maternal substitutes who did the same—he felt alive, vital, empowered. When she died, his attempt to undo that loss (by the work of mourning that I have briefly described) actually made the loss worse. Incorporating that ambivalently loved figure whose narcissistic "love" was to her (as it was to Venus) fundamentally self-involved, he acts as if *he* was lost or fatally diminished rather than his mother. He and his mother are equated. In Freud's famous formulation, "The shadow of the object [has fallen] upon the ego."[74]

Observing the extravagant self-reproaches of melancholy men and women who have lost a loved one, Freud reasoned that such self-loathing should have been repressed, rendered unconscious. The apparently meaningless (and conscious) self-reproaches have a hidden meaning if the name of the ambivalently loved (and lost) person is substituted for "I." As melancholy Stephen tries to mourn, he perceives the "bad" characteristics of his mother in himself. Saying the equivalent of, "I am a great sinner because I killed my mother," he is unconsciously saying, "*she* is the murderous sinner; *she* treated me badly as if *she* wanted to kill me."[75]

---

[73] *Ibid.*, p. 396.
[74] Freud, *op. cit.*, p. 249.
[75] Cf. Fenichel, *op. cit.*, pp. 387-406 for a useful summary of the classic psychoanalytic

Blephen: The Contransmagnificandjewbangtantiality of Father and Son

In "Circe," Joyce externalizes Stephen's sadistic self-reproaches in the person of "Mercurial Malachi." ("Self-and-other" reproaches would be more accurate since, to repeat, in his melancholy, conscious reproaches against himself are unconscious reproaches against his mother.) In the guise of BUCK MULLIGAN, a.k.a. Mercurial Mulligan, Stephen accuses himself of matricide: "She's beastly dead....The mockery of it! Kinch killed her dogsbody bitchbody" (*Ulysses*, p. 543). Stephen is calling "himself" what Nora called Joyce, a "woman killer." But, again, having unconsciously incorporated his mother, he is accusing *her* of being a woman-killer, a woman who "killed" him with what seemed to him to be her self-involved, Venus-like love, a love that was a wounding to his self-regard.

Joyce emphasizes Stephen's identification with his mother in the verbal play with "dogsbody." The harsh BUCK MULLIGAN part of Stephen elides "dogsbody" with "bitchbody." In "Telemachus," Buck Mulligan addressed Stephen (because of his second-hand clothes) as "poor dogsbody" (*Ulysses*, p. 6). Looking in the servant's mirror held up by Mulligan, Stephen accepted Mulligan's epithet: "Who chose this face for me? This dogsbody to rid of vermin" (*Ulysses*, p. 6). One answer to the question of who gave him his face is the person who created his body (and face) in the first place, his mother.

Later, in "Proteus," Stephen elaborates on his identification with a vermin-ridden dog that seems fused with a "bitchbody." To return to that image we have examined earlier, he sees a "mute," "fawning," "unheeded" dog sniffing rapidly all over the corpse of another dog—a "brother" or blood relation—and then says to himself, "Ah, poor dogsbody. Here lies poor dogsbody's body" (*Ulysses*, p. 46). In his Telemachus-like dispossession, he feels "unheeded" in his homeland; he also seems "mute" in loquacious Mulligan's company; and he fears that he might slip into fawning if he follows Mulligan's wish that he "touch [the Englishman, Haines,] for a guinea" (*Ulysses*, p. 7). But even more significant, like poor dogsbody sniffing over a corpse, Stephen has for over a year been nosing over a dead blood relation, too, the "body" of his body, his dead mother.

---

theory of depression and mania.

In the next dogsbody image (which we discussed in Chapter II), Joyce complicates our understanding of what it means to vulture the dead. He reveals that in his melancholy, Stephen is unconsciously eating up an ambivalently loved figure who has died and whom he has incorporated into himself:

> The simple pleasures of the poor. His hindpaws then scattered sand: then his forepaws dabbled and delved. Something he buried there, his grandmother. He rooted in the sand, dabbling, delving and stopped to listen in the air, scraped up the sand again with a fury of his claws, soon ceasing, a pard, a panther, got in spouse-breach, vulturing the dead. (*Ulysses*, p. 46)

Stephen is attributing his own sadistic (i.e., eroticized) eating up of his mother to poor dogsbody. Not only does he vulture the dead body of his body, but he does it with a "delving," a pard-like fury of his "claws." To delve is to dig with a spade, but it is also to put a sharp, penetrating implement into Mother Earth.[76]

When BUCK MULLIGAN derisively says that Stephen (dogsbody) "killed" his mother (dogsbody bitchbody), he is doing more than voicing Stephen's unconscious belief that he, Stephen, *did* kill his mother by refusing to pray at her bedside as she lay dying. Feeling that by dying she was killing him ("Dying on me of cancer in such a tortured and torturing way, she acted as if she wanted to kill me"), Stephen's self-accusation of matricide (again, voiced by the Malachi part of himself) is actually an accusation against his mother for infanticide.

---

[76] Once again, Joyce fuses Stephen and Bloom as Stephen connects his alter ego, dogsbody, to the "pard." As I discussed in Chapter V, at the end of "Scylla and Charybdis," Bloom leaves the library before Stephen and Mulligan: "A dark back went before them. Step of a pard. . . ." (*Ulysses*, p. 209). And in "Circe," Bloom, as *"Incog Haroun al Raschid,""* hastens on by the railings with fleet step of a pard. . ." (*Ulysses*, p. 548).

Blephen: The Contransmagnificandjewbangtantiality of Father and Son

3. Emaciated, in Leper Grey and a Torn Bridal Veil

As THE MOTHER, whom he buried in the sand and now digs up, *"rises stark through the floor"* (*Ulysses*, p. 542), Joyce dramatizes Stephen's oral incorporation of his dead mother—his unconscious eating up of her body in his depression and his vomiting out of her. Joyce also underlines the final act in Stephen's reliving of the Venus and Adonis myth, his tusking by the boar that the goddess all but identified herself with (as we saw in Chapter V). A goddess once thought that she was kissing and nuzzling the beautiful boy she loved when she, a loving swine, was actually whetting her teeth on him. Years later, her reincarnation, THE MOTHER, actually whets her claws on Stephen.

STEPHEN first calls her "lemur" (meaning ghost or spectre because of this arboreal creature's nocturnal habits), and then, increasingly terrified, he shouts at the spectre, "ghoul," "hyena," "corpsechewer." As I mentioned earlier, he is attributing his own cannibalism to this re-externalized lemur (*Ulysses*, p. 544). The retaliation that Stephen fears for *his* corpsechewing—death by cancer—obeys the *lex talionis* always alive in his unconscious:

> THE MOTHER
> (*Her face drawing near and nearer, sending out an ashen breath.*) Beware! (*She raises her blackened, withered right arm slowly towards Stephen's breast with outstretched fingers.*) Beware! God's hand! (*A green crab with malignant red eyes sticks deep its grinning claws in Stephen's heart.*) (*Ulysses*, p. 544)

Her outstretched fingers—"God's hand"—turn into the zodiacal sign of Cancer as she grinningly, malignantly claws her once beloved boy. The green crab that cancered her now cancers STEPHEN, actualizing his unconscious fear of being eaten up by the vengeful figure whom he once ate up. In the tumorous growth of remorse and guilt that he has endured for at least a year, STEPHEN inflicts a punishment on himself fitting his crime. He suffers a wound to his heart, his inability to love and to be loved that is like Adonis's wound. To both Mrs. Dedalus and

Venus, neither Stephen nor Adonis knew or could reciprocate love. Venus cannot convince chaste Adonis (whom she has dragged down on top of her) to make love, and Mrs. Dedalus (decidedly more spiritual) hopes that one day Stephen will know love, "the word known to all men" (*Ulysses*, p. 543).

We have seen other embodiments of his maternal superego, the sadism clothed in dresses lodged in the nighttown thinking of this Irish Adonis. BUCK MULLIGAN wears a *"jester's dress of puce and yellow"* as he berates Stephen for his matricidal cruelty (*Ulysses*, p. 543). Somewhat later, "Father Malachi O'Flynn" another mocking voice, is described as wearing a *"long petticoat"* (*Ulysses*, p. 560). And the most reproachful female voice of all, THE MOTHER, seems to be constantly urging Stephen to apologize and to do his Easter duty, demands that echo the demands she made in *Portrait*. "Repent, Stephen," she commands, and then, "*With smouldering eyes*," she commands again, "Repent! O, the fire of hell!" (*Ulysses*, p. 544). Whether this omnipotent force appears as the malicious, blackened, withered right arm of THE MOTHER or whether it is the dagger-bearing figure called OLD GUMMY GRANNY or the "old sow that eats her farrow," it is the source of the wound where love lies ableeding, the narcissistic injury, a tusking by a loving swine, arising from Stephen-Adonis's disappointment in love at an early age (*Ulysses*, p. 557).[77]

Like many who become depressed, Stephen may have suffered a heart wound because of the unavoidable disappointments of the birth of siblings or of relatively minor humiliations. No matter what those injuries were, he responded to those blows to his self-esteem with melancholy because his disappointment with his mother occurred when his self-esteem was bound up in his feeling of oneness with her, with a goddess-like figure. A dethroning of that seemingly omnipotent parent makes the child feel dethroned, the lowest of the low. One consequence

---

[77] Cf. William Shakespeare "Venus and Adonis," (ll. 1111-1120) in *The Complete Poems and Plays of William Shakespeare*, ed. William Allan Neilson and Charles Jarvis Hill (Cambridge, Massachusetts: The Riverside Press, Houghton Mifflin Company, 1942), p. 1345.

of such a fall from paradise is a lifelong attempt to regain it, as we have seen in Chapter II. The child might develop a kind of god—or goddess—within, in the form of the very strict and rigid superego we have been examining, and then, when that agenbite of inwit turns on him in an excessively punitive manner, or when that sadistic voice begins to make unbearable demands on him, he turns to external narcissistic supplies to help regulate his self esteem (such as turning to alcohol in "Circe" or to prostitutes and seemingly compulsive masturbation in *Portrait* or to plans to publish books).[78]

4. A Hobbyhorse Rider with a Yorkshire Girl

Let me conclude this discussion of Stephen being consubstantial with Shakespeare-in-the-mirror (and thereby with Bloom) by turning to a final pattern of images that hints at the origin of the hand wound that he shares with Bloom. Whenever Stephen's Thursdaymomun materializes, she is accompanied by images of falling hobbyhorse riders or falling harriers, along with a line from the song, "My girl's a Yorkshire girl." As we saw in Chapter V, Bloom sustained the "weal" on his hand, the mirror image of the scar Ulysses received from being tusked by a boar, while he was running with harriers. Stephen's hand wound is synonymous with falling off a hobbyhorse, and in his associations that fall is synonymous with the sadistic pandying by Father Dolan, the prefect of studies he calls a "washerwoman." Stephen merges riding a hobbyhorse with a painful fall (from the paradise he lived in at Clongowes as leader of the Yorkists)—a fall that leaves a lifelong scar. As Joyce's stage directions soon make clear, that hurt hand is a disguise for an injury to his groin, an Adonis-like injury associated with a Venus-like Yorkshire girl.

THE MOTHER comes into existence for the first time—i.e., STEPHEN'S very early experience of her as a seductress—when he falls off his hobbyhorse. As the room becomes the merry-go-round at the Mirus street bazaar with the pianola playing "My girl's a Yorkshire girl," Stephen calls his maniacally excited gyrations a "dance of death" (*Ulysses,* p. 542):

---

[78] Fenichel, *op. cit.,* pp. 387-406.

> *(....Stephen with hat ashplant frogsplits in middle highkicks with skykicking mouth shut hand clasp part under thigh, with clang tinkle boonhammer tallyho hornblower blue green yellow flashes Toft's cumbersome turns with hobbyhorse riders from gilded snakes dangled, bowels fandango leaping spurn soil foot and fall again.)* (*Ulysses*, p. 541)

As thigh-clasping Stephen falls, he "stops dead" at the terrifying sight of THE MOTHER rising through the floor, arrayed for a grotesque wedding (*Ulysses*, p. 542). She is wearing a "*torn bridal veil*" (*Ulysses*, p. 542). "(*With the subtle smile of death's madness.*)," she "(*Comes nearer, breathing upon him softly her breath of wetted ashes.*)" (*Ulysses*, p. 543). As she moves even closer to her son, "(*Her face [is] drawing near and nearer, sending out an ashen breath.*")" (*Ulysses*, p. 544). Stephen seems to be a horrified, unwilling bridegroom face to face with the "once beautiful May Goulding" (*Ulysses*, p. 544). THE MOTHER inveigles him with a "*subtle smile*" (*Ulysses*, p. 543). With the Yorkshire girl song still echoing in his ears (and in ours), he seems to perceive this bride with the ashen breath and the Giaconda smile as the seductive Yorkshire girl herself, a married woman who had two lovers.[79]

The wedding night of STEPHEN and the excessively close, importunate Yorkshire girl-Mother *is* a "dance of death." In her inviting smile—an invitation to join her in "death"—the seductive mother often seems maddeningly confusing to her son (and seductiveness, as I mentioned, can be excessive solicitude). He can be simultaneously excited and ashamed, furious and terrified. If he accepts her invitation to even deeper intimacy, for example, to share soul secrets "Tell me the word, mother, if you know now. The word known to all men" (*Ulysses*, p. 543), he risks the death of trust, along with feelings of betrayal. He also risks a moral death. If his mother indicates that what is going on between them is somehow "bad," ("Repent! O, the fire of hell!"), the child often not only feels guilty for the seduction but also interprets her love as a form of death, her seeming seductiveness as a hostile attack. He feels that she

---

[79] Gifford and Seidman, *op. cit.*, p. 232.

harbors destructive wishes towards him, even, perhaps, impulses to mutilate him. Having fallen off his hobbyhorse, Stephen dances with a ghoulish bride, THE MOTHER as a grey-eyed Yorkshire girl who is in turn the transmigrating soul of another grey-eyed seductress who once bent over a chaste boy, stooping to conquer, but unwittingly tusking him instead.[80]

5. Bella Cools herself Flirting a Black Horn like Minnie Hauck in Carmen

How does the Shakespeareness we have been studying in STEPHEN, the unconscious enactment of a Dedalean version of Shakespeare's "Venus and Adonis," appear in Bloom? On the most obvious level, as every member of the Cyclops tribe in Barney Kiernan's pub seems to know, Bloom is a cuckold. He thinks of Blazes Boylan all day, especially the time, 4 o'clock, when Molly welcomes him to her bed. As I've suggested earlier, Bloom, together with Adonis-Stephen was "overborne in a cornfield...and he will never be a victor in his own eyes after nor play victoriously the game of laugh and lie down. Assumed dongiovannism will not save him" (*Ulysses*, p. 188).

In his memory of his youthful moment in that field—the paradisiacal time when he and Molly plighted their troth mid the heather and ferns of Howth sixteen years earlier—Molly was not only Eve-like, offering her Adam a version of the apple from her own mouth, "seedcake warm and chewed. Mawkish pulp...sweet and sour with spittle" (*Ulysses*, p. 167), but she also was a seductive Venus pulling her Adonis down to her:

> well as well him as another and then I asked him with my eyes to ask again yes and then he asked me would I yes to say yes my mountain flower and first I put my arms around him yes and drew him down to me so he could feel my breasts all perfume yes and his heart was going like mad and yes I said yes I will Yes (*Ulysses*, p. 783)

---

[80] *Ibid.* "One said, My little shy little lass / Has a waist so trim and small—Grey are her eyes so bright...."

Bloom thinks of Venus immediately after he remembers Molly. She, along with Juno, is one of the "shapely goddesses" who embody the "curves the world admires," "curves" that to Bloom "are beauty" (*Ulysses*, p. 168). He then misreads "Venus and Adonis": "men too they gave themselves, manly conscious, lay with men lovers, a youth enjoyed her, to the yard" (*Ulysses*, p. 168). Although Venus does possess a "manly" consciousness—she is "like a bold-faced suitor" as she sets about wooing Adonis—and although she did "give" herself presents of men (and gave herself to men) when she desired male lovers, Adonis didn't enjoy her "to the yard."[81] Venus couldn't overcome his resistance to her.

Bloom gives himself over to an assumed dongiovannism, too, as did Stephen's Shakespeare, but it does not save him from the wound of being cuckolded. His attempts as "Henry Flower" at seducing Martha Clifford by mail is a comic dongiovannism, where he will never be victor in his own eyes nor play victorious the game of laugh and lie down. The "sting of disregard [that glows] to weak pleasure within his breast" all day *is* the blow to his self-esteem that Molly's Venus-like lust for Blazes Boylan has inflicted (*Ulysses*, p. 57).

The most significant element in Bloom's fusion with Stephen—the psychological residue of *his* disappointment in love at an early age—appears in his exchanges with Venus in nighttown herself, Bella-Bello Cohen. Even if we didn't know that Joyce used Leopold von Sacher-Masoch's *Venus in Furs* in his creation of BELLA, we could have inferred that he wanted us to think of the Venus and Adonis myth (as well as Homer's Circe) because he conflates BELLA, not just implicitly with a domineering love-goddess in furs, but also explicitly with a seductive, destructive, sexually powerful *femme fatale*.

The stage directions tell us that BELLA *cools herself, flirting a black horn fan like Minnie Hauck in* Carmen (*Ulysses*, p. 496). Many of the first readers of *Ulysses* would have known of Minnie Hauck, the American dramatic soprano who was well known in Europe in the 1870s and 1880s, particularly in the title role of Bizet's opera where the gypsy is

---

[81] Shakespeare, "Venus and Adonis", *op. cit.* p. 1333 (l. 6). Also, cf., Gifford and Seidman, *op. cit.*, p. 147.

portrayed as a "strong, ruthless, and capricious woman whose love is potentially destructive."[82] We may infer that when Leopold von Sacher-Bloom faces Bella-Venus (in furs)-Carmen, he is also the transmigrating soul of Adonis-José—a naive, potentially seducible youth confronting an imperious, manly conscious female force, goddess-like in her power.

The whoremistress then turns into her black horn fan, *"(Flirting quickly, then slowly)"* (*Ulysses,* p. 496). If a Dubliner in 1904 has the "horn," he is sexually aroused. For Bloom, powerful BELLA is seductive and exciting, but a horn can also penetrate painfully. Her seductiveness is inseparable from a distinctively feminine accouterment (like the tusk of Venus's boar) that can unman. Bloom is being given the horn and the horns. Like Shakespeare in the cornfield, facing a boldfaced goddess who is bending over him, stooping to conquer, Bloom is simultaneously being seduced and cuckolded, excited and rendered powerless.

Joyce emphasizes BELLA'S Venus-like nature in another stage direction: *"her falcon eyes glitter"* (*Ulysses,* p. 496). She is beginning to change into the hungry bird of prey to which Shakespeare likened Venus, the "empty eagle" we discussed in Chapter V, gorging on Adonis. Like Venus, the madam feeds "glutton-like," "yet never filleth."[83]

Like THE MOTHER, who seemed to be clawing, crab-wise, *her* son to death with her glittering *"malignant red eyes"* ablaze, BELLA is also poised to conquer, forcing her prey, as Venus tried to force her prey, to pay whatever ransom she willeth (*Ulysses,* p. 544). Like Stephen, who externalized in THE MOTHER an unconscious representation of an ambivalently introjected Mrs. Dedalus, so Bloom seems to be reprojecting an unconscious representation of ELLEN BLOOM, an ambivalent introjection from a time when love between him and his mother seemed vexed.

To THE FAN'S question, "Have you forgotten me?" BLOOM replies, "Yes. No" (*Ulysses,* p. 496). Consciously, Bloom has no recollection of THE FAN and its significance, but "no" is also a correct answer. Unconsciously, Bloom has not "forgotten" a trauma that seems to have occurred in infancy. As he begins to misinterpret the present in terms of

---

[82] Gifford and Seidman, *op. cit.,* p. 410.
[83] Shakespeare, "Venus and Adonis," *op. cit.,* pp. 1334, 1339 (ll.55; 548).

his psychological past, he is remembering and not remembering at the same time:

THE FAN

(*Folded akimbo against her waist.*) Is me her was you dreamed before? Was then she him you us since knew? Am all them and the same now we?

(*Bella approaches, gently tapping with the fan.*)

BLOOM

(*Wincing.*) Powerful being. In my eyes read that slumber which women love.

THE FAN

(*Tapping.*) We have met. You are mine. It is fate. (*Ulysses,* pp, 496-497)

THE FAN'S lack of differentiation between present and past ("is" and "was" merge), imperfect and perfect past ("was" and "knew"); the collapse of the distinction between now and then, here and there; and the lack of negatives, conditionals, and qualifying conjunctions—all evoke the primary process thinking that Freud attributed to the unconscious, to the dreaming mind, and to the rudimentary thought processes of the young child or the disturbed adult. Yet Joyce makes us aware that although the laws of space, time, and consecutive thought do not exist in the unconscious, there is an underlying coherence. THE FAN'S seemingly meaningless questions—"Is me her was you dreamed before?" and "Was then she him for us since knew? and "Am all them and the same now me?"—all make sense given the psychological history I have inferred in Bloom. (Again, as with my inference about Stephen's psychological history, I ask the reader to accept it for the light it may shed on these still-difficult-to-understand passages in *Ulysses*.)

With her large black horn fan and her "*deeply carboned*" eyes, "*olive face,*" and "*orangetainted nostrils,*" BELLA is like an earlier dark, powerful, costumed woman who appears before Bloom (*Ulysses,* p. 496). But since there are no representations for "like" in the unconscious, then the implicit answer to THE FAN'S first question is "Yes." The FAN-BELLA *is* "me her was you dreamed before" for Bloom. THE FAN, or "me," is "her," the domineering MARION-Molly whom Bloom met before as in a dream. In Bloom's unconscious, that is, FAN-BELLA *is* MARION-Molly:

A VOICE

(*Sharply.*) Poldy!

BLOOM

Who? (*He ducks and wards off a blow clumsily.*) At your service. (*He looks up. Beside her mirage of datepalms a handsome woman in Turkish costume stands before him. Opulent curves fill out her scarlet trousers and jacket slashed with gold. A wide yellow cummerbund girdles her. A white yashmak, violet in the night, covers her face, leaving free only her large dark eyes and raven hair.*)

BLOOM

Molly!

MARION

Welly? Mrs Marion from this out, my dear man, when you speak to me. (*Satirically.*) Has poor little hubby cold feet waiting so long? (*Ulysses*, pp. 417-418)

The not so latent dominatrix in Molly emerges in her assumption of the name Blazes Boylan impudently used to address her ("Mrs Marion") in his letter (which Bloom spotted) at 8 am. Demanding that Bloom use Boylan's designation for her, with its presumption of intimacy (as I mentioned, he mailed the letter to Mrs Marion Bloom instead of the proper Mrs Leopold Bloom), she cuckolds Poldy late at night as well as at 4 in the afternoon. Not only is MARION fused with the castrating BELLA, she seems to be the reincarnation of ELLEN BLOOM as well.

MARION takes the stage immediately after Bloom's mother appeared to him in a dreamy pantomime show. Absurdly costumed, like MARION, ELLEN BLOOM in her own comic way is just as imposing and emotionally demanding:

ELLEN BLOOM

(*In pantomime dame's stringed mobcap, crinoline and bustle, widow Twankey's blouse with muttonleg sleeves buttoned behind, grey mittens and cameo brooch, her hair plaited in a crispine net, appears over the banisters, a slanted candlestick in her hand and cries out in shrill alarm.*) O blessed Redeemer, what have they done to him! My smelling salts! (*She hauls up a reef of skirt and ransacks the pouch of her striped blay petticoat. A phial, an Agnus Dei, a shrivelled potato and a celluloid doll fall out.*) Sacred heart of Mary, where were you at all, at all? (*Ulysses*, p. 417)

In her desperate anxiety over the injured hand that Bloom got while running to harriers with his high school friends, ELLEN BLOOM'S love seems not only overly solicitous but, to her adolescent son, unmanning. He becomes crestfallen first and then silently angry: (*Bloom, mumbling, his eyes downcast, begins to bestow his parcels in his filled pockets but desists, muttering.*) (*Ulysses*, p. 417). Once again, a Thursdaymomun, ELLEN BLOOM, expresses love in a confusing and wounding manner. It is not quite a tusking ardor, but in its self-absorption, it does seem harmful to her son's belief in himself—his sense of his emerging independence, autonomy, and masculinity. Although that belief is not untimely killed, BLOOM, like Shakespeare-in-the-mirror—and thus like Stephen—seems overborne after a tumble (in a school yard-cornfield). In the presence of the final Thursdaymomun who confronts him, however, BLOOM (a.k.a Blephen) experiences in full measure a boar-like attack.

6. *A Hard Basilisk Stare*

If we accept the idea that THE FAN-BELLA is a composite "her," Bloom's fusion of unconscious images of his mother and wife, ELLEN BLOOM and MARION, women whom he has "dreamed before," then the answer to THE FAN'S second question ("Was then she him you us since knew?") is also "Yes," at least if Bloom could say what he was unconscious of. "She"—ELLEN BLOOM-MARION—"was" a "him" whom Bloom "since knew." In her forceful, emasculating "love" for him,

Blephen: The Contransmagnificandjewbangtantiality of Father and Son

his first Thursdaymomun and especially his second (a wife to whom he responded as if she were a dominating and humiliating mother and he a guilty boy)—that double Thursdaymomun often seemed as manly conscious as Venus to Bloom.

Now, very late on this Thursday night, BLOOM feels that there is another "him" within a "she" as he faces BELLA. The madam becomes the third Thursdaymomun he encounters in nighttown (she apparently has a son at Oxford). As BELLA turns into BELLO, a replica of the powerful, boar-like aspect of Venus, a "loving swine," Bloom becomes a terrified and excited, infatuated and self-emasculated little piglet, a fit consort for a boarish him/her.

As BELLA'S "falcon eyes" strike Bloom in" midbrow," "*a hard basilisk stare*," the whoremistress becomes not only the legendary reptile with the fatal glance and breath than can poison a man (*Ulysses*, p. 499),[84] but she also becomes a sexually aroused whoremaster, BELLO, a man with a "*baritone voice*" who proceeds to attack Bloom sadistically, an attack that "*Enthralled*" masochistic Bloom (*Ulysses*, pp. 499-500). Bellowing contemptuously and excitedly in Bloom's face, "Hound of dishonour," "Adorer of the adulterous rump," and, finally, "Dungdevourer," BELLO bewitches BLOOM, who is "*infatuated*" (*Ulysses*, p. 499). Smitten in a double sense, physically attacked by a hypnotic creature who unmans him, BLOOM becomes a powerless, Adonis-like youth, admiring yet desexualized by an older, manly conscious woman who simultaneously seduces and destroys, both a Circe and a Venus in the nighttown version of a Shakespeare's English cornfield.

In the endless vaudeville show that is life in Circe's den, Bloom metamorphosizes into a female pig:

BLOOM
(*Her eyes upturned in the sign of admiration, closing.*)
Truffles!
(*With a piercing epileptic cry she sinks on all fours, grunting, snuffling, rooting at his feet, then lies, shamming dead with eyes tight*

---

[84] Gifford and Seidman, *op.cit.*, p. 176.

shut, trembling eyelids, bowed upon the ground in the attitude of most excellent master.) (*Ulysses*, p. 499)

This image, along with the image of the whoremistress/ whoremaster, is Joyce's externalization of self-images and object-images in BLOOM'S unconscious. The image of a frightened, snuffling, rooting creature on all fours, with eyes shut tight and eyelids trembling, calls up a female-ized pig awaiting slaughter but also a terrified infant awaiting punishment, an echo of BLOOM abjectly waiting MARION'S pleasurable discipline. It seems that Bloom often felt castrated (and self-castrated) in the presence of MARION, THE FAN, and BELLA. Taken together, they comprise an image of a dominating, often cruel, manly conscious seductress—a Venus in drag.

It is possible that Bloom unconsciously incorporated a maternal image on which he had projected his own excrementitious hostility, his version of chokiting a Thursdaymomun. The result was the existence in his unconscious of a frightening creature named BELLO. BELLO'S sadistic pleasure in tormenting Bloom with anal name calling implies that Bloom's ambivalent introjection of a representation of his mother might very well have occurred at an early age. (At around 18 months or later, the anus comes to be the site of the most important sexual tensions and gratifications, the retention and expulsion of feces as well as pleasure in fecal odors.[85]) Joyce hints at the intense ambivalence of that period when Babby Bloom with a chubby finger counts the bronze buckles on an earlier Thursdaymomun, Zoe, "One two tlee: tlee, tlwo tlone," and THE BUCKLES suggest the game Babby is playing. When they reply, "Love me. Love me not. Love me," they seem to be saying that Bloom is asking whether mother loves him or loves him not and simultaneously whether he in turn loves her or loves her not (*Ulysses*, p. 501).

Joyce gives us the most vivid picture of Bloom's unconscious maternal identification when the masculinized madam mounts him (or her). BELLO ("*Squats, with a grunt, on Bloom's upturned face, puffing cigar*

---

[85] Charles Brenner, *An Elementary Textbook of Psychoanalysis*, rev. ed. (Garden City, New York: Anchor Press/Doubleday, 1974), p. 24.

smoke, nursing a fat leg.") (*Ulysses*, p. 502). Babby feels "(*Goaded, buttocksmothered.*"), and pleased (*Ulysses*, p. 502). It's not difficult for BELLO to read BLOOM'S mind here since he *is* part of BLOOM'S mind. Bloom got Molly to become a playful BELLO when he and Molly were newly married and living on Pleasants street. From his confession of the "most revolting piece of obscenity" in his "whole career of crime," we have learned that he apparently got himself buttocksmothered by his wife, for he "rererepugnosed in rerererepugnant" (*Ulysses*, p. 506). To be sure, Molly isn't particularly enamored of her husband's lovemaking techniques:

> if he wants to kiss my bottom Ill drag open my drawers and bulge it right out in his face as large as life he can stick his tongue 7 miles up my hole as hes there my brown part then Ill tell him I want £1 or perhaps 30/...Ill let him do it off on me behind provided he doesnt smear all my good drawers.. . .I know every turn in him Ill tighten my bottom well and let out a few smutty words smellrump or lick my shit or the first mad thing comes into my head (*Ulysses*, p. 733)

Molly might not be mollified even if she knew that Bloom is as fascinated with her rere as he is with Venus's. In the "Lestrygonians," Bloom plans to go to the museum to see if Venus has a "hole": "Never looked. I'll look today. Keeper won't see. Bend down let something fall see if she" (*Ulysses*, p. 168). He apparently followed through on his plan. Mulligan tells Stephen in "Scylla and Charybdis" that he saw Bloom looking at her: "His pale Galilean eyes were upon her mesial groove. Venus Kallipyge" (*Ulysses* p. 193). As I mentioned earlier, after his scientific curiosity was aroused about the anus of the love goddess, Bloom's streaming consciousness next flowed to the love making of Venus and Adonis, another hint from Joyce that the psychological meanings of the Venus and Adonis story comprise the substance in which Bloom is consubstantial with Stephen, and Blephen is consubstantial with Shakespeare-in-the-mirror. It is in their Shakespeare-ness that Stephen and Bloom are consubstantial.

7. *A Cockhorse to Banbury Cross*

The cockhorse imagery marks the culmination of BELLO'S sadistic anal attack on Bloom. Of course, consciously, Bloom feels that Bella Cohen—who has magically turned into a Circe-like monster—has gratuitously attacked him. At the risk of redundancy, let me repeat that, unconsciously, BELLO is BLOOM'S reprojection of an introjection, the externalization of an unconscious maternal image, a figure on whom he had first projected his own excrementitious hostility and then had incorporated. Bloom's disappointment in love, like Stephen's and like the disappointment of Stephen's version of Shakespeare, occurred early in life in the "nursery." Like them, Bloom was overborne by a goddess whose domineering love was synonymous with a fall, an expulsion from paradise, a mini-death to his emergent manhood so that he, like Shakespeare in the cornfield, could never fully be a "victor" in his own eyes:

BELLO

(*He throws a leg astride and, pressing with horseman's knees, calls in a hard voice.*) Gee up! A cockhorse to Banbury cross. I'll ride him for the Eclipse stakes. (*He bends sideways and squeezes his mount's testicles roughly, shouting.*) Ho! off we pop! I'll nurse you in proper fashion. (*He horserides cockhorse, leaping in the saddle.*). The lady goes a pace a pace and the coachman goes a trot a trot and the gentleman goes a gallop a gallop a gallop a gallop. (*Ulysses*, p. 502)

Converting BLOOM into his own private hobbyhorse, BELLO seems to be as manly conscious as Bloom imagined Venus to be earlier in the day. In fact, BELLO is even manlier than Venus. While Venus pushed Adonis backward, "as she would be thrust," BELLO places his powerful body on Bloom, pushing him down as he mounts him, and, as did Venus, "govern[ing] [Adonis] in strength" "in blindfold fury." When BELLO finishes the work of his version of a milkmaid, squeezing Bloom's testicles, he all but turns into that mythical "loving swine," piggishly, boarishly unmanning Bloom by humiliating him, first squatting "*with a grunt on Bloom's upturned face*" and then "*uncork[ing] himself behind: then, contorting his features, fart[ing] loudly."* (*Ulysses*, pp. 502-503). If there was ever a tyrant of the heart in Joyce, this castrating mother within, torturing Bloom rather than nursing him, is it.

As BLOOM explains his schemes for "social regeneration" in "Circe," Joyce's stage directions read: *"The keeper of the Kildare Street Museum appears, dragging a lorry on which are the shaking statues of several naked goddesses Venus Callipyge, Venus Pandemos, Venus Metempsychosis...."* (*Ulysses*, p. 463). Throughout *Ulysses*, Bloom and Stephen seem drawn to Venus Metempsychosis. Stephen conflates Anne Hathaway with Venus and late at night receives a tusking wound from another Venus, THE MOTHER, in a place where love lies ableeding. At lunchtime, Bloom is fascinated with the question of whether Venus's statue has an anus, and at night he has little power to resist the power of that loving swine with many names: lustful MARION, the blackhorn FAN, and BELLA/BELLO.

Consubstantial in their reliving of the Venus and Adonis story in different ways—in their embodiment of the transmigrating soul of reindeer antlered Shakespeare-in-the-mirror—Bloom and Stephen comprise a "fusion" in yet another way. In the next chapter, I want to explore how Joyce enlarges and complicates our sense of the Shakespeare "substance" which lies at the heart of Blephen or Stoom—their shared artistic nature.

CHAPTER VII

Portraits of the Artist: Consubstantiality in a Different Light

(Stephen and Bloom gaze in the mirror. The face of William Shakespeare, beardless, appears there, rigid in facial paralysis, crowned by the reflection of the reindeer antlered hatrack in the hall.)

SHAKESPEARE

(In dignified ventriloquy.) 'Tis the loud laugh bespeaks the vacant mind *(To Bloom.)* Thou thoughtest as how thou wastest invisible. *Gaze. (He crows with a black capon's laugh.)* Iagogo ! How my oldfellow chokit his Thursdaymomum. Iagogogo !

—*"Circe" (Ulysses, p. 531)*

As we have seen, in mythic or prehistoric or preverbal time, when gods walked the earth and when parents *were* gods to infants, Blephen suffered a disturbance in love because his self-esteem was bound up in his love for an all-but omnipotent, all-but omniscient goddess. Joyce found the most fruitful metaphor for this primal parent, a bisexual-seeming mothering figure, in "manly conscious" Venus loving her Adonis with a tusking ardor.[86] He shows us the consequences of that loving wounding in the highly memorable image (which we have examined before) that appears in Bella Cohen's mirror as Stephen and Bloom simultaneously gaze into it. *"The face of William Shakespeare, beardless, appears there rigid in facial paralysis, crowned by the reflection of the reindeer antlered hatrack in the hall"* (*Ulysses*, p. 531). Joyce transforms the writer he considered *the* Lord of Language into a cuckold who *"crows with a black capon's laugh"*: "Iagogo! How my Oldfellow chokit his Thurdaymomun. Iagogogo!" (*Ulysses*, p. 531)!

Just before Shakespeare's face materializes, Lynch points to the mirror and laughingly says, "The mirror up to nature" (*Ulysses*, p. 531). Joyce is asking us to catch the dramatic irony in Lynch's mocking allusion to Hamlet's caution to the players about overacting. Reindeer-antlered Shakespeare *does* hold the mirror up to nature—Blephen's psychological nature. As Stephen and Bloom look, their enraged, horned, crowing reflection symbolizes the psychological results of early empathic failures, mis-attunements that can involve excessive gratifications as well as disappointments or combinations of gratification and disappointment. Put somewhat differently, these images, I argued, symbolize the emotional effects in later years of a disturbance in *amor matris,* the love of a mother for her son and the love of the son for his mother. These disappointments arose when the child's omnipotence was wrapped up in his mother's, leaving the child hungry for the emotional warmth, sense of well being, and feelings of heightened self-worth that he had (and lost) early in his life.[87]

This wounded demigod, an Adonis-like Shakespeare, is at the heart of the consubstantiality of Stephen and Bloom. But Joyce also compli-

---

[86] Cf. Leonard Shengold, "Trauma, Soul Murder, and Change," *The Psychoanalytic Quarterly*, LXXX, no. 1 (2011), 130 n 7.

[87] By "early," I suspect that it might have occurred when Stoom was in the final stage of differentiating himself psychologically from his goddess-like mother and of consolidating various psychological structures, including his sense of his own bodily outline and integrity—the age of fifteen months to eighteen months or even earlier, according to Margaret S. Mahler, Fred Pine, and Anni Bergman, *The Psychological Birth of the Human Infant: Symbiosis and Individuation* (New York: Basic Books, Inc., 1975), pp. 76-108. The "rapprochement subphase" of the separation-individuation process is especially important.

cates our sense of their fusion. In this chapter, I want to explore another aspect of their consubstantiality. The Shakespeare "substance" that Bloom and Stephen share is more than an early injury. For Joyce, the transformation of conflicts in mother love into literary creativity, especially clear in the case of Stephen, is at the heart of their oneness as well.

First, let me look briefly at Bloom. In his serious joking, seriojocular, way, Joyce has Lenehan tell us that "There's a touch of the artist about old Bloom" (*Ulysses*, p. 225). At the beginning of his day in "Calypso," 8 am, June 16, 1904, Bloom recreates in moving prose-poetry the Mediterranean world through which he will pass (as simultaneously Odysseus will pass), for the next eighteen hours, until he falls asleep in "Ithaca" at 2 am, June 17, 1904:

> Somewhere in the east: early morning: set off at dawn, travel round in front of the sun steal a day's march on him. Keep it up for ever never grow a day older technically. Walk along a strand, strange land, come to a city gate, sentry there, old ranker too, old Tweedy's big moustaches leaning on a long kind of a spear. Wander through awned streets. Turbaned faces going by. Dark caves of carpet shops, big man, Turko the terrible, seated crosslegged smoking a coiled pipe. Cries of seller in the streets. Drink water scented with fennel, sherbet. Wander along all day. Might meet a robber or two. Well, meet him. Getting on to sundown. The shadows of the mosques along the pillars: priest with a scroll rolled up. A shiver of trees, signal, the evening wind. I pass on. Fading gold sky. A mother watches from her doorway. She calls her children home in their dark language. High wall: beyond strings twanged. Night sky moon, violet, colour of Molly's new garters. Strings. Listen. A girl playing one of these instruments what do you call them: dulcimers. I pass.
> (*Ulysses*, p. 55)

Three hours later, Bloom almost surpasses the stunning metaphor that he came up with in the morning, "their dark language." In "Hades," he creates other metaphors that seem to arise as naturally as breathing. (For Joyce, art is not compensatory; it does not arise from deficiency and neurosis but from the fullness of nature herself.) Ever alert and curious, Bloom spots a rat as he looks down into a stone crypt in Glasnevin cemetery where he is attending Paddy Dignam's funeral, "The grey alive crushed itself in under the plinth, wriggled itself in under it." He then imagines not only the busy underground work of rats but the taste of a corpse as well:

> Wonder does the news go about whenever a fresh one is let down. Underground communication. We learned that from them. Wouldn't be surprised. Regular square feed for them. Flies come before he's well dead. Got wind of Dignam. They wouldn't care about the smell of it. Saltwhite crumbling mush of corpse: smell, taste like raw white turnips (*Ulysses.*, p.110).

Astonishing as Bloom's simile- and metaphor-making is, Joyce also undercuts his artistic gifts by making Bloom comic. (If he didn't, Joyce's readers would too easily identify him with Bloom in all of Leopold Bloom's polymorphous perversity.) In fact, Bloom would probably think we were laughing at him if we told him that he had a touch of the artist about him. For middlebrowish, conventional, Edwardian Bloom, true poetry can never be a "Saltwhite crumbling mush of corpse"; nor can there be artistic beauty in "night sky moon, violet, colour of Molly's new garters." Ambitious and daring Stephen might be impressed by Bloom's simile, but he would probably think we were condescending to him if we told him that we thought that he, Stephen Dedalus, had a touch of the artist about him (he would especially object to the belittling, "touch").

Rather than a touch of the artist, Joyce wants us to see that Stephen is *the* artist-to-be in *Ulysses,* but the artist-to-be who is now grounded after his abortive, Icarus-like flight to Paris. Crashing to earth in Dublin, Stephen is now possessed by the transmigrating soul of Telemachus—dispossessed, all but unmanned in his depression, seemingly unable to create the boldly imaginative metaphors that unself-conscious Bloom seems to toss off so effortlessly. At the end of *Portrait,* however, as he prepares to fly away from Ireland, we will see him giving birth to his artist's soul and creating in the bird-like girl at the Bull a symbol of both that soul and his Irish Beatrice, his guide to the paradise of divine creativity.

And it is in *Portrait* that Joyce explores the transmigrating soul of Shakespeare within Stephen, his artistic nature, most fully. Before turning to *Portrait*, let me introduce a new term to describe Stephen's lifelong attempt to regulate his self-esteem. In Chapter I and Chapter II, I discussed his often driven search for various mothers and maternal figures who can supply that self-esteem, a hunger for a sense of heightened well being and security that was shaken, I suggested, by an early disturbances in mother love. Another way of describing this hunger is to speak of Stephen's narcissistic vulnerability.

Here let me offer a brief description of narcissism, as many psychoanalysts understand the term.[88] It refers, of course, to the Greek youth, Narcissus, who fell in love with himself. We see signs of healthy narcissism, of normal self-directed love, in infants. Their attitude toward the first objects they are aware of is exclusively self-centered. They are concerned with the gratifications and pleasures that these persons or things, animate or inanimate, can afford, whether a breast, a piece of blanket, a thumb, or a loving glance. Traumatic disruptions in those early forms of gratification and pleasure can lead to a self-absorbed life where psychic energy is invested mainly in one's self and one's projects; a relative lack of interest in, and genuine concern for, others; and a tendency to use other people instrumentally.

For our purposes here, an even more important consequence of those early disturbances is the difficulty facing such narcissistically vulnerable men and woman in "integrating into their personalities" the residue of those disturbances—an unconscious "archaic grandiose self" and an unconscious" idealized parental imago."[89] Unlike men and woman suffering from such personality disturbances, Stephen finds ways to satisfy those grandiose and idealizing impulses and thus avoids feelings of self-depletion and inner impoverishment. Said somewhat differently,

---

[88] See Charles Brenner, *An Elementary Textbook of Psychoanalysis,* rev. ed. (New York: Anchor Press/Doubleday, 1974), pp. 97ff. I am using his brief summary in what follows.

[89] Heinz Kohut, *The Analysis of the Self: A Systematic Approach to the Psychoanalytic Treatment of Narcissistic Personality Disturbances* (New York: International Universities Press, 1971), pp. 45-46.

rather than wall himself off from the "unrealistic claims" of an archaic grandiose self or against "the intense hunger...for other forms of emotional sustenance," Stephen seems almost instinctively to turn to the earliest and most rudimentary forms of imaginative activity to satisfy those claims, and as he does, he comes to realize that he himself is the most powerful source of self-esteem.[90]

Again, unlike narcissistically vulnerable patients, Stephen's heightened feelings of pleasure in himself and in the imaginary worlds he creates for himself do not lead automatically to unpleasurable excitement and anxiety, followed by feelings of dullness and passivity. Nor do those surges of creative joy get totally derailed by rebuffs or the absence of expected approval. Yet he does share a rhythm that often appears in the lives of such vulnerable men and women, an oscillation between excitement and depression, between heightened praise or interest received from others, followed by mild embarrassment and self-consciousness or severe shame and despair.[91]

Let me now focus on three portraits of the artist as a young man. We first have Joyce's portrait of Stephen's "manifest" and conscious life. This is inseparable from his more inferential portrait of Stephen's narcissistic vulnerability and Stephen's attempts to reduce his subsequent self-loss. Finally, I turn to Stephen's own portrait—his word-painting of a birdlike girl standing in a rivulet at the Bull that he composed before writing his Villanelle to the Temptress. Here we see him dying to his old fearful and guilt-ridden self and giving birth to the artist-soul that has been gestating within him all his life.

2. *Her Serious Alluring Eyes, Horse Piss, and Rotted Straw*

Let me turn now to Stephen's adolescent turmoil in *Portrait*, focusing first on how Joyce reveals his oscillating rhythm between feelings of

---

[90] *Ibid.*, p. 17.
[91] *Ibid.*, p. 20. Gabriel Conroy's gathering embarrassment and self-consciousness, leading to severe shame and despair, appears most dramatically at the end of Joyce's masterpiece, "The Dead." See, especially, Appendix.

deadness and exuberant vitality, shame and excitement and, then, on how Stephen discovers his own unique way to counteract painful feelings of self-fragmentation. As a senior boy at Belvedere, he was to play a "farcical pedagogue" in the Whitsuntide play (*Portrait,* p. 321). He felt "no stage fright" as he waited for the curtain to go up, but the "part he had to play humiliated him. A remembrance of some of his lines made a sudden flush rise to his painted cheeks" (*Portrait,* p, 334). The flush of humiliation seems due to Stephen anticipating that the audience will not look admiringly and approvingly on his theatrical exhibition of himself. Perhaps they'll even laugh at him rather than at the farcical pedagogue he is painted up to perform.[92] But this brief moment of shame quickly dissolves as he sees EC looking at him:

> He saw her serious alluring eyes watching him from among the audience and their image at once swept away his scruples, leaving his will compact. Another nature seemed to have been lent him: the infection of the excitement and youth about him entered into and transformed his moody mistrustfulness. For one rare moment he seemed to be clothed in the real apparel of boyhood.... (*Portrait,* pp. 94-95)

Stephen seems to be experiencing (although briefly, to be sure) the self-depletion that Kohut finds in his patients, the fleeting feeling that one's will is no longer "compact." One is no longer feeling fully real, in possession of a coherent self, a "real" boyhood identity. His "moody mistrustfulness," this constellation of self-conscious embarrassment and shame, soon dissolves. Stephen manages to halt the plummeting of his self-esteem and makes his will "compact." He seems to be incorporating EC visually, putting on her "nature" along with her "serious alluring eyes." With a kind of prehensile vision, he gazes into the window of her soul, her serious and alluring eyes, and takes her soul into his own. All but attributing to those eyes the soul-heartening gleam in a mother's

---

[92] It's possible that part of his anxiety might be due to the intrusion of what are, at this time of his life, frightening (because grandiose) exhibitionistic wishes.

eyes as she gazes admiringly on her son—"their image at once swept away his scruples"—Stephen reduces his painful anxiety by briefly creating a kind of fantasy-world where he is the apple of EC's eye, where "another nature seemed to have been lent him."

Joyce shows us the same "individuating rhythm" when the curtain falls. No longer fantasizing that EC is holding him all "compact" in her gaze—self-coherent and real to himself, "clothed in the real apparel of boyhood"—Stephen sees the "simple body before which he had acted magically deformed, the void of faces breaking at all points and falling asunder into busy groups" (*Portrait*, p. 95). Joyce's ambiguity implies that the "simple body" falling asunder is not only the audience (or even EC's body) that is undergoing this "magical transformation." Joyce is using a fusion of third- and first-person narration in *Portrait*—free indirect speech, an "objective" narrative often suffused with Stephen's "subjectivity," language, and viewpoint. Stephen's body, not just the audience, also appears to be "breaking" and "falling asunder" because once more he felt himself momentarily broken, fallen asunder. This fleeting repetition of self-fragmentation is perhaps due to his separation from EC, before whom he just exhibited himself or, more accurately, his separation from her alluring eyes, the source just before of his heightened self-worth, his renewed compactness of will. Angrily bypassing his family, Stephen feels anguished again:

> Without waiting for his father's questions he ran across the road and began to walk at breakneck speed down the hill. He hardly knew where he was walking. Pride and hope and desire like crushed herbs in his heart sent up vapour of maddening incense before the eyes of his mind. He strode down the hill amid the tumult of suddenrisen vapours of wounded pride and fallen hope and baffled desire. They steamed upwards before his anguished eyes in dense and maddening fumes and passed away above him till at last the air was clear and cold again. (*Portrait*, p. 96)

Disillusioned and anguished, Stephen is all but suffocated by shame, as if he has been painfully exposed in his grandiose hope of being won-

Portraits of the Artist: Consubstantiality in a Different Light

derful, of performing a lofty role before EC wonderfully. He hits on yet another way to dispel "the tumult of suddenrisen vapours of wounded pride and fallen hope and baffled desire," the injury to his self-esteem. The very act of walking "at breakneck speed down the hill" seems to be part of a self-soothing process. (How often Stephen walks, runs, and then soars, Icarus-like, in *Portrait* and then feels calmed afterwards.[93])

Joyce then dramatizes a habit from Stephen's infancy that best helps him dispel the dense, suddenrisen vapours of sunken self-worth, truly "maddening" in his frightening feeling of incipient unreality and self-fragmentation. As the vapours passed away above him, the air became clear and cold:

> A film still veiled his eyes but they burned no longer. A power, akin to that which had often made anger or resentment fall from him, brought his steps to rest. He stood still and gazed up at the sombre porch of the morgue and from that to the dark cobbled laneway at its side. He saw the word *Lotts* on the wall of the lane and breathed slowly the rank heavy air.
> —That is horse piss and rotted straw, he thought. It is a good odour to breathe. It will calm my heart. My heart is quite calm now. I will go back. (*Portrait*, p. 96)

Stephen's "anger or resentment" seems to be a mild form of narcissistic rage, a feeling, perhaps, that no one has taken him at what might have been his own very high valuation of himself during the performance, neither

---

[93] As we shall soon see, he seems to walk out of time—"How far had he walked? What hour was it?"— as the image of the "angel of mortal youth and beauty" passes into his soul at the end of Chapter IV of *Portrait* (p. 200). Although similar, Stephen is finally unlike the idealistic, intensely imaginative, and grandiose young boy in "Araby." Joyce's self-appointed priest-knight imagined that he could bear his "chalice safely through a throng of foes," hoping that he could perform love service for Mangan's sister or, more accurately, for the "image" he created out of her. Stephen, unlike the boy, is not left painfully disillusioned, "driven and derided by vanity" ("Araby," in *Dubliners*, with an introduction by Padraic Colum [New York: The Modern Library, 1926] pp. 34-35, 41). Subsequent references to *Dubliners* will appear in the text and refer to this edition.

EC, nor his family, nor (most importantly) himself. As he first gazes up "at the sombre porch of the morgue" and then at the "dark cobbled" street at its side, *Lotts* laneway, Joyce implies that Stephen is briefly experiencing a small psychological death-in-life after the Whitsuntide play. But because of his inborn "power" to incorporate the heartbalm of horse piss and rotted straw in an olfactory manner, he doesn't linger in this mental morgue. He has the ability to repair injuries to his narcissism, which makes dislocating anger or resentment "fall from him."

When we recall Stephen's first sensation of urine in *Portrait*, we can understand more fully why horse piss is so calming:

> When you wet the bed, first it is warm then it gets cold. His mother put on the oilsheet. That had the queer smell. (*Portrait*, p. 1)

Associated with his mother, who "had a nicer smell than his father," the odor is as calming as gazing into her eyes must have been when she changed his cold, wet bedding and tucked him in (*Portrait*, p. 1). Joyce seems to be describing in Stephen an adolescent derivative of what D. W. Winnicott called "transitional phenomena." These highly sensual, autoerotic experiences are heirs to the babbling songs and tunes that an infant sings to himself before going to sleep, "a defense against [the] anxiety" of being separated physically and psychologically from mother, something "absolutely necessary at bed-time or at a time of loneliness or when a depressed mood threatens."[94] They occupy "an intermediate area of experience, between the thumb and the teddy bear, between oral eroticism and the true object-relationship."[95] Put another way, such self-generated forms of self-soothing are aids in "the infant's transition from a state of being merged with the mother to a state of being in relation to the mother as something outside and separate."[96]

---

[94] D. W. Winnicott,"Transitional Objects and Transitional Phenomena," in *Playing and Reality* (New York: Routledge, 1982), p. 4.
[95] *Ibid.* p. 2.
[96] *Ibid.* pp. 14-15. Cf. Mahler, Pine, and Bergman, *op. cit.* for a fuller discussion of the "birth," the psychological separation, of the infant from the mother.

Although they originate at some time between the infant's very early use of fingers, thumb, and fist to stimulate the mouth and his all but inseparable connection to a teddy bear or a soft or a hard toy, later derivatives of these phenomena seem to reappear in looking deeply into a girl's alluring eyes or in breathing in the odor of urine. In a later discussion of an older Stephen's creation of a prose-poetic portrait of the wading girl at the end of Chapter IV in *Portrait,* we will see derivatives of Winnicott's "transitional object," an all but tangible aid in making the transition from being bound up with the Motherland and being separate from her psychologically and morally. Joyce is suggesting that in infancy and adolescence, Stephen finds old ways to bind the anxiety that arises from painful feelings of self-diminishment, abandonment, and maternal loss; and in young adulthood, when he gives birth, parthenogenetically, to his artist's soul, Stephen, no longer fearing self-loss, no longer brooding and ashamed of the "wounds" to his soul, will begin to create "proudly out of the freedom and power of his soul, as the great artificer whose name he bore, a living thing, new and soaring and beautiful, impalpable, imperishable" (*Portrait,* p. 197).

3. Fading Out Like a Film in the Sun

In the scenes following the Whitsuntide play, Joyce offers us further examples of Stephen's experiences of inner emptiness and impoverishment. He also shows us how Stephen reduces those feelings of powerlessness and despair by the use of incantatory rhythms—the repetition of simple declarative sentences that seem to be the heir to the infant's use of organized, self-soothing sounds and fragments of song at bedtime to help him go to sleep. Accompanying his father to Cork to sell Simon's property, Stephen seems momentarily to lose both himself and his hold on reality. Hearing his father's voice "break into a laugh which was almost a sob" as Simon recalls his own father, "the handsomest man in Cork" who had the women standing "to look after him in the street," Stephen becomes mentally paralyzed:

> His very brain was sick and powerless. He could scarcely interpret the letters of the signboards of the shops. By his monstrous way of

life he seemed to have put himself beyond the limit of reality. Nothing moved him or spoke to him from the real world unless he heard in it an echo of the infuriated cries within him. He could respond to no earthly or human appeal, dumb and insensible to the call of summer and gladness and companionship, wearied and dejected by his father's voice. He could scarcely recognize as his own thoughts, and repeated slowly to himself:

—I am Stephen Dedalus. I am walking beside my father whose name is Simon Dedalus. We are in Cork, in Ireland. Cork is a city. Our room is in the Victoria Hotel. Victoria and Stephen and Simon. Simon and Stephen and Victoria. Names. (*Portrait*, pp. 103-104)

Stephen seems to connect his sick and powerless feeling of self-estrangement and estrangement from reality to the "infuriated cries within him"—his "monstrous reveries," his "mad and filthy orgies" (*Portrait*, pp. 340-341). But Joyce also wants us to sense that his self-loss is connected even more deeply to Stephen's painful disillusionment with his father. Earlier, Stephen was flooded with the shame of his autoerotic fantasies when he accompanied Simon to the anatomy theater of Queen's College to search for the desk with his father's initials. The sight of the word "*Foetus*" cut several times in the dark wood, while he was thinking of Simon's initials, "startled his blood" (*Portrait*, p. 100). It stirred memories of "his secret riots," "dark orgiastic riot, its keen and humiliating sense of transgression." But perhaps it also led to fantasies that Simon also secretly succumbed to a mad and filthy autoerotic life when he was in college (*Portrait*, p. 111). If we accept the likelihood that Stephen harbors unconscious urges to idealize his father (and himself), his de-idealization of Simon could quite likely have led him to deprecate him father: "he is as fallen as I am"; "he is a failure as a provider and protector"; "his voice is wearisome and depressing, his posturing preposterous." Such thoughts could very well have led Stephen to feel that he was in danger of sailing "beyond the limits of reality."

Stephen tries to ground himself, to "recognize as his own thoughts," by slowly repeating a kind of litany of simple declarative sentences that I quoted earlier: "I am Stephen Dedalus. I am walking beside my father whose name is Simon Dedalus.... Simon and Stephen and Victoria. Names" (*Portrait*, p.104). Joyce is asking us to recall that Stephen used sentences and names in a similar self-soothing way at Clongowes: "And there were nice sentences in Doctor Cornwell's Spelling book. They were like poetry....It would be nice to lie on the hearthrug before the fire, leaning his head upon his hands, and think on those sentences" (*Portrait*, p. 5). Stephen's happiness-inducing phrase, "Nice mother," is almost an epithet. Phrases and sentences associated with home and mother suggest that as a boy Stephen was using a rudimentary kind of prose-poetry to arrest his dipping self-esteem.

After Wells frightened and humiliated him by shouldering him into the cold slime of the square ditch—and after Wells compounded Stephen's shame by asking him an embarrassing question that could not be answered with either a yes or a no, "do you kiss your mother before you go to bed?"—Stephen seemed to experience the same self-impoverishment that he experienced later while listening to his father in Cork (*Portrait*, p. 10):

He turned to the flyleaf of the geography and read what he had written there: himself, his name and where he was.
Stephen Dedalus
Class of Elements
Clongowes Wood College
Sallins
County Kildare
Ireland
Europe
The World
The Universe (*Portrait*, pp. 11-12)

Stephen then reads the flyleaf from bottom to the top till he came to his own name again—"that was he" (*Portrait*, p. 12). Although his very brief autobiographical short story makes him feel real for an instant, returns him to some place within the "limits of reality," as he reads down the page once more, he senses that what was after the universe was "nothing" (*Portrait*, p. 12). It seems that Stephen has again pressed up against those limits beyond which he can become lost to himself and pass out of existence, forgotten somewhere in the universe.

Although he does not consciously recall himself reading what he wrote in the flyleaf of his geography from top to bottom and then from bottom to top, he does remember an experience in Clongowes that is strangely like the experience of brain-sickness and impotence that overwhelmed him as he listened to the linguistic marvel that was his father praising his own past in Cork. Once again, Stephen finds a way to forestall his gathering feelings of emptiness, coldness, and paralysis. This time he transforms his seemingly inborn fascination with proper names—and with sound, language, and rhythm—into an elaborate fantasy that reveals the soul of the artist-to-be *in utero,* before Stephen gives birth to it later in his reveries at the Bull.

Stephen's narcissistic vulnerability seems to have been especially painful as he began his studies at Clongowes. When (in Cork) an older Stephen recalls that "he had been sent away from home to a college"; "sent away" suggests that Stephen remembers he had suffered from a feeling of deliberate banishment, a heartache that intensified what must have been a painful separation from his mother (*Portrait*, p. 104). Intense homesickness becomes the major theme in his early life at the college. Feeling small and weak, young Stephen thinks, "Soon they would be going home for the holidays. After supper in the study hall he would exchange the number pasted up inside his desk from seventysix to seventysix" (*Portrait*, pp. 4-5). He "longed to be at home and lay his head on his mother's lap" (*Portrait*, p. 8).

Already struggling with what seems to be an incipient depressed mood, Wells's teasing and cruelty take on a deeper significance. His first response to Wells's question (Stephen admits that he *does* kiss his mother before going to bed) underscores his neediness—his yearning for a mother's warmth, touch, and smell. His response to Wells's shouldering him into the square ditch, which left Stephen with a feverish chill, suggests that he is not just sick in his "breadbasket," as Fleming tells him: "But he was not sick there....he was sick in his heart if you could be sick in that place....He wanted to cry" (*Portrait*, p. 9).

Physical illness together with tearful heartsickness is painful enough, but wounds to his narcissism compound Stephen's suffering. His "confus[ion]" as he tries to do a hard arithmetic problem is not simply because he was "no good at sums" (he is a leader of the House of York in the Class of Elements where in some weeks he gets "the card for first") (*Portrait*, p. 7). It is a far more grievous wound to be laid low if you are a proud boy who wears the white silk of the badge of York. But it's even more ignominious to be pushed into the square and to feel "the cold slime of the ditch cover[ing] [your] whole body," slime into which a "big rat jump[ed] plop into the scum" (*Portrait*, p. 10).

Injured in soul and body, Stephen attempts to forestall his intensifying feelings of coldness and despair, to find a way to repair these injuries to his self-esteem, with thoughts of Christmas: "Going home for the holidays! That would be lovely....Holly and ivy for him and for Christmas.... Welcome home, Stephen!" (*Portrait*, pp. 17-18). Yet he is no more successful in dispelling the strange, frightening waves of cold and heat with these thoughts of home than he was earlier, when he attempted to warm himself with a fantasy of his mother "sitting at the fire with Dante waiting for Brigid to bring in the tea. She had her feet on the fender and her jewelly slippers were so hot and they had such a lovely warm smell!" (*Portrait*, pp. 5-6).

With hindsight, Stephen can feel more deeply the self-loss that he suffered as a boy in the infirmary. In the presence of his de-idealized father, feeling momentarily that *he*, Stephen, might fade out of existence or be lost and forgotten somewhere in the universe, Stephen attributes his present state to his boyhood self. He recalls his boyhood reverie of "being dead...But he had not died then. Parnell had died....He had not died but he faded out like film in the sun. He had been lost or had wandered out of existence for he no longer existed" (*Portrait*, p. 104).

With his use of the ambiguous "he," Joyce is implying that in his fever Stephen feels Parnell-like. But unlike Parnell, the schoolboy did not die physically, nor did he die psychologically, fading out like a film in the sun. As the light pales at the infirmary window, Stephen imagines a world for himself that halts the plummeting of his self-esteem, a creation with undertones of Irish history where he merges himself (and his feeling of painfully eclipsed grandeur) with a figure of the highest (yet also eclipsed) grandeur. Visited by a dream vision, Stephen fashions a rudimentary work of art that foreshadows his later creation of the "angel of mortal youth and beauty."

In his sickbed at Clongowes or walking at the Bull in adolescence, he blends the rhythms of outer and inner reality. As a sick boy, he transforms the fire that "rose and fell on the wall" to waves "rising and falling." The "voices talking" become "the noise of the waves talking among themselves" (*Portrait,* p. 25). In his free indirect style, Joyce allows us to infer that Stephen, who has been alternating between feeling cold then hot, washed over by waves of heat then cold, has found an objective correlative for his feverish state: "He saw the sea of waves, long dark waves rising and falling, dark under the moonless night" (*Portrait,* p. 25).

The soothing, hypnotic regularity of that rhythm carries over to his use of verbal repetition. "Dark" occurs three times; "waters' edge" twice; and "sorrow" is repeated two times or three, if we take "sorrowful" to be an aural equivalent. "He saw" gets repeated, too. Twice, Joyce has Stephen end a sentence with a colon followed by an independent clause beginning with "And." He concludes his prose-poem with a long sentence about Dante Riordan that also begins with "and."

Stephen repeats imagery as well. The image of the tiny light "[that] twinkled at the pierhead" reappears, and Stephen twice contrasts that pierhead light with the darkness surrounding it. The dominant "curve of an emotion" in his vision, the pervasive rising and falling, is carried through in the very subject—the rise of Ireland's greatest political leader to the heights of power in the House of Commons only to suffer betrayal and a fall. But Stephen knows that Ireland's everliving Uncrowned King has been resurrected in the imaginations of his devoted followers.

At the end of Stephen's fantasy, a "multitude of people" has gathered at the edge of the sea, waiting to see the ship enter their harbour. On the deck stands kind Brother Michael, the motherly man with the sorrowful face who had stood at Stephen's bedside with a bowl of beeftea:

> He saw him lift his hand towards the people and heard him say in a loud voice of sorrow over the waters:

—He is dead. We saw him lying upon the catafalque.
A wail of sorrow went up from the people.
—Parnell! Parnell! He is dead!
They fell upon their knees, moaning in sorrow. (*Portrait,* pp. 25-26)

Earlier, when he first entered the infirmary, Stephen realized that he could die "before his mother came" and then he imagined a "dead mass" in the chapel sung for him (*Portrait,* p. 22). All the fellows would be at the mass, even Wells, dressed in black and all with sad faces: "He would be buried in the little graveyard of the community...And Wells would be sorry then for what he had done" (*Portrait,* p. 22). Masochistically using his suffering (unto death) as a weapon, Stephen is punishing Wells for his cruelty, unconsciously punishing his mother for "sending" him away to Clongowes in the first place, and simultaneously punishing himself by identifying himself with the dead Parnell. But he is also maintaining his sorely tried belief in his own greatness. The sad boys of Clongowes, dressed in black, mourning the fallen leader of the House of York, become a sorrowful multitude mourning another fallen leader, someone who was also betrayed by former companions, followers who were as mean-minded as Wells. Stephen arrests his self-fading by identifying himself with the martyred King. Paradoxically, he brings an end to his self-depletion and melancholy by a kind of heroic self-abandonment.[97] Put another way, Stephen transforms a once-wavering belief in his grandeur, his unconscious, "archaic grandiose self," by exchanging it for another's.

It seems that when Stephen can no longer idealize his parents, no longer participate in *their* grandeur, he invents someone (or something) wonderful to worship or to blend in with. Just before he implicitly identifies himself with the dead Parnell, Stephen thinks of his father with disappointment: "he felt sorry that he was not a magistrate like the other boys' fathers" (*Portrait,* p. 24). Actually, Stephen seems to be

---

[97] In the last lines of "The Dead," Gabriel Conroy gives himself over to a similar dream-vision, a night reverie somewhere between consciousness and unconsciousness where he imagines a highly paradoxical self-abandonment. See Appendix.

feeling sorry for himself, dejected because of his failed attempt to make Simon higher than the other fathers, a powerful wish that Joyce dramatizes in the homecoming scenes at Christmas: "Welcome home, Stephen! Noises of welcome. His mother kissed him. Was that right? His father was a marshal now: higher than a magistrate" (*Portrait*, p. 18).

In fact, Simon seems to be second best for his son. Stephen tries to imagine a very good mother, but ambivalence weakens his idealizing impulses. Kissed by her, he wonders, "Was that right?" And earlier, he recalls, "The first day in the hall of the castle when she had said goodbye she had put up her veil double to her nose to kiss him: and her nose and eyes were red. But he had pretended not to see that she was going to cry. She was a nice mother but she was not so nice when she cried" (*Portrait*, p. 4).

Unable to idealize either parent fully—unable to participate in parental perfection of any sort—he finds that perfection within, a sense of his greatness that remains alive. Out of that grandiosity he fashions his Parnell-Stephen and repairs (by avenging) the various insults to his narcissism that he suffered at Clongowes.

4. The Sea-Bird at the Bull, Childhood Grandeur, and the Nature of Dedalean Creativity

We have seen a rhythm in Stephen's life that appears in narcissistically vulnerable men and women—an oscillation between excitement and depression, pleasure in themselves and in the world that fades to embarrassment, shame, and despair when they feel that they haven't received the praise and interest they expect as their due from others. At the Whitsuntide play, in Cork and in Clongowes, Stephen feels what he would feel years later, self-depleted and impoverished, as if he were "drifting amid life like the barren shell of the moon.

> "*Art thou pale for weariness*
> *Of climbing heaven and gazing on the earth,*
> *Wandering companionless. . . ?*"

> He repeated to himself the lines of Shelley's fragment. Its alteration of sad human ineffectualness with vast inhuman cycles of activity chilled him, and he forgot his own human and ineffectual grieving. (*Portrait*, p. 108)

Stephen is doing something we have seen him doing with EC's eyes, with horse piss, and with the image he creates of Parnell on his catafalque. But unlike many men and women suffering from narcissistic disorders, Stephen manages to escape his human and ineffectual grieving, the sad and lonely emptiness of drifting like the moon, by dissolving it in the work of the artistic imagination.

To be sure, Stephen's imaginative activity is elementary in Clongowes. He incorporates self-soothing but ordinary things from the outer world into what he will later call the "virgin womb" of the imagination, but he is not yet ready or able to press them back out into the world as wondrous creations (*Portrait*, p. 255). Later, Stephen uses an image from a more sophisticated imagination, the moon from Shelley's unfinished poem "To the Moon," to halt his own helpless drifting. But in either case, Joyce wants us to realize that Stephen's creativity is never simply a form of psychopathology. Unlike those suffering patients who have not integrated into their personalities the "unrealistic claims" of an unconscious "archaic grandiose self" or an idealized "parental image," Stephen *consciously* accepts his feeling that he was destined for greatness, weds talent to that conviction, and satisfies those claims in his portrait of a wading girl. As Richard Ellmann often reminds us in *James Joyce* and *Ulysses on the Liffey*, art never springs simply from neurosis, from deficit or deficiency, for Joyce (although it does seem to have its mysterious origins in narcissistic injuries, disappointments in love at an early age).

In Stephen's transformation of the girl standing before him in midstream at the Bull, we have something like the proto-Dedalean artist acting in his health. We see his irreducible powers of "perception, representation, and realization" that are as natural and non-neurotic as his "power of walking and talking."[98] In the novel's emotionally climactic scenes, Joyce

---

[98] And of sweating. Shem the Penman, the archetypal artist in *Finnegans Wake*, sweats

offers us further insights into the psychological roots of Dedalean creativity, and because Stephen seems increasingly consubstantial with his artist-father (as well as with Bloom), we get Joyce's implicit insights into his own creativity as well.

Let me turn again to Winnicott's ideas about the child's first not-me possession endowed with meaning, his use of an object or an image or a repeated sound or a pattern of behavior to help him reduce the anxiety that arises as he makes the "transition" from being merged with his mother (who seems omnipotent) to being separated from her.[99] This "transitional object" or "phenomenon" is an archaic form of creation, where the infant fashions a subjective-object out of something from the outer world that he suffuses with his own subjectivity. To him, it is neither external nor internal. His piece of wool or soothingly soft object or image or sound is not simply his mother (or her breast), nor is it simply a smelly blanket. It is a possession, yet it is not an external object either.

At the Bull, Stephen fashions a kind of transitional object out of the image of a Dublin girl that helps him manage his separation from mother (and her wish that he become a priest), from Mother Church, and from his Motherland. Instinctively rejecting the implicit offer of the director of studies to join the Jesuits, he discovers that he has a different

---

"dirty" words out of his pores. Cf., Lionel Trilling, "Art and Neurosis," in *The Liberal Imagination: Essays on Literature and Society* (Garden City, New York: Doubleday & Company, 1953), p. 177, for an eloquent discussion of the fundamental health of the artist, "the power to conceive, to plan, to work, and to bring his work to a conclusion."

[99] Anna Freud in "The Concept of Developmental Lines," *Psychoanalytic Study of the Child,* 18 (1963), p. 250, writes from a somewhat different angle about the infant's movement toward body (and psychological) independence: "the mother's narcissistic possessiveness of her infant's body is matched from the child's side by his archaic wishes to merge with the mother and by the confusion concerning body limits which arises from the fact that early in life the distinctions between the internal and external world are based not on objective reality but on the subjective experiences of pleasure and unpleasure....The mother's breast, or face, hands, or hair may be treated (or maltreated) by the infant as parts of his own organization...."

In his idea of an "intermediate area of *experiencing,* to which inner reality and external life both contribute," Winnicott is offering his view of the observable signs by which we may infer that the infant is gradually dispelling that "confusion" to gain psychological autonomy (Winnicott, *op. cit.,* p. 2).

calling. He seems literally to hear it: "a voice from beyond the world was calling" (*Portrait*, p. 429). As his classmates almost voice over that call by calling out to him in their schoolboy Greek, "Stephanos Dedalos!" Stephen apprehends his strange name as a prophecy:

> Now, at the name of the fabulous artificer, he seemed to hear the noise of the dim waves and to see a winged form flying above the waves and slowly climbing the air. What did it mean? Was it a quaint device opening a page of some medieval book of prophecies and symbols, a hawklike man flying sunward above the sea, a prophecy of the end he had been born to serve and had been following through the mists of childhood and boyhood, a symbol of the artist forging anew in his workshop out of the sluggish matter of the earth a new soaring impalpable imperishable being? (*Portrait*, p. 196)

With this sudden access of the grandiosity that we have seen before, Stephen senses his oneness with both hawklike, soaring Icarus and with Daedalus forging imperishable artifacts in his workshop. He identifies himself with these mythic forebears, and he simultaneously identifies himself with the Virgin Mary, the greatest human creator in Christian history. Stephen seems to be experiencing a Virgin birth, the birth of something as pure as the Son of God, the birth of his artist-soul:

> His heart trembled; his breath came faster and a wild spirit passed over his limbs as though he were soaring sunward. His heart trembled in an ecstasy of fear and his soul was in flight. His soul was soaring in the air beyond the world and the body he knew was purified in a breath and delivered of incertitude and made radiant and commingled with the element of the spirit. An ecstasy of flight made radiant his eyes and wild his breath and tremulous and wild and radiant his windswept limbs. (*Portrait*, p. 196).

Trembling and breathing faster—in Mary-like labor?— greekjew/jewgreek Stephen feels, finally, not just pure and powerful but miraculous as he regards the miracle he has produced:

His soul had arisen from the grave of boyhood, spurning her graveclothes. Yes! Yes! Yes! He would create proudly out of the freedom and power of his soul, as the great artificer whose name he bore, a living thing, new and soaring and beautiful, impalpable, imperishable. (*Portrait*, p. 197)

When Stephen seems most grandiose, Joyce is least ironic, almost as if he is fused with his youthful self, vicariously enjoying a moment of genuine inspiration that, it's tempting to say, he himself quite possibly experienced.[100] He also take pains to save Stephen from any suggestion of mania by making his self-consecrated priest of the eternal imagination painfully realistic about his future as an Irish artist: Icarus, after all, soared only to crash into the sea.[101]

Continuing the imagery of a miraculous parthenogenesis, Joyce intensifies our sense that Stephen feels that he is presiding over something like the divine birth of his soul: Joyce underscores the nature of the transitional phenomenon that is the first creation of that soul. In his subsequent portrait—Stephen's word painting of the girl standing before him in midstream— every one of his brush strokes, like Joyce's brush strokes in *A Portrait of the Artist as a Young Man*, reveals the "curve of an emotion," the "individuating rhythm" of his subject. Wading slowly up a "long rivulet in the strand"—moving up? down? the birth canal—the girl, all but blended in with Stephen's soul, is not yet completely free (*Portrait*, p. 198). (An obstetrician might say that it is "engaged," resting on the floor of the perineum.) As he perceives the girl, the soul that had "hung back from her destiny, to brood alone upon the shame of her wounds" is no longer hanging back (*Portrait*, p. 198).

Stephen feels that he has somehow managed to free himself from the wounding shame of his vulnerabilities, the emotional and moral death-in-life that he has often fallen into when the lofty picture that he has of himself collapses:

---

[100] See Epilogue for a discussion of the Man in the Macintosh, Joyce's Holy Ghost of creative inspiration.

[101] In substituting Daedalus and the Virgin Mary for Simon and his mother, Stephen again satisfies and integrates the claims of "unconscious" "idealized" parental imagoes.

What were they now but cerements shaken from the body of death—the fear he had walked in night and day, the incertitude that had ringed him round, the shame that had abased him within and without—cerements, the linens of the grave? (*Portrait*, p. 197)

Hoping at Belvedere College to be, perhaps, an ideal Prefect of the Sodality of Our Blessed Lady, Stephen seems to have tried to be just such a prefect in every area of his life. Incorporating those imposing duties into an already harsh and demanding conscience, Stephen suffers grievously for his sexual sins. Before his Lazarus-like resurrection—actually self-resurrection—he felt his soul was wrapped in the "linens of the grave." He was not just guilty but deeply ashamed for failing to be perfectly pious. Rejecting the director's offer, he seems to have reduced the moral and deathly fear that he had walked in day and night, the debasing shame. It came from within ("How totally corrupt I must be! God has reserved a special place in hell for my sins!") and it comes from without ("What priest could possibly hear my confession? How could he not be disgusted at my fall from such an exalted height?").

Becoming a prefect of his own sodality of one, he now feels an access of the moral freedom that allows him to delight in his omnipotent strivings rather than cloak them (because of their pridefulness) in cerements that belong to "the body of death." Like Bloom, his consubstantial father at the end of "Circe," Stephen is about to shed the humiliation and self-abasement that rose up to haunt him. He begins to satisfy the latent wish to be his own priest worshipping his own god, to be as great as the great artificer whose name he bears.

With his body "purified in a breath and delivered of incertitude and made radiant and commingled with the element of the spirit," Stephen begins to recreate life out of life (*Portrait*, p. 196). In the full flush of the power of his newly emergent, newly cleansed soul, he incorporates something from the objective world into himself and reprojects it outward, in rhythmic prose-poetry, suffused with his subjectivity—Winnicott's subjective-object. The girl becomes, in part, a mirror of his newly purified, radiant, and spiritualized body. As barelegged as Stephen, she, too, has momentarily paused, hanging back. She is equally "alone and young," perhaps equally "willful and wildhearted" (*Portrait*, p. 199). She is as birdlike as Stephen. He feels his soul is in flight, his throat aching "with a desire to cry aloud, the cry of a hawk or eagle on high" (*Portrait*, p. 197).

In the spell that Stephen casts about this Dublin girl, she seemed "like one whom magic had changed into the likeness of a strange and beautiful seabird. Her long slender bare legs were delicate as a crane's and pure save where an emerald trail of seaweed had fashioned itself as a sign upon the flesh" (*Portrait*, p. 199). Her crane-like body then becomes a dove:

> Her thighs, fuller and softhued as ivory, were bared almost to the hips where the white fringes of her drawers were like featherings of soft white down. Her slate-blue skirts were kilted about her waist and dovetailed behind her. Her bosom was as a bird's, soft and slight, slight and soft as the breast of some dark-plumaged dove. (*Portrait*, p. 199)

Stephen is connecting the girl to the Holy Ghost (the Dove of the Whitsuntide play finally does descend near a heretical Disciple), but his allusion to the Virgin Mary is even more significant. Her thighs are "fuller and softhued as ivory." Stephen heard "protestant" children mocking the allusion to the Virgin in the Litany of Our Lady (called "of Loretto"): "*Tower of Ivory*" (*Portrait*, p. 45).[102] Her "slateblue skirts," a color attribute of the Blessed Virgin, intensifies our sense of her Mary-like nature, her deep moral and spiritual significance for Stephen.[103] Stephen is now close to feeling what he felt later, at University College, after awakening from a dream-vision that he converted into his Villanelle to the Temptress: he himself possesses a secular version of the Virgin's womb—the "virgin womb of the imagination" in which not only is the word made flesh but flesh is made words.

---

[102] Don Gifford, *Joyce Annotated: Notes for Dubliners and A Portrait of the Artist as a Young Man*, 2nd ed. rev. (Berkeley: University of California Press, 1982), p.145.
[103] *Ibid.*, p. 222.

The figure who comes from without and is transformed into a creature who comes from within is not a hallucination. Stephen's intense experience with the seabird-girl involves the creation of an illusion that allows us to share that illusion. We do not to ask whether she is outside or inside Stephen. We suspend our disbelief and enjoy the liberating spectacle of Stephen converting inner reality into outer, outer into inner reality. A Daedalean artist, before our eyes, he is converting actuality into imagination, imagination into actuality.

His creation-possession-illusion embodies yet another aspect of Stephen's soul, newly freed from her house of squalor and subterfuge. The girl's long, slender, bare legs were "pure save where an emerald trail of seaweed had fashioned itself as a sign upon the flesh." Her seeming impurity is suggested again in Stephen's repetition of the compound adverb "hither and thither." Withdrawing her eyes from his, she "bent them towards the stream, gently stirring the water with her foot hither and thither. The first faint noise of gently moving water broke the silence, low and faint and whispering, faint as the bells of sleep; hither and thither, hither and thither: and a faint flame trembled on her cheek" (*Portrait*, p. 199).

Years earlier, Stephen repeated the phase three times when he fantasized about the hell "reserved for his sins" that God allowed him to see. Recreating the preacher's terrifying sermon on hell—recreating life out of life as the nascent artist that he is—young Stephen imagines an even darker, excrementitious realm, "A field of stiff weeds and thistles and tufted nettlebunches. Thick among the tufts of rank stiff growth lay battered cannisters and clots and coils of solid excrement" (*Portrait*, p. 158). His sins of impurity, lecherous "goatish creatures with human faces," are moving through the field "hither and thither," "hither and thither, trailing their long tails behind them," "winding hither and thither through the weeds, dragging their long tails amid the rattling cannisters" (*Portrait*, pp. 158-159).

However, the girl's hither and thither movement belongs to a creature in paradise, not a dweller in Stephen's private hell. In her slateblue skirts and ivory-hued thighs, Stephen makes this seemingly impure earthly creature as pure as the Virgin herself. The paradox that her long bare legs are "pure," save where a "trail of seaweed" has fashioned itself as a "sign upon the flesh," begins to resolve itself when we remember that Stephen is fashioning a self-object. He is attributing aspects of his newly "purified" body, "made radiant and commingled with the element of the spirit" to the bird-like girl.

But he also feels that *his* body (like all human bodies) is not completely purified, not pure soul. His flesh still bears the "sign" of his mortal nature, memories of the "swoon of sin" that he *once* believed consigned him to a hell of fiends, winding hither and thither through excrement-filled fields. When he lived as such a self-convicted sinner, Stephen unconsciously bifurcated women, imagining that they could be as virginal as Mary or as fallen as a prostitute, either absolutely pure or absolutely impure, but not, like the wading girl, "pure" *and* "impure" simultaneously.

No longer shame-filled because of a belief in his unchangeable nature (irreducibly fallen, irreducibly wanton), Stephen can imagine her as, paradoxically, a very human body suffused with a transcendent spirit, an "angel of mortal youth and beauty" (*Portrait*, p. 200). Registering the "worship of his eyes" with a "faint flame trembl[ing] on her cheek," she is sexually mature, perhaps even sexually experienced, but hardly wanton (*Portrait*, p. 199).[104] No longer given over to a Manichaean gynecology or to a Manichaean sense that he is either totally pure or totally corrupt, Stephen seems almost inseparable from her, a kind of

---

[104] As I mentioned earlier, Stephen seems to be an older version of the boy in "Araby" who idealizes Mangan's sister, worshipping her "image," but here he is also a younger version of James Joyce who idealized a young and beautiful Dublin woman with a somewhat different emerald sign upon her flesh diminishing her "purity," a lowly employee in Finn's Hotel, a "slightly exalted rooming house" (Richard Ellmann, *James Joyce* [New York: Oxford University Press, 1965], p. 162).

Edwardian misogyny might have regarded Nora Barnacle as someone who probably made up beds for traveling salesmen, a likely demi-vièrge, a sister to Polly Mooney in Joyce's "A Mother." While working in the rooming house run by her mother, known as the "Madame," Polly inveigled and trapped Bob Doran into proposing to her. The nameless, language-drunk narrator in "Cyclops" refers to the Madame's establishment as the "kip" [she kept] in Hardwicke street," and even more delicately, he later speaks of "the old prostitute of a mother procuring rooms to street couples" (*Ulysses*, pp. 290, 301).

psychological extension of his blushing angel-creation: "His cheeks were aflame; his body was aglow; his limbs were trembling" (*Portrait*, p. 200). Ecstatic, he experiences the most profound epiphany of his life:

> Her image had passed into his soul for ever and no word had broken the holy silence of his ecstasy. Her eyes had called him and his soul had leaped at the call. To live, to err, to fall, to triumph, to recreate life out of life! A wild angel had appeared to him, the angel of mortal youth and beauty, an envoy from the fair courts of life, to throw open before him in an instant of ecstasy the gates of all the ways of error and glory. On and on and on and on! (*Portrait*, p. 200)

This wild angel appearing before Stephen as gratuitously as the descent of the Dove, the Holy Ghost, is also the fulfillment of a wish that arose years earlier, in the first stirrings of adolescence, when a "strange unrest crept into his blood":

> He wanted to meet in the real world the unsubstantial image which his soul so constantly beheld. He did not know where to seek it or how: but a premonition which led him on told him that the image would, without any overt act of his, encounter him. They would meet quietly as if they had known each other.... They would be alone, surrounded by darkness and silence: and in that moment of supreme tenderness he would be transfigured.... Weakness and timidity and inexperience would fall from him in that magic moment. (*Portrait*, p. 71)

Though he once yearned for a sexual initiation that would lead to his physical transfiguration, Stephen now undergoes a spiritual transfiguration that still retains in a sublimated form his passive adolescent sexual longings. Without any overt act of his, something like the image that he once fantasized about encounters him. It silently enters him, "passe[s] into his soul for ever and no word [breaks] the holy silence of his ecstasy" (*Portrait*, p. 200). As weakness and timidity fall from him in a magic moment, his body glows, his limbs tremble, and his cheeks become inflamed. Out of this sexually alive yet purified body, frail flesh commingled with the spirit, he recreates life out of life. No longer filled with timidity and weakness—no longer fearful of the grandiose image of himself that he has long harbored—he now feels consciously that he *is* Daedalus's true heir. In addition, Stephen can now also integrate a previously unconscious, idealized maternal image into his personality. In his pre-Raphaelite portrait, a symbolic girl, an angelic figure suffused with Spirit and painted in Mary's blue and ivory, had summoned his newly born soul to its destiny, "an envoy from the fair courts of life, to throw open before him in an instant of ecstasy the gates of all the ways of error and glory" (*Portrait,* p. 200).

5. Tufted Sandknolls and an Opening, Unfolding Flower

In the concluding metaphor of the opening flower, glimmering and trembling, that irradiates Stephen's new world, Joyce is asking us to feel that this is the most emotionally significant experience in Stephen's life. Like the angel of mortal youth, Stephen's artist-soul, which he always refers to as "she," is arousable but not licentious, erotically alive but without shame. Hoping to "still the riot of his blood," the "pounding of his heart," Stephen lays down in a "ring of tufted sandknolls," an echo of the tufts of rank stiff growth that dotted the field in his personal hell (*Portrait,* p. 200). His mounting excitement is not completely stilled until he turns the sunset into his vision of a crimson, unfolding flower, flooding all the heavens, gradually subsides:

> His soul was swooning into some new world, fantastic, dim, uncertain as under sea, traversed by cloudy shapes and beings. A world, a glimmer, or a flower? Glimmering and trembling, trembling and unfolding, a breaking light, an opening flower, it spread in endless succession to itself, breaking in full crimson and unfolding and fading to palest rose, leaf by leaf and wave of light by wave of light, flooding all the heavens with its soft flushes, every flush deeper than other. (*Portrait,* pp. 200-201)

Portraits of the Artist: Consubstantiality in a Different Light

Rather than something "darker than the swoon of sin," which overwhelmed him when he felt pressing on his brain an "unknown and timid pressure" from something between a prostitute's lips, Stephen here is swooning (but guiltlessly) into a breaking light, a very different opening flower (*Portrait,* p. 114). On first reading, this unearthly rose of light calls up the multifoliate Rose that extends through Paradise, Dante's beatific vision at the end of *The Divine Comedy.* Stephen is perhaps remembering that with the divine aid of *his* angelic mediatrix, Beatrice, Dante sees the God of Love that *is* Light. But Stephen has also created a libidinal paradise, where the images, rhythms, and autobiographical references suggest an orgasmic unfolding. Joyce, in his free, indirect style, might be using Stephen's knowledge of the end of the final cantos of the *Paradise*—or he might be using his own—to reveal the full depth and power of the revelation that Stephen has just experienced at the Bull. He could be asking us to sense that the sublimated sexual ecstasy unfolding throughout this new world is Stephen's artistic recreation of his conscious experience of self-transcendence—the physical intensity of spiritual transfiguration.[105]

We have already noted Stephen's capacity for self-transfiguration—the flaming cheeks, glowing body, and trembling limbs. In early adolescence when he sought out a prostitute for the first time, Stephen also felt that he was in "another world" traversed by "fantastic" shapes and beings. At that time, too, a "trembling seized him" as he felt "he had awakened from a slumber of centuries" (*Portrait,* p. 113). Here, at the Bull, with eyelids "trembl[ing] as if they felt the strange light of some new world," he is enraptured by a different vision. His use of redundancy—"new world," "breaking," "unfolding," "flush," "leaf"—calls to mind the building up of the rhythm of sexual tension, and the echo of chiasmus in "glimmering and trembling, trembling and unfolding" deepens our

---

[105] In his "Ecstasy of St. Teresa," Bernini also explores that very thin osmotic membrane between orgasm and divine revelation in one of his most famous sculptures. Her face seems to be that of a deeply pious woman overwhelmed by sexual rapture, a visual metaphor in its powerful intensity for the transcendent experience of her reception of the Godhead into herself.

sense of an intensifying erotic sensation, a response that seems to go "backward" only to move "forward" to a "higher" level of arousal.

In its pulsating flooding, every pulsation deeper than the other, the "breaking light" that is "glimmering and trembling, trembling and unfolding" is simultaneously an "opening flower...breaking in full crimson." The beatific Rose of Paradise now, in Joycean fashion, simultaneously calls to mind tumescence in the female genitalia, while the de-intensifying image of crimson "fading to palest rose, leaf by leaf and wave of light by wave of light, flooding all the heavens with its soft flushes, every flush deeper than other" calls up the beginning of detumescence.

Joyce from the outside is describing from the inside (without the use of interior monologue) Stephen's experience of a kind of spiritual orgasm, his female soul in the transports of ecstasy.[106] Earlier, as a schoolboy brooding on the "great mystery of [divine] love," he felt within him a "warm movement like that of some newly born life or virtue of the soul itself. The attitude of rapture in sacred art, the raised and parted hands, the parted lips and eyes as of one about to swoon, became for him an image of the soul in prayer, humiliated and faint before her Creator" (*Portrait*, p. 174). Almost as if he is recalling a picture of Bernini's Saint Teresa of Avila. Stephen, despite his desperate wish to be purified of sin, can't help but sexualize this rapturous soul in prayer. In her "parted lips," "swoon[ing]" eyes, and the externalization of his own sin-filled "humiliation," he unwittingly converts her spiritual ecstasy into the ecstasy of sinfully erotic love.[107]

But years later, at the Bull, his soul, no longer bowed down in sin and the wish for salvation, doesn't humble herself before her creator. Filled with an image of his own creation that makes him feel he is loved purely

---

[106] Joyce's style of free indirect speech is a distant relation of Winnicott's "indeterminate area of experience," transitional objects and experiences. In Joyce, we are also presented with "objective perception" based on the deepest respect for physical reality that is inseparable from intense "subjectivity," the metaphor- and symbol-making "creativity" of the literary imagination (Winnicott, *op. cit,*, p. 11).

[107] In the exploding fireworks scene in "Nausicaa," Joyce uses waves of breaking and unfolding light to dramatize a more earth-bound orgasm, Gerty MacDowell's (and Bloom's) simultaneous arousal and climax.

and perfectly—that there is neither shame nor wantonness in the angel wading in the stream nor in him—Stephen *is* quickened by the newly born life within him. Joyce deepens our sense that Stephen has given birth to the artist-soul that has begun gestating when we first meet him in *Portrait*. Even before he composes his Villanelle to the Temptress later, he has become what he anoints himself, a "priest of eternal imagination, transmuting the daily bread of experience into the radiant body of everliving life" (*Portrait*, p. 260).

Considering the director's wish that he consider whether God had called him to join the order, Stephen realizes that "in vague sacrificial or sacramental acts alone, his will seemed drawn to go forth to encounter reality" (*Portrait*, p. 184). As he encounters his destiny at the Bull, not so vague sacramental acts and images run through the final scenes, self-created sacraments, hinting in yet another way at the deep emotional and spiritual significance of the experience for Stephen. We are meant to infer that he *has* been "drawn to go forth to encounter reality" and will likely do so again. In fact, in Stephen's penultimate diary entry at the end of Joyce's *Portrait*, he repeats his earlier apostrophe: "Welcome, O Life! I go to encounter for the millionth time the reality of experience and to forge in the smithy of my soul the uncreated conscience of my race" (*Portrait*, p. 299).

Wading slowly up the course of the stream, Stephen seems to be unwittingly engaging in those sacramental acts that, he once intuited, would strengthen his will to encounter reality. As he wades in the water barefoot, mirroring his angel, he is undergoing a kind of baptism where he feels cleansed of his lifelong burden of sin. He experiences another sacramental moment, too, a form of confirmation, as he himself confirms his faith in his destiny. And as the image of the girl "passes into his soul for ever" with "no word [breaking] the holy silence of his ecstasy," Stephen feels he is entering into an eternal union. In the sacrament of marriage, two people mysteriously become one without the necessity of words, of formal or contractual language.[108] He even participates in his

---

[108] Eloping and living without legal marriage for most of their life together, Nora Barnacle and James Joyce were practicing this kind of self-consecrated matrimony as well.

own version of penance, freeing himself by confessing (to himself) his sin of living a death-in-life. His art of converting the bread of everyday life into a radiant body is a secularized eucharist itself. Of course, the most significant of the seven sacraments for Stephen is his taking holy orders. Joyce concludes the chapter by leaving us with the image of priestly Stephen practicing his eucharistic art. We are in a congregation watching this self-consecrated priest consecrating an Irish girl with her boldly kilted skirts into an emissary of heaven, converting something ordinary into something extraordinary, an angel of mortal youth and beauty.

Waking and "recalling the rapture of his sleep, [Stephen] sighed at its joy." Newly wakened spiritually and physically, Stephen ends his moment in eternity in a memory of joy, delighting in the beauty of the fallen world, no longer fallen, but transfigured by the artistic imagination:

> He climbed to the crest of the sandhill and gazed about him. Evening had fallen. A rim of the young moon cleft the pale waste of sky like the rim of a silver hoop embedded in grey sand; and the tide was flowing in fast to the land with a low whisper of her waves, islanding a few last figures in distant pools. (*Portrait*, p. 201)

But when we next meet Stephen on a Dublin beach, he is walking more or less joylessly on Sandymount Strand in *Ulysses*. In this portrait of the artist as a young man, Joyce presents something like an obverse mirror of Stephen at the Bull. He is no longer enlivened by the artistic imagination that seems to have been inseparable from his fleshly soul. (Zoe, the prostitute with the uncanny ability to see into the souls of her clients, reads Stephen's palm in "Circe" and sees the "Mount of the Moon," the symbol of the imagination.[109]) The Irish moon which he earlier transformed into something more cleanly beautiful, less sentimental, than Shelley's pale moon—a "silver hoop embedded in grey

---

[109] Don Gifford and Robert J. Seidman, *Notes for Joyce: An Annotation of James Joyce's Ulysses* (New York: E P. Dutton & Co., Inc., 1974), p. 419.

sand"—is now reduced to a mundane walking stick poking in the sand. He takes the "hilt of his ashplant, lunging with it softly, dallying still" (*Ulysses*, p. 49). Although later, at the end of "Circe," Stephen will boldly wield his ashplant as if it was the magic sword in Wagner's *Ring* that was planted in the heart of ash, here it emphasizes his powerlessness.[110] As he lunges with it softly, desultorily, "dallying still," Joyce underscores the fact that Stephen has become the depressed young man we saw before he gave birth to his artist-soul. Once again he seems ringed about with incertitude, shame, and the cerements of the grave, the death-in-life existence he thought he escaped. High-flying Icarus, once moonstruck, has been washed up on the shore, only to be transformed into a modern Telemachus, a lost, dispossessed, and companionless son.

Later on Sandymount Strand, another would-be writer appears. Exhausted, Leopold Bloom, at the end of "Nausicaa," "gently vexed the thick sand at his foot" with a "bit of stick," a "wooden pen," writing "I. AM. A." which he effaced "with his slow boot" (*Ulysses*, pp. 363-364). For an instant, in their prodding in the sand, we sense the consubstantiality of this gentle and vexed father in black, keyless and mocked, and the brooding, despairing, disowned son (also dressed in black, also keyless and mocked). But the touch of the artist in Bloom—and what is much more than a touch of it in Stephen—is even more significant. (We know from Stephen's psychological rhythm, his oscillation between feelings of emptiness and excitement, depression and exaltation, that someday he will manage to escape the inner and outer nets that prevent him from successfully launching his career.)

Unlike Bloom, Joyce didn't regard his "sacred cold steel pen" as a worthless bit of stick, and he knew in his more exalted moments that he wasn't just writing in the sand only to erase it, poking in it, as does Stephen, in a dallying, desultory way.[111] As he energetically filled sheet after sheet of paper with all that he knew and felt about dear dirty Dublin—all the

---

[110] *Ibid.*, p. 425.
[111] Lionel Trilling, "James Joyce in his Letters," in *The Moral Obligation to be Intelligent: Selected Essays* (Evanston: Northwestern University Press, 2008), p. 473. Also see Epilogue.

while enduring more than semi-blindness—Ireland's "I," as he self-mockingly called himself, perhaps did mentally complete Bloom's unfinished opus, those three one-word sentences. Christ, after all, wrote only once in his life, and in the sand, something never to be deciphered when, with a Bloomesque piece of wisdom, he saved the adulterous woman from stoning.

Did Joyce in his more grandiose moments believe that *he* was the Alpha and Omega of modern literature? Or, perhaps, did he imagine that Bloom had somehow read *his* mind and wrote down what was in it? Perhaps Bloom's consubstantial father had a slightly less grandiose interpretation of that mysterious "A." than Alpha (and Omega). I can imagine James Joyce thinking to himself, "I. AM. that I AM," the Artist in whose Virgin womb the word, Blephen, was made flesh."[112]

Always seeking in his art to give his readers the joy of wholeness, harmony, and radiance, we might ask: where does Joyce "complete" his secularized version of the triune God? Where does he present the third figure that causes his fusion of Father and Son to epiphanize as a new holy Trinity

---

[112] When Moses asked God what His name was, God answered, "I am that I am" (Exodus 3:14). Moses was always close to Joyce's heart. The "horns" of light that Michelangelo placed on Moses's head transmigrate to the horns of cuckoldry that Bloom, along with Shakepeare-in-the-mirror, is endowed with. In *Ulysses*, Joyce made Moses the heroic opponent of the Egyptian high priest who admonishes the Jews to accept the culture and religion and, most significantly, the language of their all-powerful oppressors. See *Ulysses*, p. 137.

EPILOGUE

Middler the Holy Ghost

OLD GUMMY GRANNY

(*Rocking to and fro.*).... (*She wails.*) You met with poor Ireland and how does she stand?

—"Circe" (*Ulysses*, p. 557)

STEPHEN

How do I stand you? The hat trick! Where's the third person of the Blessed Trinity? Soggarth Aroon! The reverend Carrion Crow.

—"Circe" (*Ulysses*, p. 557)

He Who Himself begot, middler the Holy Ghost, and Himself sent himself, Agenbuyer, between Himself and others....

—Stephen, "Scylla and Charybdis" (*Ulysses*, p. 189)

Stephen's second question, as usual, is a good one. Where's the third person of the Blessed Trinity in *Ulysses*? If we can agree that in Stoom we have Joyce's heretical version of the Father consubstantial with the Son, Stephen and Bloom sharing the same Shakespeare substance, we might assume (given Joyce's delight in the wholeness, harmony, and radiance of artistic beauty) that he would find a way to complete his secular version of the triune God. In the quote above from "Scylla and Charybdis," Stephen is doing more than having fun with the Apostles' Creed. Middler the Holy Ghost, Joyce himself begot a fictionalized version of his father-self and his son-self, and he sent himself, Stoom, a kind of Agenbuyer or redeemer, between himself and others, especially us, his readers. Let's read Joyce's art here as a ghost story, with a character who is an apparition, a richly demanding art that would redeem us, he hoped, from the ordinary darkness of life by bringing us joy.

Joyce apparently enjoyed his brother's remark that the Holy Ghost was sitting in the "ink-bottle," for he repeated the image in two letters to Stanislaus Joyce, the first on August 31, 1906, and the next on September 25, 1906. In the second letter, while asserting that he cannot rewrite *Dubliners* to make it more pleasing to bourgeois taste, he writes, "I am sure I should find again what you call the Holy Ghost sitting in the ink-bottle and the perverse devil of my literary conscience sitting on the hump of my pen."[113] A "perverse" spirit that prevented him from vacillating—from compromising his attitude toward literature—the Holy Ghost was inseparable from his deepest spiritual nature. With some modifications (which I will soon speculate about), Joyce would surely have agreed with Stanislaus that "Falsity of purpose was the literary sin against the Holy Ghost"—a form of "literary simony."[114]

If we assume that Joyce is identified with Shem the Penman, the archetypal writer of *Finnegans Wake* who secretes "obscene" matter from his pores and writes over every square inch of his body with this dark effluvium, then he may very well have felt that he himself was a kind of Holy Ghost when he begot Blephen with squid-like dye, with his uncompromising pen-and-ink. In Stephen's parody of the Apostles' Creed, the phrase "He Who Himself begot, middler the Holy Ghost" takes the place of the clause attributed to James (the Elder) describing God's only Son, "Who was conceived of the Holy Ghost, born of the Virgin Mary."[115] If we also assume that Dublin's most famous writer-apostle

---

[113] James Joyce, "Letter of September 25, 1906, to Stanislaus Joyce," in Richard Ellmann (ed.), *Selected Letters of James Joyce* (New York: The Viking Press, Inc., 1975), p. 110.
[114] Stanislaus Joyce *My Brother's Keeper: James Joyce's Early Years,* ed. with an introduction and notes by Richard Ellmann (New York: The Viking Press, 1958), p. 109.
[115] Don Gifford and Robert Seidman, *Notes for Joyce: An Annotation of James Joyce's Ulysses* (New York: E. P. Dutton & Co., Inc., 1974), p. 14.

(also named James) is hinting at the "part" of himself that conceived Stephen (as well Bloom) in the phrase "middler the Holy Ghost," then we may infer that Joyce begot "Himself"—his father-self and his son-self—through the "mediating," or "mid-dealing," or "intermediating" power of pen dipped in the ink of "obscenity" *and* unbudging artistic integrity. (Although "conceived" of the Holy Ghost, Stoom was "born" of what Stephen in *Portrait* called the "virgin womb of imagination where the word was made flesh" (*Portrait*, p. 255). In dark, inky, "perverse" markings—in biologically and psychologically necessary secretions (that are also "secretive?")—we sense the presence of the Holy Ghost that is consubstantial with the Artist-Father-and Son in James Joyce.

The disembodied voice (or voices) verbalizing "Oxen of the Sun"—and spinning out the linguistic web of "Cyclops," "Ithaca," and parts of "Circe"—is the Spirit in the ink-bottle working in the world. But Joyce also externalizes the spirit of his verbal gift—this crucial aspect of his three-in-one self—in another way. In *Ulysses*, a ghost appears and disappears. Wedding artistic technique to subject, Joyce makes this transmigrating spirit of the Holy Ghost—this fusion of artistic inspiration and poetic language—the most transparently verbal construction in the book. He has no language of his own, neither spoken aloud nor spoken to himself (which would be just about right for this version of the Holy Ghost). He exists in the words that other Dubliners utter about him. Materializing (out of Bloom's language) in the morning of June 16, 1904, and disappearing (with the dying away of drunken language in a brothel in the evening), this seemingly immaterial Dubliner appears almost always in Bloom's presence: Joyce who himself begot, creating a Jewish-Catholic-Protestant father out of his already existing fatherhood, middler the Holy Ghost.[116]

Bloom first sees the Man in the Macintosh at Paddy Dignam's funeral and wonders "who is that lankylooking galoot over there in the macintosh?" (*Ulysses*, p.109). Like every reader of Joyce, Bloom is immediately curious about this stranger in Dublin: "Now who is he I'd like to know?"

---

[116] Bloom "abjured" "the tenets of the Irish (protestant) church" to which his father converted "in favour of Roman catholicism at the epoch of, and with a view to, his matrimony in 1888" (*Ulysses*, pp. 734-735).

Unlike some readers of *Ulysses*, however, Bloom would only give a "trifle to know who he is" (*Ulysses*, p. 105). Also, again like almost every reader, he answers his own questions. Perhaps Macintosh is a "symbol"—or something close to it. Since he is the thirteenth at the funeral, he is, according to Bloom, "Death's number" (*Ulysses*, p. 106). But then he tells himself "silly superstition that about thirteen" (*Ulysses*, p. 106).

Silly superstition or not—is that what ghosts are?—Macintosh enters Bloom's unconscious as an image associated with "thirteen." Existing in a somewhat different state of fusion with him than in "Hades" (where he existed in Bloom's consciousness), "*A man in a brown macintosh springs up through a trapdoor*," according to the stage directions in "Circe," in the manner of the Ghost in a turn-of-the-nineteenth-century production of *Hamlet* (*Ulysses*, p. 458). As an externalization of a part of Bloom's mind, he speaks with the voice of the punitive aspect of Bloom's superego, and in Bloom, that complex mental structure (it can be idealizing, too) is often excessively harsh.

Like Judas, the thirteenth at the gathering of the Disciples, the "*man in the brown macintosh spring[ing] up through the trapdoor*" is the unconscious betrayer within Bloom. Having just created the "new Bloomusalem in the Nova Hibernia of the future," Bloom brings about his own fall—or almost does (*Ulysses*, p. 458). In the voice within—and in "Circe," as we have seen earlier—Joyce presents the unconscious of his main characters dramatically. He accuses Bloom of lying, of being "Leopold M'Intosh, the notorious fireraiser [whose] real name is Higgins" (*Ulysses*, p. 458). The buried punisher within charges Bloom with such crimes as arson and a betrayal of not only his mother but also of his mother's family (Ellen Bloom née Higgins). When Bloom sternly commands this "dog of a Christian" to be shot, Joyce intensifies our sense that to Bloom he is similar to Judas, perhaps Christendom's worst dog. More importantly, Joyce suggests (with considerable cunning, to be sure) that Bloom and his version of Macintosh (or M'Intosh) are consubstantial. As part of Bloom's mind, he is all but synonymous with him. Bloom and the man in the macintosh are also consubstantial as Sabellius heretically understood the triune mystery: this dog-of-a-Christian ghost and this father are of the same substance.[117]

---

[117] See Chapter V, note 5.

Middler the Holy Ghost

Bloom is a "dog" to many of the anti-Semitic members of the Cyclops tribe (some more virulent than the others) in Barney Kiernan's pub. Convinced that the betrayal of Jesus is in Bloom's DNA, the Citizen seems to be convinced that Bloom and his tribe are the antithesis or inversion of "God." Not only does Bloom share a doggy substance with M'Intosh. He shares it with Stephen.

Stephen, as we have seen, is also identified with a dog, a mongrel named Tatters, rooting around a carcass on Sandymount Strand in the late morning. Eyeing him, Stephen thinks to himself, "Ah, poor dogsbody. Here lies poor dogsbody's body" (*Ulysses,* p. 46). As we have seen in Chapter II, where Stephen in nighttown offers his final version of the riddle about the fox burying his grandmother, Joyce's dispossessed son is that tattered mongrel digging in the sand, also looking for something lost in past life, "Something he buried there, his grandmother" or, in Stephen's case, a mother (*Ulysses,* p. 46). Refusing to pray at her bedside as she lay dying—abjuring Roman Catholicism—guilt-ridden Stephen constantly bites into himself with his agenbite of inwit, sometimes coming close to feeling that he, too, is one of the worst dogs of Christendom. Joyce gives us a new triune god: Father, Son, and Holy Ghost consubstantial in their potential for dogginess.

In his penultimate appearance, Macintosh once again materializes out of nowhere. Once more he exists only as a skein of words in someone's mind (a ghost has no inside, therefore no language, no desires). And, once again, he haunts a group of twelve apostles, disciples of Bacchus who are communicating with their god at Burke's before midnight. The nameless narrator says, "There's eleven of them," apparently referring to medical students, hangers-on, and roisterers who are helping to close the pub (*Ulysses,* p. 406). If we count the narrator as an *ex officio,* or Matthias-like, member of the group, which includes Bloom and Stephen, we have a dozen, a baker's dozen, with the tilly, Macintosh.

Joyce underlines Macintosh's identification with the Holy Ghost by weaving Pentecostal imagery through the scene. A rushing, mighty wind of rant does fill the house where the apostles are sitting, and with the amount of drink they are downing, tongues of fire seem to be sitting in and on each of them as well. Filled with the Spirit, they speak with other tongues, too. By the end of the scene (which is also the end of "Oxen of the Sun"), we hear only a babble of voices, each one speaking in his own idiom and rhythm, as if we were members of that original multitude that was confounded by the first simultaneous translation in recorded history, a momentous international proceeding where every language was spoken at once.

Associated with a dizzying linguistic medley that is often blasphemous and soft core pornographic, Macintosh is also a walking parody of Joyce, his spitting image. He is impoverished—"Peep at his wearables.... D'ye ken bare socks?" (*Ulysses*, p. 406). He does not have much in contrast to his needs, as the Irish slang phrase "Jubilee mutton" tells us— "Jubilee mutton. Bovril [a beef concentrate convertible into a kind of beef tea], by James. Wants it real bad" (*Ulysses*, p. 406).[118] He might belong in a lunatic asylum—"Seedy cuss in the Richmond?"—and he has had Bloomesque trouble with a wife who ran out on him:

> That, sir, was once a prosperous cit. Man all tattered and torn that married a maiden all forlorn. Slung her hook, she did. Here we see lost love. Walking Macintosh of lonely canyon. (*Ulysses*, p. 406)

Joyce's autobiographical allusions, punctuated with the startling "by James" are all but explicit. It is as if he wanted us to see that sometimes the artist is *not* like the God of creation who, as Stephen once asserted omnisciently, "remains within or behind or beyond or above his handiwork, invisible, refined out of existence, indifferent, paring his fingernails" (*Portrait*, p. 252). Joyce *was* a lankylooking galoot born into a declining family. He often did seem to himself to be a tattered tramp (like tattered-dog Stephen?) who constantly weathered tragi-comic misfortunes out of Victorian melodrama, torn, lonely, loveless. But Macintosh is not "James Joyce," finally, although the allusions ask us to realize that the once prosperous op cit exists in some sort of *unio mystica* with Joyce.

Perhaps the best answer we can give Bloom's question about Macintosh's identity is a seeming trifle, the apparent throwaway line that Joyce

---

[118] Gifford and Seidman, *op. cit.*, p. 367.

gives the narrator but that actually summarizes Macintosh-ness: "Bartle the Bread we calls him" (*Ulysses*, p. 406). As the thirteenth in the baker's dozen of pubcrawlers at Burke's, Macintosh is connected to the man who delivers the bread.[119] As an archetypal deliveryman, he is neither the Father who creates our daily bread nor the Son who is the Bread of Life. (Given his starvation diet—like Melville's Bartleby the Scrivener?—it is hard to imagine him putting bread on his own table, let alone being an embodiment of the staff of life or its maker.) A mongrel of a father and a mongrel of a son are present, though, and tattered Macintosh is very much like the suddenly descending Spirit of Pentecost. But even if we can now agree that Joyce is covertly revealing his tripartite identity here, we still face two last questions. How is the Holy Ghost within Joyce connected to the delivery of bread? And why does Joyce clothe this spirit in a macintosh?

Joyce hoped to give his readers "spiritual enjoyment," his brother tells us, "by converting the bread of everyday life into something that has a permanent artistic life of its own."[120] (Joyce gives Stephen less prosaic language in *Portrait*, p. 260: the artist is a "priest of eternal imagination, transmuting the daily bread of experience into the radiant body of everliving life.") The setting for Joyce's semi-private joke is the National Maternity Hospital, a place made for the delivery of the bread of everyday life, brought forth daily in the fresh, warm, scrumptious bodies of Dublin newborns. In this place where a father, a son, and a ghost appear, Joyce is offering us his own intuitive grasp of the mysterious gestation of his art.

The Spirit of the Word, of tongues, allows young men to see visions and old men to dream dreams, Peter tells the "eleven" and the multitude who think they are all drunk in *Acts* 2. In Joyce, the inspiring power of words allows him to see visions—and to recreate them for us. As with the artist-father so with his artist-son who himself begot middler the Holy Ghost. Stephen sees visions because of the storytelling words that

---

[119] *Ibid.* Joyce glossed this for the German translator with the remark that Bartle "delivers or eats bread usually."

[120] Stanislaus Joyce, *op.cit.*, p. 104.

seem to be indistinguishable from *his* biological father—moocows coming down along the road to meet a nicens little boy. Then, almost immediately afterward, Stephen anticipates the Joycean artist he will become. He possesses the reality of his own autonomous self as baby tuckoo—"His father told him that story.... He was baby tuckoo"—only through the Word that was with the Father, Simon's astonishing linguistic energy (*Portrait*, p. 1). We may speculate that the mother tongue mediated through a father was the Spirit that brought the bread of everyday life to Joyce, allowed him, Mary-like, to receive this gift by freely accepting it into himself, and then by reprojecting it outward from the impregnated womb of his imagination.[121]

Joyce imagined his Holy Ghost as a comic delivery man, however, as dirty as a tramp or a spilled ink bottle. He did regard the language he used in his letters to Nora (and the subject matter that it delivered to him and to her) as dirty, as excitingly shameful and depraved. The image of the macintosh itself hints at this dirtiness. Using Joyce-logic, we may define a macintosh as a combination of umbrella and cloak that protects someone from the wet. Like "umbrella"—"slang for a pessary"—and like the French "capote" or cloak— "slang for a condom"—a macintosh is an equivalent for contraception.[122] Contraception is, according to Stephen, a sin against the Holy Ghost:

> But, gramercy, what of those Godpossibled souls that we nightly impossibilise, which is the sin against the Holy Ghost, Very God, Lord and Giver of Life? For sirs, he said, our lust is brief. We are means to those small creatures within us and nature has other ends than we. (*Ulysses*, p. 372)

Stephen's is only one of the many definitions of that mysterious, hard-to-define sin. One catechism lists six; the sin of Simon Magus is yet another (as is Stanislaus Joyce's "literary simony"); but there is no real consensus among the Church fathers.[123] Of course, if he was reading

---

[121] See Chapter II.
[122] Gifford and Seidman, *op. cit.*, p. 351.
[123] Don Gifford, *Joyce Annotated: Notes for Dubliners and A Portrait of the Artist as a*

Ulysses, in the full flush of his intellectual pride, Stephen might say that Joyce was obviously symbolizing contraception, the sin against the Holy Ghost, in Macintosh, the walking contraceptive. Although he would have reservations (which I will return to), Joyce would first probably be tolerant of Stephen's reading, especially since the theme of "incomplete" carnal intercourse runs through his book.

As a comic version of the mysterious devil that foils the special kind of intercourse, conception, gestation, and birth that generates Joyce's art, Macintosh calls to mind another Dubliner who has, according to the nameless catechist in "Ithaca," foiled the ends of nature with his "limitations of activity and inhibitions of conjugal rights" (*Ulysses*, p. 691). He tells us that Bloom has not had genital union with Molly for almost ten and one-half years, during which time "carnal intercourse had been incomplete without ejaculation of semen within the natural female organ" (*Ulysses*, p. 691).

Despite being intrigued at the nervy speculation of his mythicized filial self—at times Stephen does come across as a youthful Church father—Joyce would surely believe that the sin against the Holy Ghost would have to be much more dire than literally sterilizing the act of coition. It would have to be something on the level of Simon Magus's "unforgivable" sin. To use Stanislaus's phrase, it would have to be a form of "literary simony," but different from Stanislaus's sense of "falsity of purpose" (apparently Joyce's brother was thinking of a refusal to compromise one's art at the behest of timid publishers). Joyce might say that in Macintosh's "sinful" cloak-umbrella, he was symbolizing the fact of a *literary* sin against the Holy Ghost, neither Stephen's literal one of contraception nor Stanislaus's simoniacal commercializing of one's talent.

What might "blaspheming" against the Holy Ghost be for Joyce? In his memorable review-essay, "James Joyce in his Letters," Lionel Trilling's use of Joycean imagery dramatizes an answer. He imagines Joyce "submit[ting] to the necessity of taking in hand his sacred cold steel pen and

---

Young Man, 2nd ed. rev. and enlarged (Berkeley: University of California Press, 1982), pp. 206, 212-213.

with it...sully[ing] sheet after virgin sheet of paper with the filthy words that express all that he feels in the way of delight at the dirtiness of his exalted nature."[124] Dirtying virginal sheet after sheet with his filthy words, Joyce in his mounting sexual excitement is overturning the inkbottle (and with it the Holy Ghost sitting in it).

Joyce unwittingly did use some sort of pessary one time to prevent his own "natural female organ," the virgin womb of the imagination, from being impregnated by the Spirit. But what pessary? Giving himself over totally, in 1909, to importunate demands for mutual, coprolalia-centered onanism in his Dublin letters back home to Nora in Trieste, he was perverting (even if relatively briefly) his "literary conscience" sitting on the hump of his sacred cold pen. (I am *not* using "perverting" in the popular sense of doing something "immoral." Rather, I am calling to mind its root sense of Joyce "turning away" from his devilishly exacting conscience and also in the sense of Joyce being "obstinately and stubbornly self-willed" as he dipped his cold, steel pen in the ink-bottle, an act where he "opposed" what was "true and good" in himself— the creative imagination.) Rather than seeking to convert the Word made flesh into art, Joyce seemed almost obstinately to be betraying his soul: an apostate priest of the eternal imagination, renouncing, in those 1909 letters at least, his profound commitment to the literary imagination, the source of his spiritual integrity.

Let me say this somewhat differently. In words that excited Joyce sexually, we find Joyce sinning against the Holy Ghost by devoting his pen *exclusively* to the service of an obsessive excrementitiousness. In these letters, Joyce's words retain a primitive, archaic, magical quality as if he were a child (or an inwardly compelled adult) who delights in saying "dirty" things. His words (that have become things) are almost devilish in their potency. He seems to have sensed that his "obscene" words all but force the "innocent" reader (Nora) to "visualize" the acts and the objects they denote with an "hallucinatory clarity."[125]

---

[124] Lionel Trilling, "James Joyce in his Letters," in *The Moral Obligation to be Intelligent: Selected Essays* (Evanston: Northwestern University Press, 2008), p. 473.

[125] Otto Fenichel, M. D., *The Psychoanalytic Theory of Neurosis* (New York: W. W.

When the sinned-against Holy Ghost in Joyce inspires Nora to write in reply a "'certain word'" where he found "'something obscene and lecherous in the very look of the letters'" and where the sound was like the act itself "'brief, brutal, irresistible and devilish,'" her word is not some sort of mediating symbol to Joyce.[126] It *is* the act, something close to the literal equivalent for it, just as the Word *is* God and God *is* the bread and wine for a very different priest. In fact, in his perversion of the Spirit, Joyce's words *are* bodies and body parts, bodily functions and appetites, almost as if he were "emptying out" his deepest, most "demonic" impulses "into" these linguistic objects.[127]

Would it be pressing too far to say that in writing those 1909 letters, he possibly felt that if he persisted in his compulsion, he too was in danger of becoming a "dogsbody" (like depressed Stephen), even the "worst dog in Christendom" (like guilt-ridden Bloom), a literary Judas betraying his gift? Although he delighted in dirtying Nora and himself with his filthy words, and being dirtied by hers when she replied in kind, he might have also worried that he was coming close to becoming "dogsbody's body." In other words, he might have sensed that he risked profaning not only his body-and-soul but also Nora's. By seizing and exploiting her soul—by compelling her to confess her "dirty secrets" to him and then to enact them for his pleasure—he was sinning against the Holy Ghost with his version of "falsity of purpose." He also might have feared that he was on the verge of committing what Nathaniel Hawthorne's fallen priest in *The Scarlet Letter*, the reverend Arthur Dimmesdale, called a sin "blacker" than his own—a sin that "violated in cold blood the sanctity of a human heart."

Norton & Co., Inc., 1945), p. 350. Also, see Steven Marcus's description of "pornutopia," the realm of the pornographic imagination in *The Other Victorians* (New York: Basic Books, Inc., 1966), p. 280. He extends and complicates D. H. Lawrence's insights into the autoerotic impulse in pornography.

[126] Quoted by Trilling, *ibid.*

[127] See Roy Schafer's discussion of this kind of "projection" with its overtones of a projectile-like emptying out of the self, in "The Mechanisms of Defense," *International Journal of Psychoanalysis* 49 (1968), 56. Interestingly, Joyce found ways to use this language for other purposes, for high art, in *Finnegans Wake*.

Yet Joyce also managed to avoid permanently staining his Soul, cloaking it in brown. For the Church fathers, repentance for the sin against the Holy Ghost is as difficult to define as it is to define the mysterious nature of blasphemy against it, or to explain the unforgivable nature of that blasphemy, or to say what repentance might even be.[128] Perhaps Joyce remembered Paul's "'know ye not that your body is the temple of the Holy Ghost *which is* in you, which you have of God, and ye are not your own.'"[129] Returning to Nora from Dublin, he seems to have reentered the temple of the Spirit. Freed of that driven, self-absorbed, finally exploitative need to use his inspired words in the service of pornography, he managed in the next thirty years to live artistically in all the promptings of his body (which *was* his soul), especially to find ways to satisfy his almost biological need to recreate life out of life—to delight in the feeling of Mary-like sinlessness (i.e., his freedom from guilt and shame) that accompanied the unimpeded Spirit entering the virgin womb of his imagination.

No longer a prey to that devil in the hump of his pen that prompted him to be false to his soul, to betray his priestly devotion to his imagination, he converted his excursion in the world of pornography into the high art of the climactic scene in "Nausicaa," the fireworks explosion that is also the simultaneous masturbation and orgasm of Gerty MacDowell and Leopold Bloom. Joyce's artistry removes any trace of pornographic lust. Physically distant from each other yet reciprocally aroused, Gerty's slowly gathering rhythm of tumescence and detumescence is blended in with the more rapid, almost staccato arousal and orgasm of a dark stranger who, she knows, is looking avidly at her.

When a rocket "sprang" and "bang" with a "stream" that "gushed out of it," we seem to be participating physically in Bloom's rapidly mounting sexual tension and discharge of that tension. As he is being observed by Gerty—white-faced, "his hands and face were working"— so he is observing her, leaning further and further back, "trembling in every limb," giving him "a full view high up above her knee where no one ever

---

[128] Gifford, *op. cit.*, p. 213.
[129] Quoted by Gifford and Seidman, *op. cit.*, p. 340.

not even on the swing" (*Ulysses,* pp. 349-350). Gerty's mounting excitement, inseparable from Bloom's, leads to a final explosion, as if their mutual onanism climaxes in mutual orgasm: "And then a rocket sprang and bang shot blind and O! then the Roman candle burst and it was like a sigh of O! and everyone cried O! O! in raptures and it gushed out of it a stream of rain gold hair threads and they shed and ah! they were all greeny dewy stars falling with golden, O so lovely! O so soft, sweet, soft" (*Ulysses,* p. 350).

In another marked departure from pornutopia, the realm of the pornographic imagination, Joyce's exchange of especially exciting dirty words with Nora becomes the comedy of Bloom, a.k.a. Henry Flower, engaging in "literary" correspondence with his recently acquired pen pal, Martha Clifford. Bloom recalls Martha's typo where she made *his* dirty word into "world": "Wanted smart lady typist to aid gentleman in literary work. I called you naughty darling because I do not like that other world. Please tell me what is the meaning" (*Ulysses,* p. 152). And the dirty things that Joyce all but coerced Nora to write (perhaps she didn't like that other pornographic world either) become the comic misadventure of Bloom and a prostitute: "Girl in Meath street that night. All dirty things I made her say all wrong of course. My arks she called it. It's so hard to find one who" (*Ulysses,* p. 370).

Compare Joyce's excitement at recalling the "little brown stain on the seat of your white drawers"—or his excitement at reminding Nora of "the most shameful and filthy act of your body. You remember the day you pulled up your clothes and let me lie under you looking up at you while you did it?"—with Joyce fictionalizing (by making comic) his excrementitiousness.[130] Here is Molly remembering Bloom's crazy letters:

> his mad crazy letters my Precious one everything connected with your glorious Body everything underlined that comes from it is a thing of beauty and of joy forever something he got out of some nonsensical book that he had me always at myself 4 or 5 times a day sometimes and I said I hadnt are you sure O yes I said I am quite

---

[130] See Chapter IV, note 45.

sure in a way that shut him up I knew what was coming next only natural weakness it was he excited me I dont know how (*Ulysses*, p. 724)

The unsinned-against Holy Ghost reinhabiting Joyce's body allows him to inhabit Bloom's body-and-soul but with the impersonal detachment of Dedalean art. What is the subject of the following sentences from "Lestrygonians" as Bloom walks down Grafton street at lunchtime?

A warm human plumpness settled down on his brain. His brain yielded. Perfume of embraces all him assailed. With hungered flesh obscurely, he mutely craved to adore. (*Ulysses*, p. 160)

Joyce isn't asking us to think, "Bloom is hungry." He is giving us in Joycean English something like the German or French equivalent of those three words: "Bloom hat Hunger." "Bloom a faim." Bloom possesses hunger in almost every sense and in every sense of the word, and it possesses him. Hungered flesh—and Bloom does love nuzzling in Molly's warm human plumpness, enveloped by her buttocks—is walking down Grafton street looking for a pub.[131] Middler the Holy Ghost, Bloom's sexual-psychological-and physical hunger, epiphanizes before our eyes.

Let's look again at the end of Chapter IV of *Portrait* for a final example of the descent of the Spirit unsinned against. As I discussed earlier, in section 4 of Chapter VII, the Holy Spirit animates not only Joyce's creative imagination but Stephen's as well. Joyce's combination of third-person with first-person narrative technique causes us to feel that we are outside and inside Stephen at the same time, seeing him as he sees the wading girl and listening to him as he creates a symbol out of the girl who is watching him gaze at her. Once more, Joyce who himself begot (at least his youthful self), middler the Holy Ghost, himself sent himself,

---

[131] "He kissed the plump mellow yellow smellow melons of her rump, on each plump melonous hemisphere, in their mellow yellow furrow with obscure prolonged provocative melonsmellonous osculation" (*Ulysses*, p. 690).

Agenbuyer, between himself and others. Here is Joyce's new and revised version of the consubstantial Father, Son, and Holy Ghost.

Joyce-Stephen weaves dove imagery through the scene (perhaps the most traditional symbol of the Holy Ghost) to suggest that the Spirit of literary inspiration and creativity has descended to the earth and entered both Stephen and his artist-father. Let me quote again the beginning of this famous scene but with a different purpose than before in Chapter VII. Wading slowly up a long rivulet in the sand at the Bull, Stephen pauses at a heavenly sight before him, a strikingly beautiful girl standing in midstream, whom he takes into himself visually:

> A girl stood before him in midstream, alone and still, gazing out to sea. She seemed like one whom magic had changed into the likeness of a strange and beautiful seabird. Her long slender bare legs were delicate as a crane's and pure save where an emerald trail of seaweed had fashioned itself as a sign upon the flesh. Her thighs, fuller and sofhued as ivory, were bred almost to the hips where the white fringes of her drawers were like featherings of soft white down. Her slate-blue skirts were kilted boldly about her waist and dovetailed behind her. Her bosom was as a bird's, soft and slight, slight and soft as the breast of some dark-plumaged dove. But her long fair hair was girlish: and girlish, and touched with the wonder of mortal beauty, her face. (*Portrait*, p. 199)

Joyce's-and-Stephen's, Joyphen's, repetition of the image of a dove as Stephen "worship[s] her with his eyes" suggests that the Paraclete has enveloped both the gazing girl and Stephen. As I suggested earlier, the religious imagery intensifies our sense of the transcendent and self-transcendent nature of this experience for Stephen. In the "holy silence of his ecstasy," her extraordinary spiritual essence leaps to Stephen from the ordinary appearances of Dublin life, unbidden, uncoerced (*Portrait*, p. 200). Joyce dramatizes Stephen apprehending this wonder "luminously by the mind," his mind, like Shelly's "fading coal," now enraptured (*Portrait*, p. 250).

Experiencing something like the descent of the Dove, he is allowed to envision in a Dublin girl, standing in midstream, something rich, wondrous, and strange. In other words, as he gives birth to the artist's soul that has been gestating in him throughout *Portrait*, Stephen seems to be experiencing the indwelling of the same kind of grace that has infolded the girl, the inspiriting of her and him by an almost divine force, a secularized Spirit come from without.

Inspired, Stephen recreates life out of life before our eyes, perceiving-and-creating her now as the "angel of mortal youth and beauty," not by "magic," or by any attempted corruption of the Spirit as if he were a latter-day Simon Magus, but by what seems to him to be an "insufflation." He uses this word when he thinks of how his dean, an English priest in Ireland, became a convert by an inbreathed influence that Stephen figures as the mysterious working of the Holy Ghost (also symbolized by breath or wind) (*Portrait*, p. 220):

> Her image had passed into his soul for ever and no word had broken the holy silence of his ecstasy. Her eye had called him and his soul had leaped at the call. To live, to err, to fall, to triumph, to recreate life out of life. A wild angel had appeared to him, the angel of mortal youth and beauty....(*Portrait*, p. 200)

With the inseminating power of the Spirit, the word is made flesh in the virgin womb of the imagination that Joyce and Stephen both possess.

Throughout the day, Bloom tries to comprehend the enigma of M'Intosh. In "Nausicaa," he says to himself, "Ask yourself who is he now...And that fellow today at the graveside in the brown macintosh. Corns on his kismet however" (*Ulysses*, p. 358).[132] At the end of the day, the catechist in the question-and-answer lesson that is "Ithaca" doesn't provide Bloom with enough clues to "comprehend" the "selfinvolved enigma" that is "M'Intosh" (*Ulysses*, p. 685). But he is more generous with us catechumins. Appearing out of thin air in the everyday heart of Dublin, poor, unlucky, dirty M'Intosh is Joyce's joke on his fellow Dubliners

---

[132] Gifford and Seidman, *op. cit.*, p. 327. "Corns on his kismet" is slang for "down on his luck."

and on all who would ban his "dirty" book. Like all his jokes, it is also jokoserious. Consubstantial with the father-self in Bloom (M'Intosh *is* a "selfinvolved enigma"), he is even more importantly consubstantial with James Joyce, his Artist-Father. This lanky looking galoot—this wandering cowpoke of lonesome canyon—is not just the Dubin-born hero of an American western like *The Apache Chief,* riding into a venal town, the center of paralysis, to clean it up. He is the peripatetic Spirit that shows wonders in heaven above and signs in the earth beneath. Possessed of the Holy Spirit—the Word that seemed, miraculously, to be all words—Joyce was a light shining in the darkness, though most of the darkness comprehended it not.

CADENZA

Psychoanalysis and the Study of James Joyce

(By way of Another Literary Discussion in the National Library)[133]

SCENE: The National Library, some time after Stephen Dedalus presented his interpretation of *Hamlet* which Joyce recreated in the "Scylla and Charybdis" episode

CHARACTERS: The Quaker Librarian; Stephen; a visiting lecturer at Trinity College from California; various essayists and influential figures in the Dublin literary scene somewhere between 1904 and 1922

TOPIC: A preliminary discussion of, presumably, a confusing chapter from a work in progress by Mr. James Joyce, focusing on an interpretation of that work by the visiting professor

THE LIBRARIAN
(Purring, friendly and earnest.) I think we can all agree that the views of our American colleague about this very confusing work by Mr. Joyce—is it a very modern play? the work of a French Ibsen?—are most illuminating. They say we were to have a literary surprise, and your introduction

---

[133] All references to Joyce's views of Freud and psychoanalysis are from Richard Ellmann, *James Joyce* (New York: Oxford University Press, 1965), pp. 89, 351, 368, 393, 411, 450, 486, 505, 518, 525, 537, 538, 559-60, 642, 647, 660, 706, 813.

of ideas from the new Viennese school was most instructive. Mr. Dedalus also has his view of this, shall I say, New World, form of literary appreciation. I'll be bound that I cannot comprehend the interpretation any more easily than I can comprehend Mr. Joyce.

STEPHEN

(Tired of the sound of his own voice, after recalling, with his phonographic memory, his long biographical/autobiographical reading of Hamlet, but severely, contentiously, with Jesuitical rigor.) Mr. Joyce wrote me that his version of the "Circe" episode in *The Odyssey*—and that was what we agreed to try and read for today's discussion—was "the best thing he had ever written," a "new Inferno in full sail." But he believed that psychoanalysis was "absurd," its symbolism "mechanical": a "house being a womb," a "fire a penis." And "applying" psychoanalytic ideas to literature for the purpose of generating "insights"—a strange idea that seems to be one of those other American enthusiasms that quite regularly now emanate from the Land of the Gold Rush and *The Apache Chief*—that is absurdity compounded. Psychoanalysis is neither more nor less than blackmail, Mr. Joyce once told me. Dr. Freud is the "Viennese Tweedledee" and Dr. Jung is the "Swiss Tweedledum," although he also mentioned that Jung believed that he, Mr. Joyce, knew more about women than the "Devil's Grandmother." In fact, Mr. Joyce shocked an old friend from Trieste, who was enthusiastic about psychoanalysis, when he told him, "Well, if we need it, let us keep to confession."

THE LIBRARIAN

(A meek head among them, blushing, his benign forehead enkindled rosily with hope.) I own that Dr. Freud might have been rejected by Mr. Joyce, as Mr. Dedalus enthusiastically tells us, but that doesn't necessarily mean that Mr. Joyce was so—what shall I say?—so prejudiced, so one sided. All sides of life should be represented. Perhaps our American visitor has something to add to Mr. Dedalus's comments, something more in harmony with the spirit of trans-Atlantic amity that we all have been enjoying this afternoon.

THE CALIFORNIA VISITOR
(Eyeing Stephen steadily, after smiling at the Librarian and the other Dublin literateurs.) Mr. Joyce also said "I can psoakoonaloose myself any time I want." If any of the modernist masters could enter the underside of consciousness to shake Oona loose from where she frolicked—and avoid being soaked since, as his own analyst, he wouldn't have to pay what he imagined were exorbitant fees to someone from the New Viennese School—it was James Joyce.

His serious joke stayed in my mind as I taught him to undergraduates and graduate students through the years and discovered that he was the most Freudian of all the great twentieth-century writers, the creator of a fictional universe where one thing could become many things and many things one thing. His boast became even more intriguing during my psychoanalytic training when one of my teachers mentioned that Freud was convinced the Irish were the only "race" that couldn't be analyzed. I wondered whether that was because, like Mr. Joyce, they made it into a form of secularized Catholicism, mixing it up with confession. Or was it because, like Mr. Joyce, many of them could be their own priest-analysts, blessed with an uncanny access to the unconscious?

GEORGE RUSSELL
(Oracling out of his shadow.) Unconscious? Mr. Joyce, I remember, once used in conversation the phrase "subconscious." Subconscious, unconscious, consciousness—purely academic. What do these things mean? Art has to reveal to us ideas, formless spiritual essences. It brings our mind into contact with the eternal wisdom. All the rest is the speculation of schoolboys for schoolboys.

THE CALIFORNIA VISITOR
At the risk of appearing to be a speculative schoolboy, a hairsplitting medievalist, let me say to Mr. Russell—you are known, sir, as A.E. too?—that by unconscious I am referring to the *dynamic* realm of the "unsaid and unsayable," that part of the mind where, among other things, we *repress*, where we use a variety of devices to banish (also done unconsciously) thoughts, impulses, fantasies that make us anxious or

depressed or filled with unpleasure in any way. By "dynamic," I am suggesting that these repressed wishes, memories, urges are alive, constantly exerting an "upward" pressure, a "return of the repressed," if you will, "seeking" conscious expression of *derivatives* of those urges. To make things even more complicated—and to risk seeming to be Dr. Tweedledee from America— such derivatives appear in another part of the mind that is *also* unconscious, but this is not the dynamically repressed unconscious. We participants in a contemporary version of the Viennese School call it the preconscious—the realm of the "sayable." To complete my little lecture: consciousness is the realm of the "said," the stream of consciousness that Joyce explores so richly in his interior monologues; "said aloud" is public act and utterance.

JOHN EGLINTON
(Shifting his spare body, leaning back to judge, with newgathered frown.) Upon my word, it makes my blood boil to be lectured as if we were still at University. Surely literary characters aren't patients whose unconscious or preconscious—or whatever you're trying to describe—can be analyzed or inferred or whatever.

THE CALIFORNIA VISITOR
(Gazing first at Eglinton and then slowly at the rest of the group.) Analysts can't "make" the *unconscious* conscious. No one can, nor could Joyce, nor did he intend to. But as Mr. Joyce discovered—and as Freud discovered at the time he was writing *The Interpretation of Dreams*— there is a way to become conscious of latent unconscious meanings in our conscious thoughts, dreams, symptomatic acts, and the psychopathology of everyday life—slips of the tongue, strange forgetfulness, misrememberings. We help our patients become aware of the presence of, as I said before, *derivatives* of their unconscious when we ask them at the beginning of an analysis (a few of us analysts directly) to try to say whatever comes to mind, without censoring what they are thinking or feeling or fantasizing, no matter how embarrassing or distasteful or scary. Mr. Joyce, in his stream of consciousness technique, is giving us relatively uncensored thoughts, feelings, and fantasies. These conscious associations aren't "free" in his

characters, or in our patients, since they're infiltrated both by preconscious thoughts and beliefs *and* various maneuvers to keep those thoughts and beliefs out of conscious awareness.

By learning to listen to these associations with the third ear—by listening with an even-hovering attention, by trying to remain "neutral," without favoring wishes, fears, or defensive maneuvers—we begin to infer the presence of the possible unconscious significance of *repeated* phrases, images, fantasies, and metaphors, *recurrent* themes and motifs, shifts in tone, body English. To use one of Mr. Joyce's phrases about how he intends to go about creating believable characters, we infer the "curve of an emotion," the patient's "individuating rhythm" in a given hour or sequence of hours. Indulge my use of another metaphor. It's not the notes but the melody that we begin to detect and try to communicate to the patient, the latent but perennial conflicts and frightening wishes and fantasies that are preconscious, i,e., *just about* conscious but not quite. I would submit that we can begin to fathom the full complexity of his characters by doing something along the same lines.

STEPHEN

(*Begging with a swift glance the hearing of the small assembly.*) Our American guest quotes the essay that Mr. Joyce wrote before expatriating himself, "A Portrait of the Artist," which I found intriguing as well, but he hasn't responded directly to Mr. Eglinton. You're asking us to join you in psoakoonaloosing the characters in "Circe," particularly Mr. Bloom, none of whom is on the Doctor's couch, really doing the associating, free or not, that you claim is some sort of royal road to the unconscious. Nor have you explained how you can avoid errant and wild speculation about the "associations" and "fantasies" of the characters that you imply are "true." Where do the characters (or patients) truly end and your interpretations begin?

GEORGE RUSSELL

(*Impatiently.*) And you are asking us to join you (and perhaps Mr. Joyce as well) in prying into the private life of a man, his inviolable soul, precisely the wrong way to bring our mind into contact with eternal

Truth, Plato's World of Ideas. I remember that one of your most famous American novelists wrote that the "Unpardonable Sin" is a "want of love and reverence for the Human Soul," a crime which a perversely Puritanical alienist in *The Scarlet Letter* commits, an Englishman, to be sure, a Dr. Roger Chillingworth, I believe. A fallen priest in Puritan Boston, the reverend Arthur Dimmesdale, tells his lover, a Scarlet Woman, of the torments that Chillingworth inflicted on him; that man "violated in cold blood the sanctity of a human heart."

THE CALIFORNIA VISITOR

(Smiling at the thought of a race that can't be analyzed) I'd like to respond to Mr. Dedalus first. He raises a crucial and valid point. How do I avoid excessively subjective readings? Let me repeat: the analyst is on the lookout for *repeated* and *internally consistent* patterns in his patient's associations, and sometimes he is presented with three dovetailing patterns, a verbal three-leaf clover. (*Is that going too far with an Irish audience?*) The repeated theme—let's say, anxiety about challenging authority—appears in the analytic session, often an anxious, half-buried challenge to the analyst's authority; this theme has also appeared regularly in the past, sometimes in frightening fantasies or dreams; and it also appears a third time in the present but outside the office, in a tense exchange with, perhaps, a boss. At that moment, at the reappearance of those three interpenetrating leaves, most analysts would interrupt the flow of a patient's associations by offering an "interpretation."

In Joyce's prose, the analyst-critic also tries to focus on the recurrent themes, phrases, and images in Mr. Joyce's writing and his own comments about his writing rather than focus on, and debate, the interpretations of his many commentators and admirers. I also try to follow Freud's own admonition in *The Interpretation of Dreams*: "we are justified, in my view, in giving free rein to our speculations so long as we retain the coolness of our judgement and do not mistake the scaffolding for the building."

I do prefer to refer to Mr. Joyce's words than Freud's, though. Mr. Joyce once commented that the name "Joyce" meant the same thing in English as "Freud" in German—joy. He believed that comedy was the supreme art since it brought joy, and in the comic (yet often dark) dream called "Circe," he seemed to believe that the revelation of Bloom's buried self would bring us not just laughter but joy, too—the pleasure of a character epiphanizing before our eyes, and before his own eyes as well.

I would think that Mr. Dedalus would be intrigued with a writer who believes with him (and with Aquinas) that the third quality of beauty arises when an object's soul, its whatness, leaps to us from the vestment of its appearance. As you can see, a Mr. J. F. Byrne, whom I met after one of my lectures, took some notes about your lecture, Mr. Dedalus, about the nature of beauty; Applied Aquinas someone called it.

The word "soul" never embarrassed Mr. Joyce, Mr. Russell, nor did it embarrass Freud. "Psychoanalysis" means, as you well know, the analysis of the soul, which Mr. Russell might find offensive in itself, if not downright bizarre, but Freud believed that something like the soul, the very springs of our being, though usually unknown to us, is also knowable, at least in part, psychoanalytically. As a colleague wrote recently, Freud regularly used the noun *Seele* and the adjective *seelisch,* and, like Mr. Joyce, was always concerned with the mysterious inner source of psychic movement, something he tried to treat with a physician's tact and care.

But Freud intended to do away with the supernaturalism inherent in the *seelisch* entity, the psyche, and replaced it with what he thought was the scientifically validable "mental apparatus." Mr. Joyce (and especially Chillingworth's creator, Nathaniel Hawthorne) might have balked at the idea of a "mental apparatus," the idea of a "scientific" understanding of our soul that wasn't objectifying, dehumanizing, and thus irreverent; but Mr. Joyce, too, was skeptical of traditional views of the supernatural and would certainly acknowledge that some of us, potential artists especially (*Sotto voce: it's tempting to glance at Stephen Dedalus.*), can experience the emotional reality of a painful yet liberating birth of the soul.

With our hard-earned knowledge of that hidden part of the self that can cause so much pain to ourselves and to others, there can also be moments of tragic joy. Isn't that the mysterious "moly" that Ulysses used to defeat Circe? Bloom's magic herb, his embarrassingly shameful self-knowledge, which arises from his *conscious* awareness of his formerly repressed urges, fantasies, and fears, defeats the spell of shame, guilt, and despair that BELLO, his inner Bello-self, has "cast" on him. BELLO'S bewitchment of him is basically an externalization of *Bloom's* self-loathing conscience and self-loathed body image. The madam's witchy black magic reduces him in his own eyes to pure swinishness.

Once "Circe's" spell is broken, no longer feeling that he is a "perfect pig," he can begin to mourn his dead son, Rudy, who has come back from the dead. The son no longer haunts him, no longer animates his father's guilty conscience—a nice reversal of the father, come back from the dead, haunting *his* son in *Hamlet*. (*Sotto voce: it is increasingly hard not to glance at Mr. Dedalus.*) Reading, it seems, a Hebrew book, Rudy reveals himself as a charmingly lovable "fairy boy of eleven," a "changeling." With his love for his son kindled anew, Bloom, wonderstruck, is no longer guilt-ridden and unmanned. He remains "silent," "holding his hat and ashplant stand[ing] erect." We are left with the image of Bloom "on guard"—a pacifistic yet morally brave (and thus armed) Ulysses who can defeat Circe and, with anxiety reduced and feelings of paternity restored, save a surrogate son, a consubstantial son, from a beating at the hands of English soldiers.

BUCK MULLIGAN

(*A ribald face, he comes forwards then blithe in motley towards the greeting of their smiles. Primrosevested he greets gaily with his doffed Panama as with a bauble.*) You were asked, sir, about psoakoonaloosing a book, if I mistake not? Joyce? Freud? I seem to know the names. To be sure, the Dublin chap thinks he can write as deeply as the Florentine WOG, while the Viennese doctor, I have been told, thought he was a German-speaking version of the gaseous vertebrate, the Sassenach Lord of Language, that Mr. Dedalus seems to worship.

THE CALIFORNIA VISITOR

(*Steadfast, still pedagogical, fearful of being pedantic.*) Mr. Dedalus has emphasized Mr. Joyce's distaste for Freud (and for Jung, too), but surely when Mr. Joyce said that *Ulysses* was written "'to suit the esthetic of the dream, where the forms prolong and multiply themselves, where the visions pass from the trivial to the apocalyptic, where the brain uses the roots of vocables to make others from them which will be capable of naming its phantasms, its allegories, its allusions'"—surely such a writer will seem so innately "freudened," to use Mr. Joyce's own nicely turned conversational phrase, that we are all but being asked to read him psychoanalytically.

I have tried to do this without putting Mr. Joyce or his characters through what Mr. T. S. Eliot, in another context, called the" lemon-squeezer" school of criticism—that reductionistic temptation, that mad seeking out of static (and thus pre-Freudian) psychopathic entities, isolating them, and then calling the result "literary appreciation of his psychological sensitivity."

STEPHEN

(*Nodding to the slowly departing Librarian, George Russell, and John Eglinton, who in turn nod to Stephen and bow courteously to the American visitor.*) I see our friends (*the door closing behind the outgoers*) have other, less abstruse matters to discuss. (*Sotto voce: Are they tired of the sound of his American voice as I am tired of my own?*) Again, I would like you to tell me why your listening with the third ear is anything other than the loosest kind of self-absorbed impressionism—vaguely akin to Mr. Russell's self-indulgent sentimentality about the "spiritual essences" that art depicts, the "revolutions" in the world that are "born out of the dreams and visions in a peasant's heart on the hillside." After all, to repeat myself, Leopold Bloom *isn't* on your couch or in your lecture hall; he can't agree or disagree with your reading. In fact, no one can "read" the unconscious, including Mr. Bloom, since the unconscious, by definition, *is* unconscious, as any Jesuit-educated Dubliner would tell you. And why all this fuss and bother about the mystery of the unconscious in the first place? What about the mystery of the conscious? (*Sotto voce: Tell me that my Trinity scholar.*) In fact, has *your* Viennese Prefect of his own Sodality ever answered my questions?

THE CALIFORNIA VISITOR

(*Musing to himself: they're not an unanalyzable race.*) True, only my patients (and my students for that matter) can confirm or disconfirm (by their further associations) my interpretations.

STEPHEN

(*A yankee Joycean freudened no less! Wall, tarnation strike me! A kingdom for a drink.*) Let me say it again. Bloom isn't alive. With your approach, for all your attention to repetition, you risk slipping into what the Viennese Doctor, I believe, called "wild analysis," actually wild analysis on top of literary analysis, something that is more wildly and unsupportably speculative than anything I said in this room about Shakespeare and old Hamlet's ghost.

THE CALIFORNIA VISITOR

(*So he has read some of Freud's papers*) I think you'd agree, Mr. Dedalus, that artists recreate life out of life. Is it wild to say that Mr. Joyce recreates the psychological life of his characters, especially the inner life of what seems to be his favorite character, Leopold Bloom, out of the artistic recreation of his own inner life?

Joyce's mother lost her first child a boy, in 1881, shortly after the infant's birth.[134] I suggest that with the birth of Joyce himself, in 1882, and with his survival, his mother very likely responded to him with a kind of anxious protectiveness. Is it only wildly speculative to infer that with nine further births and three still-births her anxiety was complicated by guilt and depression?

What *are* the psychological consequences to a surviving son who experienced constant disturbances in his early relationship with his mother—surely a distracted mother, regularly removed from him? The repeated trauma of her almost constant rhythm of pregnancy, childbirth, and, often, misbirth was surely deepened by the trauma of perhaps witnessing these births and misbirths in his home, if not directly then indirectly with his imagination. Is it wild analysis to think that her young son may very well have associated her body with bleeding, even with genital damage, even mutilation?

What if we apply a number of psychoanalytic ideas about the consequences of these early traumas to our understanding of Bloom's character

---

[134] Ellmann, *op.cit.*, p. 20. In addition to the three misbirths, John Joyce's family included four boys and six girls. The births of Joyce's six sisters—quite likely at home—occurred regularly from the time he was two until he was twelve.

and fantasies in "Circe" and thus to our understanding of Joyce's major themes of homelessness and isolation, the nature of love, intimacy, and marriage? What if Joyce (comically to be sure) has Bloom witness multiple births, shows us that Bloom, in fact, in giving birth himself to eight babies is thus identified with a woman in childbirth? What if Joyce's complex symbolism has Bloom *apparently* looking at the bleeding genitals of a woman who *seems* to be the transmigrating soul of his mother? And what if Joyce's art reveals, again with symbolic indirection, Bloom's confusion about his own body image and his genital integrity?

Let me repeat: Mr. Joyce *isn't* Bloom. But surely, Mr. Dedalus, this might be a path to deepening and complicating our understanding of how this seemingly impersonal artist transforms his own personal experiences into high and demanding art. After all, in your biographical reading, you do assert not only that Shakespeare is old Hamlet but that Shakespeare returns regularly in his plays to his own artistic recreation of his seduction by an older woman, her betrayal of him while he was still a young man, and his subsequent murderous rage—the heart, you tell us, of Shakespeare's emotional, and thus artistic, life.

BUCK MULLIGAN

(*Preparing to join the departing gentlemen, swinging around on his heel, exclaiming sotto voce.*) O, an impossible person! He proves by an American kind of algebra that a mosey named Bloom is Mr. Joyce's own father and that Mr. Joyce himself is the ghost of Bloom's grandfather. And this talk of a mother's damaged and bleeding genitalia! I've seen women pop off at the Mater and Richmond and cut up into tripes in the dissecting room. But we're not in the dissecting room—or in Holles street. (*Nodding to the visitor.*) That's the National Maternity Hospital. Or are we in Holles street after all? Perhaps our guest would like to ask the Librarian to come back, to consider enhancing his professional skills by studying medicine with me, with a concentration in gynecology.

THE CALIFORNIA VISITOR

(*It was Connery's, the Ship hotel and tavern, that this medical student recalled—this mocker in the primrosevest, sitting civil waiting for pints apiece.*) Mr. Joyce *is* making the most arduous demands on our powers of attention and memory, seriousness, and sensibility—and our capacity for laughter. He is often asking us to "think" of Bloom in the way our dreaming minds think, to dreamily think, and the way, perhaps, *he* thought as he psoakoonaloosed himself any time he wanted. He creates his new womanly man out of a lifetime of probably painfully acquired insights into not only his conscious, but his preconscious, maybe even unconscious, life—his sexual fantasies, dreams, reveries, symptoms.

This is not ordinary conscious thinking, that is, verbal thinking that follows the laws of syntax and logic. Instead, representation is by allusion or analogy. As one of my teachers economically put it:

> [A] part of an object, memory or idea may be used to stand for the whole, or vice-versa...several different thoughts may be represented by a single thought or image. In fact, verbal representation is not used nearly as exclusively in this way of thinking as in ordinary thought. Finally, a sense of time, or a concern with time does not exist....There is no such thing as "before'" or "after," as "now" or "then," as "first," "next," or "last." Past, present and future are all one....[135]

At the risk of redundancy, let me say that Bloom's psychological consistency, his "individuating rhythm," does *not* mean that his psychology is Mr. Joyce's. A man with an "austere, almost priestly propriety," as you might have observed, he made sure that Bloom was not too obviously Joycean.[136] Although he has more than a touch of the artist about him, Bloom is hardly a priest of the eternal imagination. Joyce takes pains to

---

[135] Charles Brenner, *An Elementary Textbook of Psychoanalysis*, rev. ed. (Garden City, New York: Anchor Press/Doubleday, 1974), pp. 48-49. His discussion of the differences between what Freud called "primary process" thinking and "secondary process" thinking is impressively succinct. Brenner is also impressive in the way he suggests that *all* of us regularly steer between the whirlpool of primary process thinking—it's the habit of children—and the rock of secondary process.

[136] Lionel Trilling, "James Joyce in his Letters," in *The Moral Obligation to be Intelligent: Selected Essays* (Evanston: Northwestern University Press, 2008), p. 474.

make him noticeably deficient in all those things that might comprise a portrait of the artist as James Joyce. (*What is Mr. Dedalus thinking as he eyes me so coldly?*)

In this basically kind man—a character Joyce described to his friend, Frank Budgeon, as *"gutmütig"*—where is the narcissistic self-absorption, even a hint of the solipsistic demands for complete attention and total admiration from his friends that we find in Mr. Joyce's *A Portrait of the Artist as a Young Man*? (*Sotto voce: Should I have mentioned this book in Stephen Dedalus's presence? Has he read it? Has he even read all of "Circe" yet?*) Where does Joyce present in Bloom the cold aloofness and lordly isolation that mask an apparent incapacity in the artist-to-be for deep and lasting relationships, especially with women? Where does he dramatize in Bloom, the passionate belief that one day he will force the world to acknowledge his own high valuation of himself by actualizing that seemingly grandiose belief, by creating lasting works of art because of his genius?

Most important, Mr. Joyce takes pains to avoid leaving us with a sense of anything terrible in Bloom's sexuality, anything "unnatural" or evil or corrupting in the full range of his unconscious polymorphous perversity. In fact, Joyce renders it as part of infantile nature itself, beyond moral judgment. Reading "Circe," we often find ourselves amused, saying with a laugh (and a sigh, even a tear), Well, there goes Poldy again, essentially as innocent as a child in his polymorphous perverse fantasies and yearnings.[137] In Leopold Paula Bloom, Joyce has given us a Ulysses who recovers his soul and finally defeats a Circe lodged within, a contemptuous, hate-filled force in the mind which would have us attack ourselves because we are all little more than embodiments of an irreducibly swinish, unredeemable psychopathology.

STEPHEN

(*What have I learned? Of them? Of me? And from another pigeonstealer? from an American's Summa contra Gentiles?*) You're offering us a treatise

---

[137] *Ibid.*, Trilling's review-essay is a graceful example of how a psychoanalytically-minded critic can move between Joyce and his art without the mindless reductionism of too much literary Freudianism.

on the Truth against unbelievers, revealed by your Viennese Medicine Man, someone like my own crafty, psychologically intuitive, semi-mind-reading Director of Studies. Yet I have to confess, from what I have read of Dr. Freud, he also reminds me of the youthful Joyce who himself seemed to embody the transmigrating soul of the youthful Moses, someone who never bowed his head to his mocking enemies. If Freud did bow his head, he would never have made me believe, somehow, *some* of what he writes, if only for a moment, now and then. And if Freud or Mr. Joyce or Moses bowed his will and spirit before all *his* arrogant detractors, we never would have believed, for an instant of course, that Mr. Joyce (along with Moses and even Freud) had spoken with the Eternal or made me believe that he had come down from Sinai's mountaintop with the light of inspiration shining in his countenance, bearing in his arms the tables of a new dispensation, graven in the language of the outlaw.

APPENDIX

Gabriel Conroy's Individuating Rhythm and Joyce's use of Autobiography

Throughout "The Dead," Joyce focuses our attention on Gabriel's shame-filled reactions to his recurrent *faux pas*. This series of gaffes begins with his attempt at a jocular remark to Lily, the house servant, about her "young man." Then, he humiliates himself with his old friend from University, the nationalist "enthusiast," Miss Ivors, and, finally, Joyce gives us the most devastating mistake of all—a humiliating misreading of his wife's mood as he fantasizes making love to her. He hopes that their lovemaking will erase the dullness of their marriage. These recurrent moments of shame constitute Gabriel's "individuating rhythm" or "curve of an emotion." To Joyce in 1904, that rhythm is the very heart of a character, and the job of a writer of the future, namely James Joyce, is to "liberate" that curve of an emotion from the "personalized lumps of matter," the "fluid succession of presents," that is a life in Joyce's fiction.

Gabriel shares Stephen Dedalus's individuating rhythm, the oscillation we have seen in Chapter I between excitement and depression, pleasure in himself and in his world that fades to embarrassment, shame, and despair when he feels that he hasn't received from others the praise and interest he expects as his due, especially from a woman. Like Stephen, he seems to be the transmigrating soul of the narcissistically vulnerable patient whom Heinz Kohut describes, a patient flooded with shame and anxiety because of the *faux pas* he felt he had committed. His pain seems to have arisen from his feeling that he was rejected, suddenly and unexpectedly, just when he had expected to shine and win acclaim in his fantasies:

> [He] tends to react to the memory of a *faux pas* with excessive shame and self-rejection. His mind returns again and again to the painful moment, in the attempt to eradicate the reality of the incident by magical means, i.e., to undo it. Simultaneously the patient may angrily wish to do away with himself in order to wipe out the tormenting memory in this fashion.[138]

Let me turn to Gabriel's increasingly humiliating self-consciousness that finally begins to dissolve in a stunning epiphany when he falls asleep at the end of the story. As he slips into unconsciousness, he erases his excessive shame and self-rejection, not by magical thinking, but by presenting us with something like a product of the creative imagination—an all-encompassing dream-vision of the oneness of his life, the life of Ireland, and the life of the universe. (Gabriel's creation seems to serve the same function as Stephen's creation of "the angel of mortal life and beauty" that I discussed earlier, especially in Chapter VII.)

Even before the Misses Morkan's annual post-New Year's dance begins, Gabriel remembers an unexpectedly painful rejection from his mother when he was apparently expecting acclaim. Rather than praise his wife—in effect confirming him in his admiration for Gretta (and quite likely confirming him in his self-admiration)—his mother disparaged her. With a shadow passing over his face, he recalls her "sullen opposition to his marriage":

> Some slighting phrases she had used still rankled in his memory; she had once spoken of Gretta as being country cute and that was not

---

[138] Heinz Kohut, *The Analysis of the Self: A Systematic Approach to the Psychoanalytic Treatment of Narcissistic Personality Disorders* (New York: International Universities Press, 1971), pp. 230-231.

true of Gretta at all. It was Gretta who had nursed her during all her long last illness in their house at Monkstown.[139]

Gabriel is still hurt by her rejection of Gretta and of him, his choice of a country cute wife. Later in the evening, he returns to that moment with his friend, Molly Ivors, when she asks whether Gretta is from Connacht. He tells her "shortly" that her "people are" (p. 242). We may infer that the dignified and educated son of Ellen Morkan is still rankling from the slighting phrases of the "brains carrier of the Morkan family" (according to Aunt Kate), a woman who was always "very sensible of the dignity of family life" (p. 239). It's almost as if Gabriel is arguing with his mother (and with himself) over whether he *did* make a mistake by marrying someone beneath him, a man who took his degree in the Royal University.

2. Gabriel Coloured as if He Had Made a Mistake

Let me turn now to Joyce's even more explicit markers for Gabriel's psychological rhythm, his persistent experiences of shameful self-consciousness when he feels that he has made a "mistake." At the start, he makes what he feels is a "friendly" remark to Lily the maid, a young woman whom he knew when she was a child nursing her doll: "I suppose we'll be going to your wedding one of these fine days with your young man, eh?" (p. 227). But his attempt at gay banter falls flat when Lily replies "with great bitterness" that "The men that is now is only all palaver and what they can get out of you" (p. 227):

> Gabriel coloured, as if he felt he had made a mistake and, without looking at her, kicked off his galoshes and flicked actively with his muffler at his patent-leather shoes. (pp. 227-228)

---

[139] James Joyce, "The Dead" in *Dubliners,* with an introduction by Padraic Colum (New York: The Modern Library, 1926) p. 239. Subsequent references will appear in the text and refer to this edition.

A minute later he is "still discomposed by the girl's bitter and sudden retort" (pp. 228-229). His discomposure quickly becomes a feeling of humiliation and self-dissatisfaction, even self-disparagement, as if he sensed fleetingly that being considerate to a housemaid at Christmastime might very well have been only all palaver to get something out of her (such as gratitude for him condescending to be interested in the life of a servant).

Gloomily listening to the sounds of the other partygoers, he goes over his after dinner speech:

> The indelicate clacking of the men's heels and the shuffling of their soles reminded him that their grade of culture differed from his. He would only make himself ridiculous by quoting poetry to them which they could not understand. They would think that he was airing his superior education. He would fail with them just as he had failed with the girl in the pantry. (p. 229)

We seem to be eavesdropping on Gabriel's flow of consciousness here, but Joyce isn't using an interior monologue. Let me pause for a moment to discuss, once again, his narrative technique. In the opening sentence, Joyce alerts us to his use of the first-person-third-person style: "Lily the caretaker's daughter was literally run off her feet" (p. 224). Literally (rather than figuratively) run off her feet would make poor Lily a somersault artist on top of her duties as a housemaid. The adverb, of course, is Lily's, not Joyce's, and alerts us to her confusion when she tries to use the language of an educated woman. It also urges us to pay attention in the rest of the story to how Joyce will speak in a character's diction to reveal that character's rhythm.

Throughout "The Dead," Joyce uses Gabriel's words to suggest some of the roots of his shamefulness, his plummeting self-esteem when he feels he has failed when he has not garnered the praise he feels he deserves. Gabriel's language is either excessively self-critical or excessively self-admiring. He did not "fail" disastrously with Lily, although he did make a *faux pas*. (Was Lily, in reality, even as "bitter" as Gabriel felt her to be? It was Gabriel, after all, who used the phrase, not an omniscient third-person author.) Nor is Gabriel so "superior" to his fellow partygoers as he assumes. Although his grade of culture and education is higher (he is probably right in assuming that they would not understand allusions to Browning), his platitudinous speech later in the evening is not so sophisticated as he imagines. He first alludes to Aunt Kate, Aunt Julia, and their niece, Mary Jane, as the "Three Graces," and then mixes up the Graces with the three principal goddesses of Olympus whom Paris was asked to judge in a beauty contest.[140] Taking his degree in the Royal University is a long step below taking his degree in the much older and much more renowned institution, Trinity College, Dublin's version of Oxford's Balliol or King's College, Cambridge.[141]

It seems that Gabriel's mortification arises from an unconscious sense of his superiority, even grandiosity, an overly high picture of himself as, perhaps, the current "brains carrier" of the family. When Lily fails to confirm him in that picture—when his self-admiration is not met by hers—he "colour[s] *as if* he felt he had made a mistake" (italics mine). In the recurrent phrase "as if," Joyce implies that Gabriel is not fully and consciously feeling that he *has* made a mistake; Joyce doesn't write, "Gabriel coloured as he felt he had made a mistake" (p. 227). Quite self-consciously, Gabriel seems to be all but acting ashamed, distancing himself from his anxiety-producing proneness to humiliation. He tries to distance himself even further, attempting to undo the shame by kicking off his galoshes and "flick[ing] actively with his muffler at his patent-leather shoes" (p. 228). As if that wasn't enough to reduce the flood of "gloom," torment, and anxiety, he tries to eradicate

---

[140] "Agalia (Brilliance), Euphrosyne (Joy), and Thalia (Bloom)" are "the inspirers of those qualities which give charm to nature and to wisdom, love, social intercourse, etc." The Three Graces are very different from the Olympians' Hera, Athena, and Aphrodite: Don Gifford, *Joyce Annotated: Notes for Dubliners and A Portrait of the Artist as a Young Man,* 2nd ed. rev. and enlarged (Berkeley: University of California Press, 1982), pp. 118. Thalia (Bloom) seems to be another serious Joyce joke.

[141] Although he attended University College, Dublin, Gabriel's mother was probably instrumental in having him take his degree in the decidedly non-Catholic and more "prestigious" Royal University, which was "not an institution of learning but an examining and degree granting institution": Gifford, *ibid.,* p. 116.

the painful moment by thrusting a coin into Lily's hands, saying "Christmas-time! Christmas-time! ...almost trotting to the stairs and waving his hand to her in deprecation" (p. 228). As we will see, Joyce repeats "as if" when he describes what Gabriel almost feels during his later experiences of rejection—or what to him is even the slightest hint of rejection.

Gently mocking her husband about what he makes her wear—his "solicitude was a standing joke with them"—Gretta breaks into a peal of laughter, saying, "Galoshes!....That's the latest. Whenever it's wet underfoot I must put on my galoshes. Tonight even he wanted me to put them on, but I wouldn't. The next thing he'll buy me will be a diving suit" (p. 231). After laughing "nervously" and patting his tie "reassuringly," Gabriel barely suppresses his anger at being the object of Gretta's affectionate joking, her laughter over the excessive solicitude that he seems proud of: "He's really an awful bother, what with green shades for Tom's eyes at night and making him do the dumb-bells and forcing Eva to eat the stirabout" (p. 230). Responding to his aunts's ignorance about what galoshes are and how popular they are on the continent, Gabriel knits his brows and says, as if he were slightly angered: "It's nothing very wonderful but Gretta thinks it very funny because she says the word reminds her of Christy Minstrels" (p. 231). Although he seems to be pretending to be angry, what isn't funny for Gabriel is mockery (to him) of his wished-for worldliness and of his solicitude (no matter how intrusive and excessive that solicitude, that Bloom-like mathering, can feel to his wife and children).

3. An Ordeal making a Blush invade his Forehead

Prone to humiliation when he feels he has been rejected, especially when he expected to shine, Gabriel is even more tormented with his next failure, once again with a gently teasing woman. His increasingly agitated exchange with "frank-mannered" Miss Ivors is as comic as it is painful. Friends of "many years' standing, [their] careers had been parallel first at the University and then as teachers" (pp. 203-204). Joking with him for his lack of proper nationalistic ardor (she is deeply committed to the Gaelic League), she perplexes Gabriel when she asks, "Who is G. C.?" (p. 240): "Gabriel coloured and was about to knit his brows, as if he did not understand. . . ." (p. 240). Understanding and not understanding her question (he knows that he signed his literary columns in the pro-British *Daily Express* with his initials), Gabriel cannot feel her playfulness, even her mild flirtatiousness, as he struggles with what seems to be an emergent and empathy-clouding shamefulness.

> —O, innocent Amy! I have found out that you write for *The Daily Express*. Now, aren't you ashamed of yourself?
> —Why should I be ashamed of myself? asked Gabriel, blinking his eyes and trying to smile.
> —Well, I'm ashamed of you, said Miss Ivors frankly. To say you'd write for a paper like that. I didn't think you were a West Briton.
> (pp. 240-241)

Even more perplexed and inattentive, he is taken aback when they cross (in the dance of lancers) and she "promptly [takes] his hand in a warm grasp," explaining "in a soft friendly tone" "Of course I was only joking" when she called him a West Briton (p. 241). Bewildered, and increasingly self-conscious, Gabriel apparently didn't catch her tone. Later, after asking him why he prefers to vacation in Europe rather than in the Aran Isles, to his surprise and increasing nervousness, she presses her warm hand on his arm once more, "eagerly" (p. 243). Still anxious, blushing, and embarrassed at what is to him an "ordeal, Gabriel mistakenly feels that Miss Yvors has broken a lance with him and been harshly critical of him, his writing, his politics. He can't fathom her mood any more than he could fathom Lily's (nor will he be able to fathom his wife's mood in the climactic scenes at the end of the story).

Joyce emphasizes Gabriel's intensifying torment in what to him is a cross-examination by Miss Ivors. Expecting, perhaps, praise for his literary journalism from his only intellectual equal at the party, he feels suddenly and unexpectedly turned upon:

> Their neighbors had turned to listen to the cross-examination. Gabriel glanced right and left nervously and tried to keep his good humor under the ordeal which was making a blush invade his forehead. (p. 243)

Increasingly agitated, he misreads her as he projects his sour feelings on her:

> Gabriel tried to cover his agitation by taking part in the dance with great energy. He avoided her eyes for he had seen a sour expression on her face. But when they met he was surprised to feel his hand firmly pressed. (p. 243)

Miss Ivors is as surprised at his agitated and nervous behavior as he is surprised at her warmth. She looks at him from under her brows, not sourly, but "quizzically" until he smiles (p. 243).

After the dance is over, Gabriel does not recall her warm hand on his arm or his hand being firmly pressed. Nor does he sense the affection in her mockery or recall her "immense" admiration for his review of Browning's poems in *The Daily Express* (p. 242). All he remembers is that he didn't shine with her (as he expected to shine all evening) and his painful feeling is that she humiliated him publicly in her unexpected questioning. He feels perfectly justified in depreciating her as (he feels) she depreciated him, even going so far as to desexualize her as he felt she desexualized him (by making him feel unmanned):

> Of course the girl or woman, or whatever she was, was an enthusiast but there was a time for all things....But she had no right to call him a West Briton before people, even in joke. She had tried to make him ridiculous before people, heckling him and staring at him with her rabbit's eyes. (p. 244)

4. *A Shameful Consciousness of his own Person Assailed Him*

Underscoring Gabriel's hypersensitivity to perceived rejections and deepening our sense of Gabriel's hypercriticism of his "mistakes" and "failures," Joyce has been preparing us for his most painful failure all night. It again arises from Gabriel's unconscious wish to win acclaim, to shine in the presence of a woman whom he misreads. As he returns with Gretta to the Gresham after the party, their children cared for by Bessie at home, he anticipates "moments of ecstasy" (p. 275). Again using the free indirect style, Joyce allows us to eavesdrop on Gabriel's consciousness:

> Moments of their secret life together burst like stars on his memory....A wave of yet more tender joy escaped from his heart and went coursing in warm flood along his arteries. Like the tender fire of stars moments of their life together, that no one knew of or would ever know of, broke upon and illumined his memory." (pp. 274-275)

Although given to clichés and bourgeois pieties in his after dinner speech, Gabriel, like Bloom and Molly, does have a touch of the artist in him. He likes his tired similes, repeating the imagery of bursting stars and of joy "coursing in warm flood along his arteries." Despite, or, better, because of, the unwitting sentimentality of his metaphors, his love—love as the narcissistically vulnerable and highly conventional Gabriel experiences it—somehow shines through.[142] Repeating his image of the tender fire of stars and souls, he fantasizes that he can "make her forget the

---

[142] Although usually used to describe various middlemen of culture in twentieth-century American life—anti-intellectual intellectuals who mediate between high culture and the mass mind by simplifying and vulgarizing various cultural goodies—Gabriel, an intellectual manqué, is a kind of Edwardian middlebrow, a broker of culture, in his after dinner oration. Along with Miss Yvors, James Joyce, W. B. Yeats, and John Millington Synge would surely belong to that "new generation" that Gabriel (with Joycean irony) damns with faint praise—a "sceptical" and "thought-tormented" generation, "educated or hypereducated as it is" (p. 261).

years of their dull existence together... For the years, he felt, had not quenched his soul or hers. Their children, his writing, her household cares had not quenched all their souls' tender fire." (p. 275)

Joyce then reveals the heart of Gabriel's fantasy as he imagines himself an ardent bridegroom on his wedding night, calling his bride softly:

—Gretta!
Perhaps she would not hear at once: she would be undressing. Then something in his voice would strike her. She would turn and look at him....(p. 275)

When they reach their hotel room, Gabriel believes that with his soul's tender fire he will glow in Gretta's eyes, that he will win her love anew by passionately dispelling the dullness that has enveloped their marriage:

His heart was brimming over with happiness. Just when he was wishing for it she had come to him of her own accord. Perhaps her thoughts had been running with his. Perhaps she had felt the impetuous desire that was in him and then the yielding mood had come upon her. Now that she had fallen to him so easily he wondered why he had been so diffident. (p. 280)

When he realizes that Gretta's thoughts are not running with his, that she is feeling again the impetuous desire that was in a seventeen-year-old boy she knew as a girl in Galway, Gabriel feels the most burning shame he has experienced all evening. Joyce intensifies our sense of Gabriel's torment by his play on the phrase "distant music." On their way to the hotel, Gabriel recalls a letter that he had written to Gretta years before, part of their secret life together: "Why is it that words like these seem to me so dull and cold? Is it because there is no word tender enough to be your name?" (p. 275). He likens his words to "distant music" that were "borne towards him from the past" (p. 275). (With dramatic irony, Joyce has Gabriel call his word-painting of Gretta "Distant Music.") But the distant music from the past that transfixes Gretta is the song she was listening to at the end of the party, "The Lass of Aughrim," the song that Michael Furey sang to her in Galway. And, poignantly, it is this music she is remembering in the hotel room as Gabriel imagines making love to her.

Gabriel's humiliation becomes all but overwhelming when Gretta tells him she feels that Michael Furey "died for me" (p. 283). She recalls him standing outside her window in the winter rain and telling her that he did not wish to live since she was leaving—and then dying within a week of her coming up to Dublin. The image of Michael Furey that Gretta has been harboring floods Gabriel with the shameful self-consciousness that he has felt all evening, humiliation that broadens out into devastating self criticism:

> Gabriel felt humiliated...by the evocation of this figure from the dead, a boy in the gasworks. While he had been full of memories of their secret life together, full of tenderness and joy and desire, she had been comparing him in her mind with another. A shameful consciousness of his own person assailed him. He saw himself as a ludicrous figure, acting as a pennyboy for his aunts, a nervous, well-meaning sentimentalist, orating to vulgarians and idealizing his own clownish lusts, the pitiable fatuous fellow he had caught a glimpse of in the mirror. Instinctively, he turned his back more to the light lest she might see the shame that burned upon his forehead. (p.283)

Ashamed of his shame, he is suffering from the most intense feeling of humiliation that he has experienced all evening. It is compounded by the collapse of his belief that he and his wife created something precious in the past and that she will join him in vivifying their (to him) dull marriage by recreating that ardent past in the present. But Gretta, he now feels, has had something more precious in the past than anything he and she ever shared. He responds to her memory of Michael Furey's love with almost paranoid suspicion. He is convinced that while he had been full of memories of their secret life together, Gretta was comparing him in her mind with another—a very different "secret life" with a lower-class boy who worked in the gasworks.

Feeling that she broke faith with him even *before* they were married, Gabriel seems close to becoming unglued.[143] As if to underline the gap between Gabriel's hopes for an evening of passionate lovemaking and the reality of what Gretta is thinking about, Joyce makes it painfully clear that Gabriel is neither sleeping literally with his wife nor figuratively as well. To his attempted tone of "cold interrogation," which is actually a tone "humble and indifferent"—"I suppose you were in love with this Michael Furey, Gretta"—she replies, "I was great with him at that time" (p. 283). To Gabriel, she seems almost to be ready to fall asleep with Michael Furey, still as "great with him," still as warmly friendly with him, as when they used to go out walking in Galway, but now grief-stricken at the memory of his burial in Oughterard.

> She was fast asleep. Gabriel, leaning on his elbow, looked for a few moments unresentfully on her tangled hair and half-open mouth, listening to her deep-drawn breath. So she had that romance in her life: a man had died for her sake. It hardly pained him now to think of how poor a part he, her husband, had played in her life. He watched her while she slept as though he and she had never lived together as man and wife. His curious eyes rested long upon her face and on her hair: and as he thought of what she must have been then, in that time of her first girlish beauty, a strange friendly pity for her entered his soul. He did not like to say even to himself that her face was no longer beautiful but he knew that it was no longer the face for which Michael Furey had braved death. (pp.285-286)

Gabriel first unconsciously reacts to his resentment by turning it into its opposite, telling himself that he is looking "unresentfully" on her. He then turns "the dull anger" that has been gathering "at the back of his

---

[143] Gabriel's overwhelming anxiety (together with depression) echoes Joyce's near break with reality in 1909 when he became convinced that Nora was not a virgin when they fled Dublin for Europe five years earlier. As I mentioned earlier, he attempted to reduce that anxiety by writing letters to her to insure that she shared her most intimate autoerotic fantasies only with him (see Chapter IV, note 45). Although he doesn't set pen to paper, Gabriel's prose-poetic reverie that concludes "The Dead" also seems to calm his identity-disorganizing agitation, allowing him to drift into a much-desired snow-filled oblivion.

mind" on Gretta (p. 281). He seems to be annulling their marriage, imagining that he and she had "never lived together as man and wife." (Ironically, Joyce makes it painfully clear that Gabriel is, in fact, not now, in the Gresham, living together with Gretta as man and wife; he is not sleeping with her.) Gabriel then annuls Gretta as if she really were an opposing party in an acrimonious dissolution. Consciously feeling a "strange friendly pity," unconsciously he makes Gretta as unattractive as he consciously made Miss Ivors, with her "rabbit eyes" and ambiguous gender. He disparages the wife he formerly romanticized. He "[did] not like to say even to himself that her face was no longer beautiful," but he does say it to himself—"it was no longer the face for which Michael Furey had braved death."

Still trying to erase his mortifying feelings of inferiority and failure, he all but accuses Gretta of lying to him, in effect betraying him sexually with Michael Furey before she even met Gabriel. She didn't answer him directly when he asked (twice) whether she was in love with Michael Furey. Gabriel seems to have been mulling over her reply, "I was great with him at that time," suspecting that it might have meant something less innocent than a girl going out walking in the country with a close friend. As he glances about their room, he notices the signs of a woman "overcome by emotion" at bedtime, so overcome as to "flin[g] herself face downward on the bed, sobbing in the quilt" (p. 240).

> Perhaps she had not told him all the story. His eyes moved to the chair over which she had thrown some of her clothes. A petticoat string dangled to the floor. One boot stood upright, its limp upper fallen down: the fellow of it lay upon its side. (p. 285)

In his maddening humiliation, anger, and suspicion, he seems to be transforming Gretta's despair-filled undressing in the present into sexual abandon with Michael Furey in the past. She *was* entranced as she listened to Bartell d'Arcy sing "*The Lass of Aughrim*," the ballad from the west of a "peasant-born" woman who, with her child in her arms, goes to the castle of the lord who seduced and abandoned her, only to be turned away by his mother, a mother who, like Gabriel's mother, was also deeply aware of the "dignity of family life."[144] It's as if Gabriel were saying, "Perhaps Gretta was not a virgin when I married her. Perhaps she had been "great with" him sexually, if not great with child, then great with all of Michael Furey."

5. *A Few Light Taps upon the Pane*

As he stretches himself "cautiously along under the sheets and lay[s] down beside his wife," Gabriel begins to understand himself and everyone he knows in a profoundly different way: "One by one they were all becoming shades. Better pass boldly into that other world, in the full glory of some passion, than fade and wither dismally with age" (p. 287). He no longer seems to be tormented by the adolescent love that joined Gretta and Michael Furey together so many years earlier. Rather, in his despairing knowledge and self-knowledge, he seems sadly but clearly to perceive them in the full glory of their passion: "He thought of how she who lay beside him had locked in her heart for so many years that image of her lover's eyes when he had told her that he did not wish to live" (p. 287). Now laying down beside his wife, he no longer seems overcome by the humiliation we have just seen and the subsequent rage at those who made him feel a fool, a pitiable fatuous fellow idealizing his own clownish lusts: "Generous tears filled Gabriel's eyes. He had never felt like that himself towards any woman but he knew that such a feeling must be love" (p. 287).

With "generous tears"—perhaps a new found generosity of spirit, at least consciously—he begins to experience this Epiphany week the deepest and most wide-ranging epiphany of any of Joyce's Dubliners, a profoundly realistic awareness of himself and of others that will expand outward until, in the last lines of the story, it includes his whole time and place. (We learn early on that the Misses Morkan's annual dance takes place after New Year's Eve when Freddy Malins' mother "made him take the pledge" (p. 237).) Gabriel can now acknowledge that a common, lower class boy, working in the gasworks, felt genuine love. Aware that he was unable to live so deeply and so instinctively in his heart, Gabriel is aware at least intellectually that

---

[144] Gifford, *op.cit.*, p. 123.

Gabriel Conroy's Individuating Rhythm and Joyce's use of Autobiography

"He had never felt like that himself towards any woman but he knew that such a feeling must be love" (p. 287).

As the tears "gather more thickly in his eyes and in the partial darkness," he is visited by a dream-like vision of a mysterious region where dwell the "vast hosts of the dead" (p. 287). Gabriel becomes aware of their flickering existence and imagines that he sees "the form of a young man standing under a dripping tree":

> Other forms were near. His soul had approached that region where dwell the vast hosts of the dead. He was conscious of, but could not apprehend their wayward and flickering existence. His own identity was fading out into a grey impalpable world: the solid world itself which these dead had one time reared and lived in, was dissolving and dwindling. (p. 287)[145]

The young man standing under the dripping tree is, of course, Michael Furey. Approaching, Gabriel appears to wish to join him in death. A moment later, when he says "The time had come for him to set out on his journey westward," Gabriel seems to be repeating this wish (p. 287). Westward, the land of the setting sun, is the region where Ireland and Irish life ends. It is also the Oughterard churchyard where Michael Furey is buried. There *is* a lingering urge in Gabriel to erase his overwhelming mortification, to erase the reality of Gretta's seeming rejection of him by erasing himself, by dying all but literally of mortification. But Joyce is also implying that Gabriel is attracted to a different kind of death. With his "identity fading out into a grey impalpable world," Gabriel's once solid identity—uxorious husband, mathering father, devoted nephew, serious journalist—is dissolving, dwindling. He seems to be dying to his old self.

---

[145] Beginning to live in something like the visionary imagination of Stephen Dedalus, Gabriel seems to be on his way to shedding the stiff, stilted, pompously oratorical language he used earlier when he spoke of a "thought-tormented age," a "hypereducated" generation, "spacious days" "gone beyond recall," "the memory of those dead and gone great ones whose fame the world will not willingly let die" (pp.261-262).

If we assume that Gabriel wants unconsciously to abandon the identity that he seems to have inherited from his archangel namesake—the herald of good news, someone who feels all but compelled to administer sympathy and comfort to everyone—then we can infer the identity he hopes to be born into.[146] Dead and reborn as Michael, Gabriel seems to be fantasizing about recapturing the boldness and passionate energy of the other archangel while simultaneously abolishing the painful distance that opened up between himself and his wife.[147] At one with Michael Furey, he will fulfill his earlier wish to be at one with Gretta in whose womb of imagination, Michael Furey lies dead yet alive.

Joyce summarizes our sense that Gabriel is seeking not just death, but death and rebirth in his image of Michael Furey's burial place, a "lonely churchyard on the hill" that is like Golgotha (p. 288). Taking his night journey to that Oughterard churchyard, with its "crooked crosses and headstones," its "spear" of a little gate, its "barren thorns," Gabriel appears to imagine joining Michael Furey in a Galway Golgotha. Somewhere beyond time and space, he can actualize a Christ-like, self-sacrificing love that is simultaneously a resurrection. In this semiconscious fantasy of dying into the "full glory of some passion," he would also permanently undo the torment of his flood of shame at Gretta's rejection.

At the beginning of his dream-vision, Gabriel feels that he cannot "apprehend" the wayward and flickering existence of the vast hosts of the dead, but at the end, he does just that. "Apprehension" has a special meaning for Joyce, or at least it does for his mythicized alter ego, Stephen Dedalus. In his lecture on aesthetics to Lynch, Stephen offers what seems to have been young Joyce's belief that the supreme phase of "artistic apprehension" is when the *"whatness"* of a thing is "apprehended luminously by the mind which has been arrested by its wholeness and fascinated by its harmony."[148] In the last paragraph of "The Dead," which

---

[146] Gifford, *op.cit.*, p. 113.
[147] *Ibid.*, p. 125.
[148] See *Portrait op. cit.*, p, 250, for Stephen's discourse on aesthetics. Also, see Epilogue, above.

is also the last paragraph of *Dubliners* itself, Gabriel seems to have apprehended the "whatness" of himself, of his fellow Dubliners, and even of all of mankind: he is newly "arrested" by the "wholeness" and "harmony" of those hosts of the dead who are inseparable from himself and from all of those who act as if they are living.

Devastated by the realization that he has been living their death-in-life existence unwittingly—that the living are even more dead than the dead and that the dead, like Michael Furey, are even more alive than the living—he begins to shed his sense of superiority. Frustration in his attempts to shine all evening has caused him a shameful consciousness of his own person. But now, not so plagued by his narcissistic anxieties, he can feel, rather than become merely "conscious," that there is no difference between his existence and the wayward and flickering existence of the dead and the living dead. Paradoxically, with this newfound identity, Gabriel seems to be more secure, perhaps less likely to be puzzled by "the face whose expression always puzzled him when he saw it in a mirror" (p. 281).

Joyce implies that with his painfully earned grounding in reality, Gabriel can begin to give voice to something like an artist within, a voice that he has inhibited by his compulsion to solicitude and caution, to a kind of driven generosity and dutifulness—pressured performances that he expected would bring him praise and acclaim. Put another way, the impulse to artistic creation seems to have sprung in Gabriel from his making a radical psychological break with everything he had thought about himself, Gretta, and his whole world.

6. Joyce and the Uses of Autobiography

It is just about impossible to say who is speaking in the last paragraph of "The Dead."[149] Although he is still using the first-person-third-person style, Joyce wants us to hear a very different voice in Gabriel. He suggests this in a number of ways. First, he makes Gabriel's language indistinguishable from his own. Gabriel's late Victorian diction—

---

[149] Cf. Lionel Trilling, *The Experience of Literature: A Reader with Commentaries* (New York: Holt, Rinehard and Winston), p. 655.

sentimental, decorous, euphemistic—disappears. All but gone are the Poetic and Beautiful phrases: "There was grace and mystery in her attitude" (p. 270); "He had felt proud...of her grace and wifely carriage" (p. 276); "But now after the kindling again of so many memories, the first touch of her body, musical and strange and perfumed, sent through him a keen pang of lust" (pp. 276-277).

Joyce also emphasizes Gabriel's emergent artistic gift in the marvelously "intricated" nature of the last paragraph, Marianne Moore's phrase for the organic unity of a great poem or prose-poem. (Although he offers a worshipful word-painting of Gretta listening to Bartell d'Arcy's singing "*The Lass of Aughrim*," the title Gabriel gives it, "*Distant Music*," is as sentimental as his faux-pre-Raphaelite style.) In the conclusion of "The Dead," Joyce allows us to infer that Gabriel is intuitively fashioning a small but intricately integrated work of art, a mini-creation where imagery and mood, tone and diction, theme and atmosphere are all inseparable one from the other. Let me indulge myself by quoting it at length:

> A few light taps upon the pane made him turn to the window. It had begun to snow again. He watched sleepily the flakes, silver and dark, falling obliquely against the lamplight. The time had come for him to set out on his journey westward. Yes, the newspapers were right: snow was general all over Ireland. It was falling on every part of the dark central plain, on the treeless hills, falling softly upon the Bog of Allen and, farther westward, softly falling into the dark mutinous Shannon waves. It was falling, too, upon every part of the lonely churchyard on the hill where Michael Furey lay buried. It lay thickly drifted on the crooked crosses and headstones, on the spears of the little gate, on the barren thorns. His soul swooned slowly as he heard the snow falling faintly through the universe and faintly falling, like the descent of their last end, upon all the living and the dead. (pp. 287-288)

We have examined the complex meaning of Gabriel's belief that it was time for him to set out on his journey westward, his drifting in a dreamy, semi-conscious world between impulses to die—to die, to die to his old way of life, and to be reborn. Here I would like to focus on how he has been all but inseparable from the snow all evening and then how he uses snow imagery to recreate life out of life in a Dedalean fashion. Just as snow beckons him, laying "like a cape on the shoulders of his overcoat and like toecaps on the toes of his galoshes," he later finds himself drawn to it (p. 226). He imagines himself walking outside his aunts's home, seeing "a bright cap [of snow] on the top of the Wellington Monument" (p. 246). Then as he and Gretta drive to their hotel, crossing O'Connell Bridge, he points to the snow-clad statue of Daniel O'Connell and nods familiarly to it, waving his hand (p. 276). Here, Joyce uses snow to suggest the political tensions in Gabriel, a West Briton as Molly Ivors teasingly mocks him. Joyce connects decidedly unheroic Gabriel first to the snow-capped Wellington, the famous English patriot-soldier, and then to O'Connell, "The Liberator" of the Irish people.

But it is Gabriel himself who seems to be artfully repeating the snow imagery as he falls asleep. As he recreates his early connection to it, we infer a different polarity within him, a tension between his wish to die and his wish to live. One can effortlessly drift off to a sleepy death in the snow, especially if, highly unusually, it is "general all over Ireland." It gently obliterates the difference between the living and the dead. Gabriel is also connecting the lightly tapping snow with a passionate, death-defying tapping a moment earlier. He had heard another kind of window tapping just before he slipped cautiously into his cold bed with Gretta. She recalled Michael Furey, shivering at the end of the garden, throwing gravel up against her window the night she left her grandmother's house in Nun's Island for the convent in Dublin.

In addition to repeating a psychologically and thematically significant image, there is also a touch of the artist in Gabriel's use of other resources of poetry, especially his use of a prose-poetic version of chiasmus, a reversal of word order in successive parallel clauses, especially as he describes the snow in soft, gradually subsiding, falling rhythms: "It was falling on every part of the dark central plain, on the treeless hills, falling softly upon the Bog of Allen and, farther westward, softly falling into the dark mutinous Shannon waves."

We get that reversal again in the famous concluding line, "His soul swooned slowly as he heard the snow falling faintly through the universe and faintly falling, like the descent of their last end, upon all the living and the dead." The reversal in style embodies an abiding theme in Joyce that we have been exploring in *Tyrants*—the reversal in Stephen and Bloom of psychological death-in-life into passionate life and the reversal of passionate life into death-in-life.

Along with chiasmus, Gabriel uses alliteration in his grouping of the "s" words, creating the effect of onomatopoeia where the drifting "s" sounds in "soul swooned slowly" and the combination of "s" with "f" sounds in "snow faintly falling" seem to reflect the meaning of the words (and the words seem to "imitate" the quietly swishing sounds).

Finally, dreamily thinking, Gabriel is fashioning an early version of T. S. Eliot's "objective correlative." In the omnipresent snow falling faintly through the universe, faintly falling upon all the living and the dead, he is half-consciously correlating details in the outer world with his inner world, the physical landscape mirroring the psychological landscape. The snowy oneness of the living and the dead is also his own life-in-death.

In the last image of snow filling the whole universe, Gabriel's epiphany extends beyond Dublin, beyond Ireland, to the very edge of space and time. Like Molly, in her moment in eternity that concludes *Ulysses*, Gabriel's prose-poetry carries us with him to the darkly mysterious realm of spacelessness and timelessness—the "everchanging tracks of neverchanging space" toward which both Bloom and Ulysses are also "carried," as the nameless narrator-catachumin answers in "Ithaca" (*Ulysses*, p. 692). In that image, Joyce has allowed Gabriel to come up with a metaphor that summarizes Joyce's own radically new collection of short stories, his indictment of a stricken culture. Joyce wrote that his intention in *Dubliners* was to "write a chapter in the moral history of [his] country, and [he] chose Dublin for the scene because that city seemed to [him] the centre of paralysis."[150] At the end of "The Dead," we are asked to infer that Gabriel has intuited that his paralysis is synonymous with Dublin's emotional, spiritual, and physical paralysis, and that Dublin's paralysis is the paralysis of us all.

---

[150] James Joyce, "Letter to Grant Richards, May 5, 1906, in *Selected Letters of James Joyce*, ed. Richard Ellmann (New York: The Viking Press, 1975), p. 83.

Gabriel Conroy's Individuating Rhythm and Joyce's use of Autobiography

As Gabriel drifts between consciousness and unconsciousness, the state of mind necessary for the creative act for Joyce, Joyce is also offering us a semi-disguised self-portrait, something like El Greco's self-portrait in "The Burial of the Count of Orgaz," or Rembrandt's in "The Elevation of the Cross," or Michelangelo's, twice, in "The Last Judgment." He gives the words he wrote to Nora in a 1904 letter directly to Gabriel. Reminiscing about the past before going to their hotel, Gabriel recalls a letter he wrote to Gretta filled with what he felt was his soul's "tender fire," lines I quoted earlier: "'Why is it that words like these seem to me so dull and cold? Is it because there is no word tender enough to be your name?'" (p. 275).[151] He also gives Gabriel other details of his own life. Joyce wrote book reviews for the *Daily Express*, too, was also a language teacher, wore rimmed glasses, and parted his hair in the middle.[152] He creates Gabriel out of his father as well as himself. His platitudinous after dinner speech is delivered in John Joyce's florid oratorical style, and Gabriel's argument with his mother "suggest[s] John Joyce's quarrels with his mother, who never accepted her son's marriage to a woman of a lower station."[153]

Giving Gabriel John Joyce's voice as well as his own, at twenty-five or two-years old Joyce is offering us an early portrait of the artist as a young man. At the beginning of *Portrait*, listening to his father tell him the story about the moocow, Stephen's voice is inseparable from *his* father's, almost as if the mother tongue was mediated to him by the father. Stephen seems to have his very being in that paternal verbal nimbus. From the beginning of Stephen's life, father and son are fused in Joyce's version of the artist. As he falls asleep, Gabriel, as I have suggested, has more than a touch of the Dedalean artist in him. He, too, seems to be a fusion of father and son.[154]

---

[151] Quoted by Richard Ellmann, *James Joyce* (New York: Oxford University Press, 1965), p. 255.

[152] Ellmann, *op.cit.*, pp. 255-256. In his cautious middle-class existence, Gabriel also seems to be a double, an embodiment of Joyce's negative potential, what might have happened to him if he did not flee Ireland.

[153] *Ibid.*

[154] At the time of John Joyce's death, Joyce, grief-stricken, wrote that his "'talent'" sprang

As I have mentioned, Gabriel's individuating rhythm appears to be a rhythm in Stephen's life, but it is a rhythm in Joyce's life as well. When Gabriel's yearnings for acclaim are not met, he is plunged into the deepest anger, suspicion, and despair, just as Joyce seemed close to losing himself completely when he felt that his Galway-born wife had betrayed and abandoned him in 1909. The impulse to creativity seems to have sprung in part from a blow to his narcissism, a blow that lead to some sort of foreswearing of his previous way of life. Other artists have experienced similar soul-stunning upheavals and transformations. Rilke, pondering Cézanne's radical self-transformation, describes this leap in a letter to his wife in 1907:

> Surely all art is the result of one's having been in danger, of having gone through an experience all the way to the end, to where no one can go any further....Therein lies the enormous aid the work of art brings to the life of one who makes it.... that is the knot in the rosary at which his life recites a prayer, the ever-returning proof to himself of his unity and genuineness....[155]

In the letters we discussed earlier, which he exchanged with Nora from Dublin in 1909, Joyce managed to repair the terrible injury where he felt that he could go no further psychologically. He bound his presumably rejecting wife to him by means of a mutual sharing of their most shameful sexual secrets. In his second word painting, at the end of "The Dead," Gabriel also repairs a narcissistic injury where he feels that he has gone all the way to the end. He erases the separation from Gretta that all but unmanned him by creating out of the ordinariness of an Irish winter landscape something extraordinary, a cold Dedalean jewel where snow is extraordinarily general all over Ireland. Out of the creative

---

from his father, a man whose unforgettable voice he heard all his life. "'Hundreds of pages and scores of characters in my books came from him.'" Quoted by Ellmann, *op.cit.,* pp. 656-657.

[155] Rainer Maria Rilke, Letter to his Wife, June 24 1907, in *Rainer Maria Rilke Letters on Cezanne*, ed. Clara Rilke, trans. Joel Agee (New York: Fromm International Publishing Corporation, 1985), p. 4.

imagination, he reunites himself and Gretta, "a knot in the rosary at which his life recites a prayer." He and she are at one with each other in their oneness with a beckoning, host-haunted, snow-filled universe.

In "The Snow Man," Wallace Stevens offers an image that unites Gabriel and Joyce more beautifully than I can: "One must have a mind of winter / To regard the frost and the boughs / Of the pine trees crusted with snow; / And have been cold a long time…and not to think / Of any misery in the sound of the wind, / In the sound of a few leaves…." To the mind that has shed sentimentality—and the distortions of reality in the self-obsessed—the sound of a few leaves is "the sound of the land / Full of the same wind / That is blowing in the same bare place / For the listener, who listens in the snow…." Gabriel is that listener in the snow; Joyce is that listener in his own version of the snow; and he hopes that each of us can be that listening snow man, too: "And, nothing himself, beholds / Nothing that is not there and the nothing that is."[156]

---

[156] Wallace Stevens, "Snow Man," in *The Collected Poems of Wallace Stevens* (New York: Alfred A. Knopf, 1965), pp. 9-10.

Bibliography

Balint, Michael. *The Basic Fault: Therapeutic Aspects of Regression.* London. Tavistock Publications Ltd. 1968.

Brenner, Charles. *An Elementary Textbook of Psychoanalysis.* Garden City, New York. Anchor Books. 1974.

Brivic, Sheldon. *Joyce Between Freud and Jung.* Port Washington. Kennikat Press. 1980.

Chasseguet-Smirgel, Janine. "Loss of Reality in Perversions With a Special Reference to Fetishism." *Journal of the American Psychoanalytic Society.* 29: 1981.

Ellmann. Richard. *The Consciousness of Joyce.* Toronto and New York. Oxford University Press. 1977.

———. *James Joyce.* New York. Oxford University Press. 1972.

———. *Ulysses on the Liffey.* New York. Oxford University Press. 1972.

Ellmann, Richard (ed.), *Selected Letters of James Joyce.* New York. The Viking Press. 1975.

Faber, M. D. "Oedipus Rex: A Psychoanalytic Interpretation." *Psychoanalytic Review.* 62: 1975.

Fenichel, Otto. *The Psychoanalytic Theory of Neurosis.* New York. W. W. Norton & Company, Inc. 1945.

Frazer, Sir James George. *The Golden Bough: A Study in Music and Religion.* New York. Macmillan Paperback. Macmillan Publishing Co., Inc. 1978.

Freud, Anna. "The Concept of Developmental Lines." *The Psychoanalytic Study of the Child.* 18: 1963.

Freud, Sigmund. "The Dream Work," in "The Interpretation of Dreams," in *The Complete Psychological Works of Sigmund Freud,* vols. IV-V. trans. James Strachey. London. The Hogarth Press. 1981.

Gifford, Don. *Joyce Annotated: Notes for Dubliners and A Portrait of the Artist as a Young Man.* 2nd ed. revised and enlarged. Berkeley. University of California Press. 1982.

Gifford, Don and Robert J. Seidman. *Notes for Joyce: An Annotation of James Joyce's Ulysses*. New York. E. P. Dutton & Co. Inc. 1974.

Greenacre, Phyllis. *Emotional Growth: Psychoanalytic Studies of the Gifted and a Great Variety of Other Individuals, vol. I*. New York: International Universities Press, Inc. 1971.

Joyce, James. *Dubliners* with an introduction by Padraic Colum. New York. The Modern Library. 1926.

———. *A Portrait of the Artist as a Young Man* with an introduction by Herbert Gorman. New York. The Modern Library, Inc. 1928.

———. *Ulysses*. Shakespeare and Company. Paris. 1926.

———. *Finnegans Wake*. The Viking Press. New York. 1939.

Joyce, Stanislaus. *My Brother's Keeper: James Joyce's Early Years*. ed. with an introduction by Richard Ellmann. New York. The Viking Press. 1958.

Kohut, Heinz. *The Analysis of the Self: A Systematic Approach to the Psychoanalytic Treatment of Narcissistic Personality Disturbances*. New York. International Universities Press. 1971.

Mahler, Margaret, Fred Pine, and Anni Bergman. *The Psychological Birth of the Human Infant: Symbiosis and Individuation*. New York. Basic Books, Inc. 1975.

Marcus, Steven. *The Other Victorians*. New York. Basic Books, Inc. 1966.

Matthews, William and Ralph W. Rader. *Autobiography, Biography, and the Novel*. Papers read at a Clark Library Seminar, May 13, 1972. Los Angeles. University of California at Los Angeles: William Clark Memorial Library. 1973.

Rilke, Rainer Maria. "Letters to his Wife," in *Letters on Cezanne*. ed. Clara Rilke. trans. Joel Agee. New York. Fromm International Publishers Corporation. 1985.

Schafer, Roy. "The Mechanisms of Defense." *International Journal of Psychoanalysis*. 49: 1968.

Scholes, Robert and Richard M. Kain. *The Workshop of Dedalus: James Joyce and the Raw Materials for A Portrait of the Artist as a Young Man*. Evanston, Il. Northwestern University Press. 1965.

Schwaber, Paul. *The Cast of Characters: A Reading of Ulysses*. New Haven and London. Yale University Press. 1999.

Shakespeare, William. *Hamlet,* in *The Complete Plays and Poems of William Shakespeare: A New Text Edited With an Introduction and Notes by* William Allan Neilson and Charles Jarvis Hill. Houghton Mifflin Company, The Riverside Press Cambridge. Cambridge, Mass., 1942.

Shechner, Mark. *Joyce in Nighttown: A Psychoanalytic Inquiry into Ulysses.* Berkeley. University of California Press. 1974.

Stevens, Wallace. "The Snow Man," in *The Collected Poems of Wallace Stevens.* New York. Alfred A. Knopf. 1965.

Trilling, Lionel. "Art and Neurosis," in *The Liberal Imagination.* Garden City, New York. Doubleday & Company. 1953.

———. "James Joyce in his Letters," in *The Moral Obligation to be Intelligent: Selected Essays.* Evanston, Il. Northwestern University Press. 2008.

Weiss, Jules. "Commentary on Alan Z. Skolnikoff, 'Creativity and Therapy.'" *Dialogue: A Journal of Psychoanalytic Perspectives.* Spring. 1977.

Winnicott, D.W. "Transitional Objects and Transitional Phenomena," in *Playing and Reality.* London and New York. Routledge. 1982.

www.ingramcontent.com/pod-product-compliance
Lightning Source LLC
Chambersburg PA
CBHW070604300426
44113CB00010B/1394